DISCRIMINATION LAW:

Concepts, Limitations and Justifications

Edited by
JANET DINE and BOB WATT

DISCRIMINATION LAW:

Concepts, Limitations and Justifications

LONGMAN
LONDON AND NEW YORK

Addison Wesley Longman Limited,
Edinburgh Gate,
Harlow, Essex CM20 2JE, England
and Associated Companies throughout the world

Published in the United States of America
by Addison Wesley Longman, New York

First published 1996

ISBN 0 582 28909.2 PPR

British Library Cataloguing-in-Publication Data

A catalogue record for this book is
available from the British Library

Library of Congress Cataloging-in-Publication Data

Also available

Set by 8 in 10/12pt Plantin Light
Produced through Longman Malaysia, LWP

CONTENTS

PREFACE

This book grew out of a discussion at a Joint Session of the European Law and Labour Law Sections at the SPTL Conference at Queen Mary and Westfield College in 1993. Following that discussion, the University of Essex hosted a symposium entitled 'Justifying Discrimination' in October 1994. This attracted papers from speakers with expertise in a wide range of legal disciplines. Over two days the delegates were challenged by presentations covering major themes in discrimination law from a variety of critical perspectives. Many of these papers provided the basis for chapters which appear in this book, though these have been supplemented by a number of new contributions so as to ensure a balanced and comprehensive coverage of the key issues involved. We trust that readers will find the book a valuable and stimulating as the oroginal symposium.

We would like to thank our contributors for their prompt submission of manuscripts and for their patience with our editing.

From a personal perspective we would like to thank Gill Watt and Keith Band for their support, and send our love to them and our respective children – Graham, Elaine and Fiona Watt and Robert, Helen and Elizabeth Band.

Janet Dine & Bob Watt
University of Essex
October 1995

ACKNOWLEDGEMENTS

For permission to reproduce the following essays in a slightly amended and updated form, the publishers would like to thank:

Butterworths for 'The Cost of Removing Discrimination From Social Security Systems' by Christopher McCrudden which originally appeared in *Equality of Treatment Between Men and Women in Social Security*, edited by Christopher McCrudden (Butterworths, 1994).

Martinus Nijhoff/Kluwer Academic for 'The Protection of Minorities Under the European Convention on Human Rights' by Geoff Gilbert which originally appeared as 'The Legal Protection Accorded to Minority Groups in Europe' in 23 *Netherlands Yearbook of International Law* 67–104 (1992).

Sweet & Maxwell for 'Gender Discrimination Law in the European Community' by Evelyn Ellis which originally appeared as 'The Definition of Discrimination in European Community Sex Equality Law' in 19 *European Law Review* 563 (1994).

NOTES ON CONTRIBUTORS

STEVE ANDERMAN, B.A. (CUNY), LL.B. (Yale), M.Sc. (Lond). Birkett Long Professor of Law, University of Essex. Steve Anderman has published widely in the areas of labour law, commercial law and competition law. He is the Consulting Editor of the Industrial Relations Law Reports. Amongst his most recent publications is *Labour Law: Management Decisions and Workers Rights* (Butterworths, 1993 (second edition)).

NICHOLAS BAMFORTH, B.A., B.C.L. (Oxon). Lecturer in Laws, University College London. Nicholas Bamforth has published extensively in the areas of discrimination on the grounds of gender and sexuality. He is the author of *Sexuality, Morals and Justice* (Cassell, 1996).

CATHERINE BARNARD is Lecturer in Law at the University of Southampton, Assistant Dean and Jean Monnet Chair of European Integration. She specialises in EC Law, Employment Law and discrimination law. She is the author of a recent book entitled *EC Employment Law* (Wiley Chancery, 1995).

NICOLAS BERNARD, Maitrise en droit (Paris XI), B.A. (Kent) DEA (Paris I). Lecturer in Law, University of Essex. Nicolas Bernard's research interests include EC law. He has a number of published works in this area.

COLIN BOURN, B.Sc. Barrister. Senior Lecturer in Law and Director of the International Centre for Management, Law and Industrial Relations. University of Leicester. He has written extensively on discrimination issues and other aspects of labour law, and is the joint author (with John Whitmore) of *Race and Sex Discrimination* (Sweet & Maxwell, 1992).

RYSZARD CHOLEWINSKI LL.B. (Leicester), LL.M. (Saskatchewan), LL.D. (Ottawa), Lecturer in the Faculty of Law at the University of Leicester. Ryszard Cholewinski is the author of a forthcoming monograph for Oxford University Press on *International Protection of the Rights of Migrant Workers and their Families in Countries of Employment* (1996) and of articles on the rights of economic migrants and ethnic minorities in international human rights law. Ryszard is also the editor of and contributor to a volume on

Human Rights in Canada: Into the 1990s and Beyond (Ottawa: Human Right Research and Education Centre, 1990).

JANET DINE, LL.D., Ph.D. (Lond), AKC, Barrister, Commissioner for Friendly Societies. Professor of Law and Head of the Department of Law, University of Essex. Janet Dine has published widely in the fields of criminal law, company law, EC law, insolvency law and discrimination law. Her recent books include *Company Law* (Macmillan, 1994 (second edition)) and Criminal Law in the Company Context (Dartmouth Publishing Co. Ltd, 1995).

EVELYN ELLIS, M.A., LL.M. (Cantab), Ph.D. (Birm), Barrister. Reader in Public Law, University of Birmingham. Evelyn Ellis has written extensively on European Community Law and sex discrimination law. Her major works include *European Sex Equality Law* (OUP, 1991) and, with P. Tridimas, *Public Law of the European Community* (Sweet & Maxwell, 1995).

GEOFF GILBERT, LL.B. (Leics), LL.M., S.J.D. (Virginia), Barrister. Senior Lecturer in Law, Director of LL.M. in Human Rights Law, University of Essex. Geoff Gilbert's research interests in the field of human rights relate to the position of individuals and groups in international law. His publications include *Aspects of Extradition Law* (Martinus Nijhoff, 1991) and several articles on international criminal law, the causes of refugee flows and the rights needed by minority groups. He is a member of the editorial board of the *World Report on Freedom of Thought, Religion, Conscience and Belief* (Routledge, 1996).

SHELDON LEADER, B.A. (Yale), M.A., D.Phil. (Oxon), Barrister. Professor of Law, University of Essex. Sheldon Leader's interests include labour law, company law and legal and political theory. He has published *Freedom of Association* (Yale University Press, 1992) and other writing in labour law, jurisprudence and company law.

CATHERINE LITTLE, B.A., M.A., Lecturer in Law, Manchester Metropolitan University. Catherine Little lectures in socio-legal studies and criminology, and is a member of the Centre for Advanced Legal Studies at Manchester Metropolitan University. Her current research interests are in the area of gender, policing and police organisation.

JOANNE LUNN, B.A., M.Phil., Solicitor, Senior Lecturer in Law, Manchester Metropolitan University. Prior to entering academic work Joanne had practiced as a Solicitor both in the private sector and in industry. Her research interests include employment law and human rights law and centre upon issues in occupational health where she has published extensively.

PAULINE MATTHEWS has been a Principal Legal Officer at the Equal Opportunities Commission for six years. She conducts sex discrimination and equal pay litigation in the Industrial Tribunals and the County Courts, and specialises in the law relating to pregnancy and maternity. She has previously worked for a law centre and lectured part-time at the University of Salford.

CHRISTOPHER MCCRUDDEN, LL.B. (QUB), LL.M. (Yale), D.Phil. (Oxon). Fellow and Tutor in Law, Lincoln College Oxford, CUF Lecturer University of Oxford. Christopher McCrudden was a member of the Standing Advisory Commission on Human Rights and is currently a member of the European Commission's Expert Network on the Application of Equality Directives. Christopher McCrudden was a Visiting Professor at Queen's University Belfast during 1995. He has published extensively in the area of human rights and anti-discrimination law.

GWYNETH PITT, LL.B. (Leeds). Professor of Law and Head of the Department of Law, University of Huddersfield. Gwyneth Pitt's main research interests are in the areas of employment law, discrimination law and business ethics. She has published extensively in these areas and is the author of *Employment Law* (Sweet & Maxwell, 1995 (second edition)) and *Cases and Materials on Employment Law* (Pitman, 1994).

PETER STONE, M.A., LL.B. (Cantab), Barrister. Jean Monnet Professor of European Union Law, University of Essex. Peter Stone has published widely in the fields of European Law and the conflict of laws. He is the author of *The Conflict of Laws* (Longman, 1995).

BOB WATT, B.A. (CNAA), B.C.L. (Oxon). Lecturer in Law, University of Essex. Bob Watt's main interests are in anti-discrimination law, labour law and legal theory. He has published several papers on sexual harassment and discrimination against persons infected with the HIV. He is an editor of *Childright*.

BRIAN WILKINSON, B.C.L. (NUI), LL.M. (Osgoode Hall), Barrister. City Solicitors' Educational Trust Lecturer in European Law, University of Nottingham. Brian Wilkinson was educated at University College Cork, Osgoode Hall Toronto, and the University of Oxford. He was appointed to the City Solicitors' Trust Lectureship in 1993.

Part I

THE FUNDAMENTALS

I

INTRODUCTION
Janet Dine and Bob Watt

This book contains a wide-ranging exploration of the diverse areas of debate about discrimination. The authors consider the legal framework which seeks to regulate discriminatory practices, and the extent to which and the means by which discrimination, may be justified. A number of the authors discuss the issues of political theory which underlie the legal debate.

EQUALITY OF OPPORTUNITY?

If liberalism could be said, like molecular biology, to have a 'central dogma'[1] it would surely include, at least at a preliminary stage, the provision that all citizens irrespective of gender, origin or other irrelevant characteristics should have an opportunity to secure for themselves, in reliance upon their own merits and endeavours, their choice from among the goods available in a given society.

This statement, like all dogmas, requires considerable explanation and clarification before it can present any useful framework for discussion. First it must be emphasised that the value which is being promoted, as an alternative to discrimination, is equality of opportunity, not equality of distribution. This distinction, and the reasons for the promotion of equality of opportunity as a primary good, may be analysed in the following way.

Where an individual, or *a fortiori* the state, has a good to distribute, for example, the chance of a place at a selective school,[2] we would naturally say that the distributor discriminated were he to award the benefit upon the basis of the recipients' gender rather than upon their academic achievement. This is because academic achievement is regarded as a relevant quality, while gender is seen as an irrelevant quality in these circumstances. Merit, the definition of which depends upon the circumstances under consideration,

---

[1] See generally the works of Francis Crick, who with JD Watson first published the idea that the genetic material DNA had a physical structure in the form of a double helix, who advanced the brocade, now somewhat modified, that 'DNA makes RNA makes protein'. This was termed the 'central dogma' of molecular genetics.

[2] *R v Birmingham City Council ex parte EOC* [1981] AC 1155.

3

is viewed, even by liberals, as a reason for derogating from the equality principle. This may remain so even where we cannot say that the merit attaches to the person because of their own efforts. If a person is of above average intelligence because of some genetic predisposition it seems rather odd, or unfair, to further reward them by giving them superior schooling. Intuitively it seems simultaneously fair and unfair. Some way out of this *impasse* is needed.

Clearly scarce resources must be rationed and choices made between persons. This is true even when one acknowledges that people are equal in value, for they remain differently situated, both in terms of what they have and what they are. The making of a social security payment to a very wealthy person with secure employment is wasteful when others could benefit. The granting of maternity leave, as opposed to parental responsibility leave, to a man is senseless. Any failure to distribute goods equally among persons seems, at fist sight, to be a derogation from equality. This is, however, not the case as a deeper analysis shows.

In his work Ronald Dworkin distinguishes between 'equal treatment' and 'treatment as an equal'.[3] 'Equal treatment' means dividing the available goods between everyone and giving them similar shares, while 'treating people as equals' means treating them in accordance with their own requirements or aspirations, while preserving fairness between the shares. It may be that the difference between 'equality' and 'non-discrimination' may be expressed by reference to ideas of this sort. If this suggestion is correct it could be argued that 'equal treatment' or 'equality' was the aim of the Employment Appeal Tribunal in *Hayes v Malleable Working Men's Club*.[4]

In this case, the Employment Appeal Tribunal took the view that a pregnant woman dismissed from her job, because she was absent, should be compared with a sick man in order to resolve whether unequal treatment was afforded. This careful, though insulting, selection of a comparitor to ensure that which Lacey[5] terms 'formally equal treatment' ensures that men and women absent from work receive equal treatment. Even though Ms Hayes has been treated equally with an absent man there is no doubt that she was discriminated against. The treatment of an instance of dismissal of a pregnant woman in the *Dekker*[6] case demonstrates that the concept of 'treatment as an equal' provides a much surer foundation for anti-discrimination law than for 'equal treatment'. In *Dekker*, the European Court of Justice held that discrimination against a woman because she was pregnant amounted to discrimination against her as a woman and thus was an offence within the terms of the Equal Treatment Directive.[7] This view not only acknowledges the obvious biological differences between females and males, but also treats them both as worthy of treatment as equals. It is not immediately clear,

---

[3] Ronald Dworkin, *Taking Rights Seriously* (Duckworth, London 1978) at p 227.
[4] [1985] ICR 703, see also the dissenting judgment in *Turley v Allders Dept Stores* [1980] ICR 66.
[5] 'Dismissal by reason of pregnancy' (1986) 15 Industrial Law Journal 43 at p 45.
[6] [1990] ECR I-3941 Case 177/88 *Dekker v VJV Centrum 'Plus'*.
[7] EC Council Dir 76/207.

however, what it means to 'treat people as equals' as this implies that they should be treated differently depending upon their circumstances. To treat them equally and differently seems oxymoronic. In order to fill this apparent gap all that is needed is a recognition that individuals have different incommensurable abilities, goals and aspirations, and that treating people as equals' means giving equal weight to each person's own 'plan of life', ie treating people as equals means recognising their autonomy.

As Joseph Raz points out,[8] if we hold personal autonomy[9] to be an essential element of the good life, there are two political principles to which we must hold. These are:

(a) the principle that the state has a duty not only to provide protection from the denial of freedom, but also to provide the conditions for autonomy; and

(b) the principle that goals may not be pursued by means which infringe people's autonomy unless such action is justified to protect the autonomy of such people or others.

Joseph Raz also makes it plain that these principles are to be regarded as having primary importance.[10] If Raz's identification of the importance of the autonomy principle is correct it suggests that the focus of any debate on anti-discrimination law should be shifted from the distribution of goods to the distribution of opportunities. One might then suggest that 'equality' should be applied to certain distributions of goods, while 'non-discrimination' should be applied to similar distributions of opportunities. The debate as to whether the second of Raz's principles set out above does, or should, form a rationale for derogations from the general rule against discrimination is embedded in many of the contributions to this book.

In addition to the questions of distribution of opportunities, and the limitations which may rightly be placed upon their fair distribution, the contributors further discuss methods of promoting equality and non-discrimination. The authors discuss, for example, the validity of classifying people into groups by identifying a common characteristic eg race, gender, national origin, ethnicity etc. Some contributors consider the merits of 'affirmative action' to redress perceived discrimination.

CHOICES

As previously mentioned this book is about making choices. There are two ways in which one might examine choices. These might well be termed the 'reason-centred' and the 'effect-centred' approaches. In the reason-centred approach one looks at the character of the decision-making process, and

---

[8] Joseph Raz, *The Morality of Freedom* (Clarendon, Oxford 1986) pp 424–5.

[9] We take this to mean *dispositional* autonomy as opposed to merely *occurrent* autonomy. For discussion of these terms see Dine and Watt 'Sexual harassment: moving away from discrimination' 1995 MLR 343 at 357.

[10] See *Morality of Freedom* at p 425.

enquires whether the process is tainted by some bias against a particular gender or race. If the choice made between persons was seen to be tainted by some unacceptable, discriminatory reason it would then be struck down. This amounts to an examination of the motive underlying the discrimination and asks whether it has been done intentionally. For example, the Court of Appeal held in *Skyrail Oceanic Ltd v Coleman*[11] that an employer's assumption that a woman's job was of less value to her than her husband's job was to him amounted to such bias, and was, therefore, unlawful discrimination.

On the other hand, the choice may be subjected to scrutiny by examining its effect. The majority of the House of Lords gave this method of analysis its *imprimatur* in *James v Eastleigh Borough Council*[12] where three of their Lordships, led by Lord Goff, looked at the result of the Council's policy as allowing persons of pensionable age to swim without payment in their swimming pool and asked whether women and men would be equally treated 'but for' their respective gender. Lord Goff was clear that this test was appropriate because it avoided 'complicated questions ... such as intention, motive, reason or purpose'.[13]

A third approach may be emerging. Lord Ackner, in one of the two minority judgments in *James*, analysed the nature of the reasons for the Council's policy and, in particular, focused upon whether questions of gender had played a part in their reasoning. He held that since the Council had not considered questions of gender their action could not amount to discrimination. This approach also encompasses the situation where the alleged discriminator does not wish to discriminate – the motive is absent – but the method of making the decision in the prevailing circumstances makes the discrimination inevitable. It also focuses upon the decision-making process as well as its effect and is, perhaps, a better way of promoting equality of opportunity in the longer term because it is more likely to lead to an improvement in decision-making mechanisms and underlying institutional discriminations.[14] This approach may be seen as consistent with that of the US Supreme Court in *City of Cleburne Texas v Cleburne Living Center*.[15]

The relative merits of the 'effects' and 'reason'-centred approaches are discussed by a number of our contributors. The emphasis given to the different approaches may vary according to whether direct or indirect discrimination is the issue in case.

In direct discrimination cases judicial policy seems firmly established and is rooted in examining the effects of the practice. In matters of indirect discrimination the situation is altogether less certain. The Employment Appeal Tribunal held in *Bhudi v IMI Refiners Ltd*[16] that, in order for the presumption of unlawful discrimination to be raised the

---

[11] [1981] ICR 864.
[12] [1990] 3 WLR 55; [1990] IRLR 288.
[13] See para 39 of the report in IRLR.
[14] Christopher McCrudden 'Institutional Discrimination' (1982) 20 JLS 303.
[15] (1985) 473 US 432, 105 S Ct 3249, 87 L Ed 2d 313.
[16] [1994] IRLR 404.

putative discriminator must have applied some requirement or condition having a disparate and adverse impact upon an identified group. This gives weight to the reasoning behind the alleged discriminator's decision rather than relying exclusively upon an analysis of the effect. This follows the line of the US Supreme Court in *Atonio v Wards Cove Fish Packing Co*[17] rather than the European Court of Justice in the equal pay case of *Enderby v Frenchay Health Authority*,[18] and seems to be a move in the direction of the third approach outlined above.

JUSTIFICATION

The symposium at which these papers were originally presented was entitled 'Justifying Discrimination'. It is, therefore, not surprising that the concept of justification is a major concern in a number of the essays published in this book. Not only is the operation of the justification rule considered in depth, but also several of the authors consider whether justification is a defence which obviates redress or makes the original decision lawful. The fundamental concept of justification may be illustrated by the *Panesar* case. The use of a facially neutral rule[19] in *Panesar v Nestlé Co Ltd*,[20] where the respondent employer forbade the wearing of beards in a chocolate factory. The application of this rule acted so as to prevent the employment of certain ethnic[21] groups to whom the wearing of beards formed part of their ethnic identity. This amounted to, *prima facie*, unlawful discrimination and, examined from an 'effects' viewpoint it is discrimination based upon race or ethnic origin. However, the judgment in *Panesar* makes it plain that the rule, and the resulting employment practice, may be legally justified where the employer demonstrates that the rule is necessary for some reason and is untainted by discrimination.[22] The process of justification makes that which seems to have an unfair effect, and hence is unlawful, into a fair and lawful practice by an exposure and examination of the reasoning behind the practice.

THE CONTRIBUTIONS

The book falls into three sections. First, a number of papers deal with the foundational and conceptual issues. The second part is concerned with discrimination as it affects selected groups in society as a whole.

---

[17] 490 US 642, 104 L Ed 2d 733.
[18] [1993] IRLR 591.
[19] No pun intended, see, for the origin of this term, the judgment of Burger CJ in *Griggs v Duke Power Company* 401 US 424 (S Ct 1971).
[20] [1980] ICR 144.
[21] See *Mandla v Dowell-Lee* [1983] 2 AC 548.
[22] See s 1(1)(b)(ii) of both the Sex Discrimination Act 1975 and the Race Relations Act 1976 for the legislative provision and eg the *Panesar* case for its application.

In the third part, discrimination as it occurs in specialised fields or sectors is examined, eg the police service. The intention of this section is to illuminate the ways in which particular institutions cope, or fail to cope, with discrimination and to see what broader lessons may be gleaned from them.

The discussion of whether a reason-centred or an effect-centred approach by the courts is most appropriate is carried further by Evelyn Ellis in the first of the papers contained in this book. She concludes that the robust purposive, teleological or to use the terminology adopted here – effect-centred – approach adopted by the European Court of Justice, and indeed by the British courts in direct discrimination cases, is more effective in promoting equality of opportunity. Her analysis of the case reveals that the courts view the defence of 'justification' not as an exculpatory factor making a *prima facie* act of discrimination legally acceptable, but as a factor wholly removing the act in question, its damaging effects, and its disparate impact from the sphere of discrimination.

Pauline Matthews continues the investigation commenced in the previous paper. However, she shifts the focus to a consideration of the extent to which discrimination, upon the grounds of gender, is acceptable in society. She begins her paper by questioning the Genuine Occupational Qualification (GOQ) provisions of the Sex Discrimination Act 1975[23] which allow discrimination in certain situations. She examines whether some of these discriminatory provisions do, in fact, amount to genuine qualifications for the job.

On the other hand she asks whether social practices which have grown up in the provision of single-sex services, such as taxi services run exclusively by and for women, and which are of dubious legality, ought not to attract legal protection in the light of rising levels of violent crime against women. To place this in terms which may be suggested by Raz's second principle,[24] the restriction of males' occurrent autonomy (the refusal to allow males to use particular taxi-cabs) may be justified by the countervailing benefits to the dispositional autonomy of females. The latter may now be able to plan evening activities and commitments secure in the knowledge that their safety in travelling is assured.

The contributions from Colin Bourn, Nicholas Bamforth and Nicolas Bernard each draw comparisons between different forms of discrimination, and focus upon the differing considerations of public policy which underlie the various forms of discrimination, while Catherine Barnard seeks to expand the scope of the notion of non-discrimination which lies behind gender discrimination into other areas.

Catherine Barnard argues that the main European Union Treaty provisions are underpinned by the notion of 'non-discrimination'. Although this is particularly clear in the context of Art 1119, she argues that this notion

---

[23] Contained in s 7 of the Act, see also the equivalent provisions in s 5 of the Race Relations Act 1976.

[24] See above p 5 and n9.

should be attached to all the other main Treaty provisions – which are couched in the 'obscure jargon' of 'distinctly and indistinctly applicable measures', 'mandatory requirements' and 'public interest requirements'.

Colin Bourn shows how the provisions of discrimination law attempt to draw a balance between the economic interests of employers and society in general, on the one hand, and, upon the other, individuals whose rights are under threat and the social groups from which these individuals come. Bourn views discrimination law as a tool for the use of disadvantaged groups to protect and advance their claims for fair participation in society. These claims to participate may have economic disbenefits to other groups, not because they directly challenge their dominance, but because of the costs of implementation of fair participation procedures. He views the concept of justification with suspicion. He sees it as a means by which certain economic interests, those of employers which are currently in the ascendant, may defeat legal provisions designed to protect and advance the claims of disadvantaged groups.

Nicolas Bernard doubts that the 'anti-discrimination principle' can be recognised as a unitary principle. While he agrees with Bourn that the political principle underlying the European legislation outlawing discrimination on the grounds of gender is the promotion of equal participation in society for women and men, he argues that other policies come to the fore in other fields. He considers that, in the judicial control of economic policy making, the courts are far more concerned in ensuring the effectiveness of Community policy rather than to promote the fair treatment of particular economic actors. Discrimination law in this field seems to focus upon equality of opportunity to compete in the market irrespective of the starting point of the actors. When Nicolas Bernard looks at discrimination on the grounds of nationality within the European Union, he discerns an integrationalist policy – the forging of an ideal of European citizenship. It is possible to argue, if one accepts the premises of his contribution that the anti-discrimination principle has three facets: fair competition, equality of starting point, and integration.

The last of these raises a number of problems which are addressed in this book. A distinction has been made between assimilationist and pluralist theories of anti-discrimination law.[25] Stated briefly, an assimilationist argues that the purposes of anti-discrimination law include a commitment to assimilating all the parties in a polity to a common outcome, while a pluralist recognises that there may be a number of different, but fundamentally equal outcomes or positions arising from the operation of anti-discrimination law. (Ryszard Cholewinski's paper addresses this issue later in the book.[26])

Nicolas Bamforth looks at a more fundamental point – whether we should consider a person's membership of an identifiable group as essential to

---

[25] For discussion of this distinction see O'Donovan and Szyszczak 'Equality and Sex Discrimination Law'.
[26] See pp 134–149.

discrimination law, by way of examining whether any single continuous principle can serve to justify anti-discrimination law. He observes that John Gardner suggests that the purpose of laws prohibiting direct discrimination is to 'foster a public culture which enables people to take pride in their identity as members of . . . groups',[27] and the harm which is done to a person's autonomy by discrimination is preventing them from taking pride in group membership. Bamforth questions whether this is the specific harm done to victims of discrimination, because there may well be those who had, 'prior to the (discriminatory) act itself, no sense of identity attaching to their (eg) gender or race, and that the hurt inherent in the act was being made aware that others ascribed a derogatory identity to them because of their sex or racial origins'. He asserts that objectification of a person by identifying them as a member of a despised group is the harm done by direct discrimination, while indirect discrimination – in his view – is the denial to them of the opportunity of consideration as a person with their own merits.[28]

Sheldon Leader and Steve Anderman conclude this section of the book by considering the means by which a discriminatory practice can be said to be 'justified'. Anderman considers the factors which the courts will accept as objectively justifying discrimination, and discusses the relationship between various courts which will determine this question. The second stage test of proportionality forms the basis for Sheldon Leader's analysis. The contested ground is between 'a *prima facie* discriminatory practice can be said to be justified when it is reasonable' and 'a *prima facie* discriminatory practice can be said to be justified when the harm done by the practice is less than the good achieved by permitting the practice'. Our authors explore this ground. These essays can be seen as providing a link between a number of the contributions in the book and should be read in conjunction with those from Evelyn Ellis, Pauline Matthews, and Christopher McCrudden.

In the second part of the book we turn to a consideration of the impact of discrimination upon specific groups in society. We turn also to arguably different meanings of 'discrimination' and 'justification'. Two of the papers (those by Ryszard Cholewinski and Geoff Gilbert) advance the view that specially advantageous treatment is, or should be, directed towards disadvantaged groups. That such treatment is, in its way, discriminatory cannot seriously be doubted.[29] However, both authors argue that not only are there justifications for positive discrimination, but also that it has a legal basis, and that there is evidence that such measures are being undertaken.

The second part of the book commences with Brian Wilkinson's examination of the extent to which member states may legally discriminate against the nationals of other member states when they seek to exercise their rights of free movement under Art 48 of the Treaty of Rome. He concludes

[27] Citing Gardner 'Liberals and Unlawful Discrimination' (1989) 9 OJLS 1 at 18–19.

[28] Bob Watt's contribution in Chapter 13 below continues the discussion of this particular theme.

[29] See the dissenting judgments of Burger CJ and Rehnquist J in *United Steelworkers of America AFC-CIO-CLC v Brian F Weber* (1979) 61 L Ed 2d.

that the European Court of Justice gives priority to the policy of European integration and the forging of European citizenship over the concerns expressed by the governments of member states over national sovereignty and the maintenance of a public service staffed by nationals.

Cholewinski argues for the adoption of legal measures promoting the integration of non-EC national immigrant workers into the fabric of the societies of member states. He argues for a conception of integration based upon a mode of participation in society essentially consistent with that proposed by Joseph Raz.[30] The contrast between notions of integration and assimilation is sharply made in this paper, together with arguments for a strong notion of European citizenship and for Community action.

Geoff Gilbert's contribution examines how the position of national minorities has been enhanced under the European Convention on Human Rights and Fundamental Freedoms. There is no positive Convention provision guaranteeing minority rights, there exists only the right to be free from discrimination on the ground of association with a national minority when exercising rights otherwise guaranteed under the Convention. The right to non-discrimination is contained in Art 14. Gilbert argues, however, that in deciding cases both under Art 14 and under other substantive Articles that the Court has, with little evidence of jurisprudential contortion, both succeeded in protecting minority groups from discrimination, and in promoting their identity and standing. He suggests that in deciding that differences between groups should be recognised, the court has given protection to the customs and cultural identity of the minority group. Furthermore, he identifies situations in which the Court has gone further and permitted states to favour minority groups and to promote democratic participation, even where this apparently discriminates against the majority. Gilbert continues that since both the court and the Commission have been prepared to hold that a national minority's culture may be protected within the meaning of Art 8 (which secures for citizens the right to respect for their private and family life) discrimination in favour of national minorities has been used creatively in order to guarantee minority rights, even in the absence of an express provision.

In the first section of the book Nicholas Bamforth[31] makes it plain that there are those who may well feel aggrieved at being identified as members of a group. Clearly those who are seropositive for the human immuno-deficiency virus (HIV) can derive little that is positive or pleasing from their group identity, and it is clear that those who are seropositive are widely stigmatised and despised. Bob Watt makes an argument against group membership as a basis for ascribing rights against discrimination, and with reference to US cases, argues instead for certain activities – such as dentistry or obstetric surgery – to be closed to those who exhibit seropositivity. This amounts to a process whereby direct discrimination against seroconverts may be justified in a small, though significant, number of situations. Watt

[30] Above p 5.
[31] See p 49.

also argues that in the vast majority of situations the fact that a person is, or is not, seropositive for the HIV is irrelevant. In the course of his paper he identifies one particular case where seropositivity, and the experience of seropositivity, could be used to the immediate advantage of the individual.

In the third part of the book the discussion turns to consider the impact of discrimination within specific sections of society. (This contrasts with the second section where the focus was upon discrimination within society as a whole.) The reason for the separation is that the second part of the book deals with the problems faced by identifiable groups within society as a whole, while here we look at the problems faced by majorities – for example, 51 per cent of the British population is female – when they engage with identifiable segments of society or the economy.

First, Christopher McCrudden's paper contains a detailed analysis of the economic costs of providing equality between men and women in social security provision. It is a truism that the *Barber* case[32] and the cases following[33] have not only caused difficulties for the court, but also for academics, policy makers and the providers of pension funds. These issues were debated at a conference in Oxford early in 1994 and we are grateful to Messrs Butterworths for allowing us to reprint part of Christopher McCrudden's contribution to that debate.[34] His paper considers the extent to which the costs of implementing equal provisions between women and men should be taken into account when fixing the boundaries of the right to equal treatment. He concludes that while budgetary considerations alone do not, and should not be permitted to, allow unequal treatment; that costs of implementation must be taken into account.

Gwyneth Pitt's contribution explores the acceptability and utility of one of the very few instances of positive discrimination which is lawful under British law – the Genuine Occupational Qualification (GOQ) – contained in the Sex Discrimination Act 1975, s 7 and the Race Relations Act 1976. She discusses whether the use of the 'authenticity in dramatic performances'[35] provisions is truly justified in the theatre. She argues that, if patrons are required to suspend their belief to such an extent that they find themselves in, say, a South Vietnamese brothel rather than in a theatre, why is a Eurasian man needed 'for reasons of authenticity' to play the part of the pimp?

While Pitt's piece centres upon the theatre it is clear that the GOQ provisions affect much wider situations, and we suggest that a very valuable debate has been opened by her article. The police service is a good example of a 'society within a society' having, as Roger Graef has shown,[36] a particular

---

[32] Case C-262/88 *Barber v Guardian Royal Exchange Assurance Group Ltd* [1990] ECR I-1889.
[33] Cases C-109/91 *Ten Oever v Stichting Bednifspensioenfonds voor het Glazenwassers-en Schoonmaakbednif* [1993] IRLR 601; C-132/92 *Birds Eye Walls v Roberts* [1994] IRLR 29; C-152/91 *Neath v Hugh Steeper Ltd* [1994] IRLR 91; and C-110/91 *Moroni v Firma Collo GmbH* [1994] IRLR 130 to say nothing of the *Coloroll* case C-200/91.
[34] *Equality of treatment between women and men in social security* (Butterworth, London 1994).
[35] See Sex Discrimination Act s 7(2)(a), Race Relations Act s 5(2)(a).
[36] See Roger Graef, *Talking Blues* (Collins Harvill, London 1989).

culture of its own, generally known as the 'canteen culture'. Catherine Little considers the effects of the 'canteen culture' and the history of women's employment in the police as barriers to women's recruitment and promotion within the service. She concludes that, while there is a formal mechanism for eliminating discrimination within the service, there remain less formal institutional and cultural barriers to entry and promotion. Some of these barriers are produced by an abiding institutional perception of police work which are not in accordance with the realities of modern policing.

Peter Stone, in a timely and controversial piece, argues that the continuing extension of European equality legislation should continue into areas of social legislation which are, at least at first sight, unconnected with pay. He argues that the burdens of the Child Support Act 1991, which clearly fall most heavily upon men – as the majority of 'absent parents' – are incompatible with the provisions of European law.

Our final contribution, from Joanne Lunn, surveys the extent to which job applicants may be subjected to health checks by employers. This essay is especially important because the Disability Discrimination Bill 1995 will undoubtedly pass into law during the lifetime of this book, and her piece provides a useful survey of the barriers to employment which may be erected against those suffering from some form of disability.

2

GENDER DISCRIMINATION LAW IN THE EUROPEAN COMMUNITY[1]

Evelyn Ellis

OBJECTIVES OF ANTI-DISCRIMINATION LEGISLATION

Legislation outlawing discrimination, whether it be on the ground of sex, race, religion, political opinion or any other factor, is usually precipitated by a varied cocktail of political influences. However, its primary expressed purpose is always to redress perceived injustices or disadvantages being experienced by a particular group within a particular community. Certain sections of the population, for example, women, ethnic minorities, or Catholics, become identified as participating to a disproportionately and unfairly small degree in such areas as employment and educational opportunities. The legislature furthermore generally appreciates that such deprivation inevitably leads to these sections of the community becoming underprivileged in terms of wealth and overall status, and sometimes also, as in Northern Ireland in recent times, to political protest and violence. So, for instance, in the White Paper 'Equality for Women', which preceded the United Kingdom Sex Discrimination Act of 1975, the government explained that:

> 'The status of women in society, the disabilities and disadvantages imposed on women, and their consequences, are social questions. They are legitimate subjects of the public interest and are appropriate matters for government action.'[2]

Similarly, in the European Community context, the preambles to the equality directives,[3] the statements of the Council and the Commission, and the remarks of the Court of Justice all frequently reveal a perception of women as at least an *economic* underclass; and they, therefore, emphasise the importance of the objective of raising the standard of treatment received by women in the workplace and in vocational training, so as ultimately to give them equality of employment opportunity with men.

---

[1] I am indebted to my colleague, Professor David Feldman, who read an earlier draft of this article and offered many valuable comments on it.

[2] Cmnd 5724 (1974), para 3.

[3] These are: the Equal Pay Directive, Directive 75/117, [1975] OJ L45/19; the Equal Treatment Directive, Directive 76/207, [1976] OJ L39/40; the Social Security Directive, Directive 79/7, [1979] OJ L6.24; the Occupational Social Security Directive, Directive 86/378, [1986] OJ L225/40; the Self-Employed Persons Directive, Directive 86/613, [1986] OJ L359/56.

All sorts of explanations can be advanced for differing success levels in different groups of people. However, before enacting the sex, race, and religious and political anti-discrimination legislation of the mid-1970s, the United Kingdom legislature seems to have been particularly convinced by two specific explanations. The first, and less palatable, notion was that there was active prejudice in operation against these disadvantaged sections of society. The second, and more subtle, was that discrimination had become 'institutionalised' in certain sectors, so that traditional and unquestioned practices were having the effect of unnecessarily and unfairly excluding equality of opportunity. Probably the most graphic and now the most famous articulation of this latter principle is to be found in the judgment of Chief Justice Burger in the United States Supreme Court in *Griggs v Duke Power Company*, where he said:

> 'Congress has now provided that tests or criteria for employment or promotion may not provide equality of opportunity merely in the sense of the fabled offer of milk to the stork and the fox. On the contrary, Congress has now required that the posture and condition of the job-seeker be taken into account. It has – to resort again to the fable – provided that the vessel in which the milk is proffered be one all seekers can use. The [United States] Act proscribes not only overt discrimination but also practices that are fair in form, but discriminatory in operation.'[4]

Three vital deductions follow from such an understanding of the origins of anti-discrimination laws. The first is that the anti-discrimination laws were created as devices for the relief of disadvantage; it was not intended to be in any sense criminal or punitive in nature. The logic underlying it is the compensation for the victims of the prior system and, by doing so, the deterrence of others in the future from repeating the injustices of the past. Thus, however this may become disguised as a result of technical legal definition and judicial interpretation, it is at the very heart of the notion of discrimination that it is the *effect* on its victims with which the law is truly concerned, not the precise nature of the conduct of its perpetrators.

The second deduction is that the legislation has to recognise two different situations in which discrimination can occur; this has been reflected by the law's general acceptance of the twin concepts of direct and indirect discrimination, an acceptance made both by domestic systems and by the European Community system. Thirdly, however, it has to be concluded that these concepts are indeed twins, in other words that they are very closely related and have both sprung from identical roots.[5] Their underlying rationale is the same and this means that they must both consist essentially of the same two elements: some sort of adverse impact on their victims and a prohibited classification underlying that impact. Adverse impact and causation, at least

---

[4] 401 US 424, (1971) at p 431.
[5] For a recent articulation of this principle, see the opinion of Lenz A-G in Case C-127/92, *Enderby v Frenchay Health Authority and the Secretary of State for Health* [1993] ECR I-5535; [1994] 1 CMLR 8.

in a broad, non-technical sense, must, as a matter of basic logic, be the constituent elements which underpin all systems of anti-discrimination law. The question then becomes whether the definition of discrimination provided by a particular system of law, and thereupon applied by the relevant group of judges, adequately recognises this logic. This is the question which the present chapter seeks to address in the European Community context.

DIRECT DISCRIMINATION

Taking United Kingdom legislation in this area first, direct discrimination is specifically defined by s 1(1)(a) of the Sex Discrimination Act 1975:

> 'A person discriminates against a women in any circumstances relevant for the purposes of any provision of this Act if on the ground of her sex he treats her less favourably than he treats or would treat a man'.[6]

For the purposes of European Community law, direct discrimination is referred to but not defined by the secondary instruments on equality. The Court of Justice itself has also developed the notion that Art 119 on equal pay is to be interpreted as forbidding both direct and indirect discrimination.[7] Does direct discrimination mean the same thing in both systems, or can it be said that European law has approached this matter in a more effective fashion than United Kingdom law? In order to examine this issue fully, the two constitutive elements of discrimination, namely causation and adverse impact, must be looked at separately.

Causation

As regards causation, although the Court of Justice and the United Kingdom courts appear to have taken a similar approach, the Court of Justice has pursued the issue somewhat further in analytical terms. What sometimes leads to confusion in cases of direct discrimination is the fact that the clearest instance of its occurrence is provided where the perpetrator makes plain an intention to disfavour the victim, in other words, the case of intentional direct discrimination. The temptation here is to extrapolate from the malign motive and to conclude that it is this element which renders the conduct offensive. This, however, is to fall into the trap of analysing discrimination as quasi-criminal in nature rather than treating the notion as essentially remedial in character. An intention to disfavour the victim simply helps to prove the case. It is *not* a necessary ingredient of the statutory tort. This has been becoming clearer with the development of case law, both United Kingdom and European Community, on the subject. The Court of Appeal

---

[6] The Act applies *mutatis mutandis* to discrimination against men: s 2(1).
[7] The starting-point of this development came in Case 96/80, *Jenkins v Kingsgate (Clothing Productions) Ltd* [1981] ECR 911; [1981] 2 CMLR 24.

explained in *R v CRE ex parte Westminster City Council*[8] and the House of Lords in *R v Birmingham City Council ex parte the Equal Opportunities Commission*[9] that a motive or desire to injure persons on the ground of their membership of a particular group was not essential for direct discrimination. However, it was not until, *James v Eastleigh Borough Council*[10] that the difficult boundary between intention and causation was fully explored by the United Kingdom courts. The issue is: can it ever be said that action is *grounded* upon sex or race, where the actor has never consciously taken that factor into account? Mr James, who was 61, had been charged 75p for entry to a Council swimming-pool; his wife, who was the same age, had not, because the Council's policy was to grant entry free of charge to anybody who had reached state pensionable age. Mr James argued that he had been discriminated against on the ground of his sex contrary to s 29 of the Sex Discrimination Act and the House of Lords, by a majority, agreed. There was no suggestion that the Council's motives were other than benign; they had merely sought to benefit persons on low incomes. However, they had chosen as their criterion the state pensionable age, which itself discriminates between the sexes over the age of entitlement. Lord Bridge explained that the expression 'pensionable age' is no more than a 'convenient short-hand expression which refers to the age of 60 in a woman and to the age of 65 in a man.'[11] He said that, in considering whether there has been discrimination against a man on the ground of his sex, it cannot possibly make any difference whether one uses the shorthand expression or spells out its full meaning. And the House of Lords went on to hold that the test for causation in this area of the law is an objective one: would the complainant have received the same treatment as his wife *but for* his sex? If the answer is yes, as Lord Bridge put it, 'the purity of the discriminator's subjective motive, intention or reason for discriminating cannot save the criterion applied from the objective taint of discrimination on the ground of sex'.[12]

The Court of Justice seems to have arrived at a similar conclusion to the United Kingdom courts in *Dekker v Stichting Vormingscentrum Voor Jonge Volwassen Plus*.[13] *Dekker* concerned a refusal to employ a pregnant woman who would otherwise have been appointed to a job of training instructor in a youth centre. The employers explained that, as Ms Dekker was already pregnant when she applied for the job, the employer's insurers would not reimburse the sickness benefits paid to Ms Dekker during her maternity leave. It would, therefore, be impossible for the employers to employ a replacement during Ms Dekker's absence, which would mean in the end that they would lose some of their training places. The first question which the Court of Justice had to answer was whether this situation amounted to

8 [1985] ICR 827.
9 [1989] AC 1155.
10 [1990] 3 WLR 55.
11 *Ibid*, at p 60.
12 *Ibid*, at p 62.
13 Case 177/88, [1990] ECR I-3941; see also Shaw (1991) 16 ELRev 313.

direct sex discrimination. They held that this depended on whether the most important reason for the refusal to recruit Ms Dekker was a reason which applied exclusively to one sex. Since employment can only be refused because of pregnancy to a woman, such a refusal, the court held, *must* be direct discrimination on the ground of sex. And a refusal to employ because of the financial consequences of pregnancy must be deemed to be based principally on the fact of the pregnancy. In other words, the Court was saying that, *but for* Ms Dekker's sex, she would have been appointed, so that her adverse treatment must be grounded on her sex; there was no need to prove any subjective consideration of Ms Dekker's sex on the part of the employers. The Court of Justice's conclusion here thus seems to be substantially the same in theory as that of the House of Lords in the *James* case.[14]

However, the Court of Justice added a further point in *Dekker*, which indicates its fundamental grasp of what the law in this area is seeking to achieve. It had been urged to hold that the employers could escape liability if they could establish a 'legal justification' for their action. This it refused to do, saying that the only defences to unlawful sex discrimination were those contained in Art 2 of the Equal Treatment Directive. It is highly significant that the Court did not allow itself to be muddled by the introduction of a notion of justification into *direct* discrimination[15] (as distinct from *indirect* discrimination where, as will be explained below, it plays a vital role in relation to causation). In effect, it took a very clear-sighted view of direct discrimination, accepting that Ms Dekker would win her case if she could show simply that she had suffered detrimental treatment and that that treatment was grounded on her sex; if the employers could not rely on one of the listed defences, that was the end of the matter for them. Once causation had been established, the discrimination could only be excused for one of the specific reasons articulated by the directive. Looking at this from a different angle, the Court is focusing here on the *effect* of the impugned treatment, rather than being diverted by subjective inquiries into *why* the employers behaved as they did. The important thing which the court keeps uppermost in its mind is the *remedial* function of the anti-discrimination law, and it is not thrown off course by arguments about culpability which would be appropriate in a criminal law context.

[14] However, the practical application of the principle enunciated both by the Court of Justice and the House of Lords will vary, depending on the level of abstraction focused on by the court in question. This, of course, is a problem inherent in the nature of all law, but it can lead to difficult distinctions in practice. Thus, in Case 179/88, *Handels-OG Kontorfunktionaerernes Forbund I Danmark (acting for Hertz) v Dansk Arbegdgsgiverforening (acting for Aldi Marked K/S)* [1990] ECR I-3979, the Court of Justice differentiated between a decision taken on the ground of pregnancy (unlawful discrimination) and a decision taken on the ground of an illness which was a consequence of an earlier pregnancy (not unlawful discrimination). At one level of abstraction, a 'pregnancy-related illness' can be said to be something from which a person cannot suffer *but for* her female sex; at another level of abstraction, it can be said that 'illness' can be suffered alike by either sex.

[15] Described as a 'dangerous heresy' by Hepple in 'Can Direct Discrimination be Justified?' (1994) 55 EOR 48, but see Watt in Chapter 13.

Similar sensitivity, though arguably with less satisfactory results, was shown by the court in *Birds Eye Walls Ltd v Roberts*[16] and in *Neath v Hugh Steeper Ltd;*[17] there both the Commission and Van Gerven AG urged it to accept the argument that direct discrimination could be justified.[18] In *Roberts*, Ms Roberts had retired early because of ill health and complained that the 'top-up' payments she received from her ex-employer's occupational scheme discriminated unlawfully against her on the ground of sex, since they were diminished by the amount of state pension receivable by her between the ages of 60 and 65; had she been a man of the same age, she would not yet have become eligible to a state pension and thus no deduction would have been made from the 'top-up' payments. Advocate-General Van Gervern argued that the discrimination here was justified because the employer's actions were 'designed to ensure' ultimate equality of take-home pay as between the sexes. This, it is submitted, is to fall into the double trap of not realising that, once causation has been demonstrated, the defendant's only way out is to rely on a substantive defence to discrimination and also of suggesting that justification is a subjective rather than an objective concept.[19] The court, perhaps uncomfortable with the results dictated by state pension legislation which actively perpetuates sex discrimination over pensionable age, escaped its consequences by holding that Ms Roberts's situation was not identical to that of her male comparator and that there was thus no discrimination at all:

> '[A]lthough until the age of 60 the financial position of a woman taking early retirement on grounds of ill health is comparable to that of a man in the same situation, neither of them as yet entitled to payment of the state pension, that is no longer the case between the ages of 60 and 65 since that is when women, unlike men, start drawing their pension. That difference as regards the objective premise, which necessarily entails that the amount of the bridging pension is not the same for men and women, cannot be considered discriminatory.'[20]

In the view of the present writer, such an analysis can be criticised on the basis that two wrongs do not make a right: Ms Roberts did not receive as large a 'top-up' payment as her male comparator *because of her sex* and she was thus the victim of direct sex discrimination. That this could occur was entirely attributable to the United Kingdom's state pension legislation and

---

[16] Case C-132/92, [1993] 3 CMLR 822; [1994] IRLR 29.

[17] Case C-152/91, [1994] 1 All ER 929.

[18] See also the view of Lenz AG in *Enderby v Frenchay Health Authority and the Secretary of State for Health*, n 5.

[19] As to which, see discussion below.

[20] [1994] IRLR 29. at p 32. Notice also the Court of Justice's remarks in Case C-421/92, *Habermann-Beltermann v Arbeiterwohlfahrt, Bezirksverband Ndb./Opf eV* [1994] 2 CMLR 729, in which it discussed the possible 'justification' of the dismissal of a pregnant woman night-worker; it explained that in this case, unlike the position in *Dekker*, the unequal treatment was not based *directly* on the woman's pregnancy but was an *indirect* consequence of it since national legislation imposed a ban on night-time working during pregnancy. See also the court's judgment in Case C-32/93, *Webb v EMO Air Cargo (UK) Ltd* [1994] 3 WLR 941, discussed below.

the discrimination contained therein should not be 'cured' by an artificial factual distinction intended to obscure causation. However, in being prepared to make such a distinction in an attempt to produce justice in the case, the Court of Justice showed its real dislike of the argument that direct discrimination can be justified; it would have been relatively simple to accept the Advocate-General's submissions here and, in looking for its own route out of the difficulty it perceived in this case, the Court once again demonstrated firmly that it was not prepared to follow such a line.[21]

Adverse impact

Turning to the other element of direct discrimination, adverse impact, all the United Kingdom anti-discrimination legislation defines this in terms of *comparison*. The Equal Pay Act requires the complainant to be able to produce an actual comparator, a person of the opposite sex, placed in similar circumstances (as defined by the Act), who is receiving better contractual terms than the complainant. The Sex Discrimination Act is broader and allows comparison with the treatment which a member of the opposite sex either *is* receiving or *would* receive, the so-called 'hypothetical comparator'. In both situations, however, it is not merely adverse treatment which is outlawed; it is treatment which is more adverse than a member of the opposite sex is receiving or would receive.

Difficulties have nevertheless arisen in United Kingdom domestic law from the restrictions placed by our legislation on the nature of the comparison which can be carried out for this purpose. The Sex Discrimination Act provides in s 5(3): 'A comparison of the cases of persons of different sex . . . must be such that the relevant circumstances in the one case are the same, or not materially different, in the other.' The critical word is 'relevant'; what circumstances are relevant for the purposes of such a comparison? If too much detail is required for the comparison, the spirit and purposes of the legislation will be undermined because comparison will become impossible. Courts have expressed differing views in this area over the years. The low-water mark came in *Turley v Allders Department Stores*,[22] where a woman was dismissed on account of pregnancy and sought to prove that this constituted unlawful direct discrimination. The majority of the Employment Appeal Tribunal held that it did not because no comparison could be envisaged with the treatment a man might have received. In the now-immortal words of Bristow J, 'When she is pregnant a woman is no longer just a woman. She is a woman, as the Authorised Version accurately put it, with child, and

---

[21] It should, however, be noted that the Court of Justice has not been wholly consistent in its approach to this issue. In the *Webb* case (*op cit* n 20) it said that 'termination of a contract for an indefinite period on grounds of the woman's pregnancy cannot be justified by the fact that she is prevented, on a purely temporary basis, from performing the work for which she has been engaged' (at p 40), thus suggesting that such termination of a fixed-term contract *might* be justifiable.

[22] [1980] IRLR 4.

there is no masculine equivalent'.[23] The woman wing-member 'of the Tribunal sharply disagreed, pointing out that the relevant thing for the purposes of this comparison was that the pregnant woman would require time off work to have her baby and that a comparison could, therefore, be made with a man who similarly required time off work for a minor medical reason. The Employment Appeal Tribunal subsequently endorsed that dissenting view,[24] but further complications arose as a consequence of the decision of the Court of Justice in *Dekker*.

After holding in *Dekker* that, where a person receives adverse treatment for a reason which can only apply to one sex, that treatment must necessarily constitute direct sex discrimination, the Court of Justice went on to say that it did not matter for this purpose that no men had applied for the job in question, so that no comparison could actually be made. This statement was interpreted as meaning that no comparative element is required at all under European Community sex discrimination law, a conclusion which has seemingly since been upheld by the Court of Justice in *Webb v EMO Air Cargo Ltd*.[25] This latter case concerned the dismissal on account of pregnancy of a woman employed on an indefinite basis but taken on specifically to cover for another employee who was going on maternity leave. The evidence presented revealed that the employers dismissed Ms Webb because she would be absent from work for substantially the same period of time as the woman whose services she was supposed to be going to replace. The case was referred by the House of Lords to the Court of Justice, after the House had held that this was not unlawful direct discrimination under United Kingdom law because the dismissal was not on account of pregnancy but on account of its consequences.[26] Since a man in comparable circumstances would have been treated similarly, there was no unlawful discrimination. The reference sought to determine whether this situation amounted to direct discrimination under European Community law.[27]

The Court of Justice held that it did. It began by reiterating its earlier rulings that the dismissal of a female worker on account of pregnancy constitutes direct discrimination on grounds of sex, and emphasised the importance attributed by the Community legislature to protection of the health of pregnant women. It went on to hold:

'there can be no question of comparing the situation of a woman who finds herself incapable, by reason of pregnancy discovered very shortly after the conclusion of the employment contract, of performing the task for which she was

[23] *Ibid*, at p 5.
[24] *Hayes v Malleable Working Men's Institute* [1985] ICR 703.
[25] Case C-32/93, [1994] 3 WLR 941; [1944] 2 CMLR 729; [1990] ICR 442 (Employment Appeal Tribunal); [1992] ICR 445 (Court of Appeal); [1993] 1 WLR 49 (House of Lords); see also Arnull (1992) 17 EL Rev 265.
[26] This neatly illustrates the point made in n 14.
[27] The directive on health and safety in pregnancy (Directive 92/85, [1992] OJ L348/1) renders dismissals of pregnant employees generally illegal, but the *Webb* case nevertheless remains of interest because of the light which it sheds on the principles underlying direct discrimination which continue to apply to forms of pregnancy discrimination other than dismissal.

recrutited with that of a man similarly incapable for medical or other reasons . . . [P]regnancy is not in any way comparable with a pathological condition, and even less so with unavailability for work on non-medical grounds, both of which are situations that may justify the dismissal of a woman without discriminating on grounds of sex.'[28]

In the opinion of the present writer, although the Court of Justice's strenuous protection of pregnant women employees is to be welcomed, it is unfortunate from the point of view of the underlying components of Community anti-discrimination law that it analysed the position in the way it did in *Webb*. It is submitted that an element of comparability is important to the component of adverse impact; if direct discrimination is defined simply as 'nasty treatment' on the ground of sex, enormous discretion is placed in the hands of Courts and tribunals, who remain overwhelmingly male in composition, to decide what is to the detriment or advantage of complainants, the majority of whom are female. For reasons of objectivity, it is preferable if the adversity of the treatment received by the complainant is measured by means of a comparison with the treatment received or receivable by a member of the opposite sex, placed in broadly the same circumstances as the complainant.[29]

INDIRECT DISCRIMINATION

As discussed earlier, it seems logical to regard indirect discrimination as consisting of essentially the same two elements as direct discrimination, namely, adverse impact and causation. Admittedly, the two elements have to be presented somewhat differently in the context of indirect discrimination. Indirect discrimination, it must be recalled, was invented in order to cater for the situation of institutionalised discrimination, the situation where the way in which we order our society impacts adversely on a particular group of people. What the law must be aiming at catching, therefore, is behaviour (taking that word very loosely) which has a detrimental effect on a particular group of people and for which there is no other explanation than discrimination.

In the United Kingdom, domestic anti-discrimination law undoubtedly reflects these two elements, but unfortunately in a complicated and technical way. Section 1(1)(b) of the Sex Discrimination Act requires proof that a 'requirement or condition' has been imposed which a considerably smaller proportion of women can comply with than men and which is to the detriment of the woman complainant. This is the element of adverse impact (defined once again in comparative terms). The legislation also creates the concept of *justifiability*, requiring the defendant to explain away the adverse

---

[28] [1994] 3 WLR 941, at p 968.
[29] At the time of writing the final decision of the House of Lords in the *Webb* case has not been delivered.

impact on some non-discriminatory ground. In other words, presumably because of the defendant's peculiarly close relationship with what has been going on, the burden of proof is placed by United Kingdom legislation on the defendant to *disprove* causation; the law assumes the adverse impact to have been on the ground of sex,. where a greater number of women than men have been affected by it, *unless and until* the defendant can disprove this.

European Community legislation does not as yet define indirect discrimination, although the equality directives refer to its prohibition. A draft directive attempting to provide a definition was recently rejected by the member states,[30] so the actual definition of indirect discrimination for the purposes of European Community law remains the creation of the Court of Justice. This has had the enormous advantage that the over-technical aspects of the United Kingdom definition have not presented problems for Community law and that the Court of Justice has been able to proceed purposively, with an eye clearly on the objectives to be served by the law. This is evident when one examines the element of adversity.

Adverse impact

The United Kingdom courts have faced an insuperable obstacle in the words 'requirement or condition'. They have hitherto been driven to hold that, as a matter of United Kingdom law, the element of adverse treatment is only satisfied when the defendant has imposed a 'must' on the complainnant, a requirement which invariably has to be complied with, and not merely a preference or a practice.[31] As a matter of United Kingdom law, it is therefore not enough to show simply that the way things are organised within a particular enterprise works to the disadvantage of women; it is essential to be able to point to a particular hoop through which women are required to jump. This of course can be extremely difficult to identify, and to prove. European Community law is unencumbered by this technicality. It remains free to find adverse impact proved in whatever way seems appropriate in the circumstances. Admittedly, the Court of Justice has not yet devoted a great deal of attention to this matter; this is because the vast majority of indirect discrimination cases which have been presented to it have involved part-time workers. For this group, a requirement or condition in the United Kingdom sense is imposed, namely, the requirement or condition that they work full-time in order to receive better treatment. The issue of other detrimental situations has not yet often been clearly presented to the Court of Justice. However, it has several times expressed itself in quite broad terms nevertheless, demonstrating its sensitivity to the purposes intended to be achieved by the legislation and its intention not to be deflected from such

[30] COM (88) 269 final.
[31] *Perera v Civil Service Commission* [1983] ICR 428; *Meer v London Borough of Tower Hamlets* [1988] IRLR 399.

purposes by legal niceties. For example, in both *Bilka-Kaufhaus GmbH v Weber Von Hartz*[32] and *Handels-OG Kontorfunktionaererernes Forbund I Danmark v Dansk Arbejdsgiverforening (acting for Danfoss)*,[33] the Court referred to pay 'practices' which were illegal because they were indirectly discriminatory. Indeed, in *Danfoss*, the Court was satisfied simply with statistical evidence which created the suspicion that there was sex discrimination going on, accepting that because of the 'non-transparent' nature of the computation of pay in the organisation concerned there was really no way in which the women employees could discover *how* they were being prejudiced. The element of adversity thus being broadly satisfied, the Court was content to go straight to the issue of causation.

More recently, in the *Enderby* case,[34] the Court of Justice held that:

> '[W]hen a measure distinguishing between employees on the basis of their hours of work has in practice an adverse impact on substantially more members of one or other sex, that measure must be regarded as contrary to the objective pursued by Art 119 EC, unless the employer shows that it is based on objectively justified factors unrelated to any discrimination on grounds of sex.'[35]

It is strongly arguable that the Court did not intend this statement to be confined to the equal pay situation, but rather that it meant that, whenever and however a plaintiff establishes a '*prima facie*' case of sex discrimination, the burden shifts to the employer to prove that discrimination has not occurred. If this is correct, the United Kingdom's restrictive formulation of the circumstances in which indirect discrimination arises is contrary to Community law. Such a view was rejected by the Employment Appeal Tribunal in *Bhudi v IMI Refiners Ltd*,[36] but may yet be accepted by the higher courts.

Causation and justification

As far as causation or justifiability are concerned, the Court of Justice has been developing its jurisprudence ever since *Jenkins v Kingsgate (Clothing Productions) Ltd*.[37] It is quite clear that, just as United Kingdom anti-discrimination law places the burden of proving justification on the defendant, so does European Community law. The forward thrust of Community law in this area has concerned the *ways* in which justification can be established. This of course is absolutely vital to the utility of the law. If it is going to have the remedial effect intended for it, it must not allow employers the chance of exonerating their practices too easily. The law in practice must impose a rigid requirement on employers to examine exactly how and why their practices are essential for them; and, if they are not essential, then they should

---

[32] Case 170/84, [1986] ECR 1607.
[33] Case 109/88, [1989] ECR 3199; see also Shaw (1990) 15 EL Rev 260.
[34] Above, n 5.
[35] At p 161.
[36] [1994] IRLR 404.
[37] Case 96/80, [1981] ECR 911.

be forbidden because of their discriminatory effect. The nub of the matter is, after all, to show that the *root* of the practice is not discrimination; at base, there is another and non-objectionable reason for the behaviour in question.

Although the United Kingdom courts began well enough in this field in the early sex discrimination cases, holding that justifiable really meant 'necessary',[38] they were thrown off course by the courts interpreting the identical provisions of the race relations legislation. The judges in race discrimination cases began to hold justification to be established on very frail grounds, in particular where the practice was acceptable to 'right-thinking' people.[39] They recoiled from saying that it had to be proved to be absolutely necessary. The Court of Justice, however, did not and in its famous decision in *Bilka-Kaufhaus*,[40] it held that the employer must demonstrate 'objectively justified factors which are unrelated to any discrimination based on sex'. It went on to explain that it would demand a high degree of proof for such justification:

'It falls to the national court', it said, 'which has sole jurisdiction to make findings of fact, to determine whether and to what extent the grounds put forward by an employer to explain the adoption of a pay practice which applies independently of a worker's sex, but in fact affects more women than men may be regarded as objectively justified [on] economic grounds. If the national court finds that the measures chosen by Bilka correspond to a real need on the part of the undertaking, are appropriate with a view to achieving the objectives pursued, and are necessary to that end, the fact that the measures affect a far greater number of women than men is not sufficient to show that they constitute an infringement of Art 119.'[41]

This sets up a formidable obstacle for an employer, although it does not address at all the difficult balance which has to be recognised between the commercial profitability of an organisation and the elimination of sex discrimination. The employer must prove a genuine need on the part of the enterprise for the discriminatory factor, that the means chosen are suitable for attaining the objective and that they are *necessary* for attaining that objective. In other words, if reasonable alternative means are open to the employer to achieve the objective, the defence is not made out. Nor, obviously, is it enough if the employer just points to his or her subjective beliefs or intentions. It is essential to be able to prove that the discriminatory factor really is the only way of achieving the permissible objective.[42]

The Court of Justice's decisions in this area since *Bilka-Kaufhaus* have developed the concept of justifiability in three separate but related ways, all of which contribute substantially towards furthering the effectiveness of the concept of indirect discrimination. These are:

[38] See in particular *Steel v Union of Post Office Workers* [1978] ICR 181.
[39] *Ojutika v Manpower Services Commission* [1980] IRLR 418.
[40] Case 170/84, *Bilka-Kaufhaus GmbH v Weber Von Hartz* [1986] ECR 1607.
[41] Ibid, at p 1628.
[42] See the contribution by Sheldon Leader in Chapter 9.

(a) the actual bases on which justification will be held to be established;
(b) the extent to which the Court of Justice will be prepared to intervene; and
(c) the activities which are subject to the test of justification.

In *Rinner-Kuhn v FWW Spezial-Gebaudereinigung GmbH*[43] the issue was the legality as a matter of European Community law of German legislation governing the payment of sick pay, which excluded part-timers. After an extraordinarily ungenerous submission by Advocate-General Darmon, the Court of Justice held that the German legislation in question created two classes of employees, full-timers and part-timers. Since it was established that there were many fewer women than men in the full-time category, the Court concluded that the legislation contravened Art 119 on equal pay. It went on to hold that this would only be legitimate if it could be proved that the distinction between the two categories of employees was justified by objective factors unrelated to sex discrimination. The first point of interest to notice in this case is that it was *legislation* which was being challenged in the case, not the mere unilateral action of an employer. The Court made it quite clear, because of the principle of the primacy of European Community law, that national legislation is to be scrutinised according to the equality standard, as well as private action. This is extremely important in the United Kingdom, where employment legislation has traditionally distinguished between full-timers and part-timers.[44]

The Court in *Rinner-Kuhn* went on to deal with the kind of reasoning which it will accept as justificatory. The significance of this to the effectiveness of the notion of indirect discrimination lies not merely in the rigour of the test applied, but also in the fact of the Court of Justice being prepared to intervene at all. The question of whether justification is proved is a matter of fact and, therefore, for the *national* court in a preliminary ruling. However, the situation resembles that in relation to the determination of the limits of public policy for the purposes of the free movement of workers: although the matter is essentially one for national law, there are certain limits beyond which the European Court will not allow the national courts to stray. The European Court, therefore, exercises a supervisory jurisdiction.[45] It is thus prepared to state certain general principles for the guidance of the national court, and this it did in *Rinner-Kuhn*. The German government had argued that its legislation was justified because part-time workers are not as integrated in, or dependent on, the undertaking employing them as other workers. The Court of Justice was thoroughly dismissive of this argument, calling it a mere 'generalisation'. It went on to say that justification could only be established in circumstances such as these if the member state could

[43] Case 171/88, [1989] ECR 2743; [1993] 2 CMLR 932; see also Szyszczak (1990) 19 ILJ 114.
[44] The Equal Opportunities Commission successfully challenged the legality of various provision of the United Kingdom legislation in *R v Secretary of State for Employment, ex parte EOC* [1994] 2 WLR 409; [1993] 1 CMLR 915.
[45] See, for example, Case 41/74, *Van Duyn v Home Office* [1974] ECR 1337; [1975] 1 CMLR 1.

show that the means chosen met a necessary aim of its social policy and that they were suitable and requisite for attaining that aim.

Such justification was established by the Belgian government, to vindicate certain of its social security provisions. *Commission v Belgium*[46] was a prosecution of Belgium by the Commission for an alleged breach of the Social Security Directive.[47] As has been evident in earlier litigation,[48] the Court of Justice appears to be much more readily convinced that conduct is justified in the field of social security than in the field of employment.[49] In social security cases, the balance has to be struck between the principle of equality of opportunity between the sexes and the relief of poverty, and the latter frequently seems to win. It appears to be more difficult to establish justification where the competing consideration is the profitability of a commercial organisation, although the logic of this distinction has not been explored by the Court.[50]

Ruzius-Wilbrink v Bestuur van de Bedrijfsvereniging Voor Overheidsdiensten[51] concerned the Dutch social security system which discriminated against part-time workers in relation to disability allowances; in particular, it restricted the disability allowance receivable by part-timers to the amount previously earned by them, while other categories of people received a full minimum subsistence payment. The question was whether this was a form of indirect discrimination prohibited by the Social Security Directive. Once again, the issue was the applicability of national legislation, when judged against the European Community standard, and once again the Court showed itself prepared to take strict line on justifiability. It observed that the only reason put forward in the proceedings to justify the difference in treatment between part-time workers and other groups of people was that it would be unjust to grant them a disability allowance larger then the amount of their previous wages. However, the Court rejected this argument because it found that there were other groups, such as students, for whom this was also true. This is further evidence of the Court of Justice's willingness to look critically into a case presented to it and even to involve itself in the facts, in order to monitor the use to which justification is put.

In the *Danfoss* case,[52] the respondent employer tried to justify pay discrimination on the basis that incremental payments were made to its employees as a reward for what it called 'mobility', for vocational training and for seniority. The Court examined each separately. Mobility had a special meaning and did not merely cover a willingness to work at different

[46] Case C-229/89, [1991] ECR I-2205; [1993] 2 CMLR 403; see also Banks (1991) 20 ILJ 220.
[47] Directive 79/7, [1979] OJ L6/24.
[48] In particular, Case 30/85, *Teuling v Bedrijfsvereniging Voor de Chemische Industrie* [1987] ECR 52497.
[49] See the contribution by Steve Anderman in Chapter 8.
[50] For further discussion of this point, see Francis Herbert 'Social Security and Indirect Discrimination' in *Equality of Treatment Between Women and Men in Social Security* (Ed McCrudden, Butterworths, 1994).
[51] Case C-102/88, [1989] ECR 4311.
[52] Case 109/88, [1989] ECR 3199, also discussed above.

hours; it involved the employer making an overall assessment of the quality of the work carried out by the employees and took into account their zeal, initiative and amount of work done. The Court of Justice observed that there is an important distinction to be made according to whether mobility refers to the quality of work carried out by the employee or whether it means adaptability to different work schedules and the like. In the first place, meaning quality of work, the Court thought the criterion was totally gender-neutral so that, if it resulted in systematic unfairness to female workers, that could only be because the employer was operating it in an abusive manner. 'It is inconceivable', said the Court, 'that the quality of work done by women should be generally less good. The employer cannot therefore justify applying the criterion of mobility so understood where its application proves to work systematically to the disadvantage of women.'[53] If mobility meant adaptability, on the other hand, the Court thought that could work to the disadvantage of female employees because of their domestic commitments and it stated, therefore, that in this case it would only constitute acceptable justification if it could genuinely be shown to tbe of importance in the performance of the specific duties entrusted to the particular worker concerned. It said much the same about vocational training; in other words, that could provide justification if it could genuinely be shown in individual circumstances to enhance performance. However, in relation to seniority, it held somewhat weakly that seniority goes hand in hand with experience which generally places a worker in a better position to perform his or her duties. Thus, there is no need for the employer to produce specific evidence about the importance of seniority to particular jobs and its importance can simply be assumed. This does not make much sense because there must be many dull and repetitive jobs in which seniority might easily undermine performance. However, the court was probably afraid to go too far on this point in *Danfoss*, believing that it had gone quite far enough already and that it did not want to upset established collective bargaining arrangements.[54] In any event, as will be discussed below, it reconsidered the matter within a short time.

In *Kowalska v Freie und Hansestadt Hamburg*[55] the notion of indirect discrimination was applied to a collective agreement which disadvantaged part-time workers in relation to severance pay, This is yet another important practical development in the useful scope of the doctrine, since it provides a vehicle not merely for the avoidance of discriminatory provisions contained in collective agreements, but also for their replacement by non-discriminatory provisions.[56] However, on this occasion the Court of Justice was noticeably reticent about justification. It noted in its judgment that the City of

[53] Ibid, at p 3227.
[54] This view has been expressed in particular by the editors of the Equal Opportunities Review: see (1990) 29 EOR 41.
[55] Case C-33/89, [1990] ECR I-2591; see also Reiland (1991) 20 ILJ 79 and More (1991) 16 EL Rev 58.
[56] Cf. The Trade Union Reform and Employment Rights Act 1993, s 32.

Hamburg had argued that part-timers do not provide for their needs and those of their famililes exclusively out of income from their employment and, therefore, that employers have less responsibility towards them. This, one might be tempted to think, is precisely the type of generalisation which the court would find unacceptable, but instead it merely observed that it was up to the national Court to assess justification. It reverted to its old, more critical style however in *Nimz v Freie und Hansestadt Hamburg*.[57] Another allegation of indirect pay discrimination against part-timers contained in a German collective agreement, the employers argued that full-time workers were more valuable to them because they acquired job-related skills more quickly than part-timers. The Court of Justice replied:

> 'Such considerations, in so far as they are no more than generalisations about certain categories of workers, do not make it possible to identify criteria which are both objective and unrelated to any discrimination on grounds of sex ... Although experience goes hand in hand with length of service, and experience enables the worker in principle to improve performance of the tasks allotted to him, the objectivity of such a criterion depends on all the circumstances in a particular case, and in particular on the relationship between the nature of the work performed and the experience gained from the performance of that work upon completion of a certain number of working hours.'[58]

This clearly informs national courts that they cannot simply accept length of service, by itself, as sufficient justification for better treatment; they are required to look further and to ask whether length of service actually makes the employee better at the job and only if this is established will the employer escape liability.

In *Arbeiterwohlfahrt der Stadt Berlin eV v Botel*[59] the Court of Justice again displayed considerable sensitivity and perception. Ms Botel, who was president of a staff committee in Germany, took advantage of a statutory right to paid time off work to attend some industrial training courses. Her employer only paid employees taking such courses for their normal working hours which meant that Ms Botel, a part-time worker, received less pay for attending the courses than a full-timer would have received. She claimed that this constituted indirect discrimination. Her employers maintained that the difference in treatment was entirely attributable to the number of hours worked and that all that was being paid was compensation for hours *not* worked. Since Ms Botel did not work as many hours as a full-timer, she was entitled to less compensation. However, the Court of Justice refused to accede to this argument. It held that it did not alter the fact that part-timers who attended the courses received less money than full-timers. Furthermore, it pointed out that the continuation of this situation would put part-timers off becoming members of staff committees.

---

[57] Case C-184/89, [1991] ECR I-297; see also More (1991) 16 EL Rev 320 and Adinolfi (1992) 29 CML Rev 637.

[58] *Ibid*, at p 319.

[59] Case C-360/90, [1992] IRLR 423.

CONCLUSION

The track record of the Court of Justice in sex discrimination cases does on the whole demonstrate that it understands better than the United Kingdom courts what sex equality law is seeking to achieve and the devices which it employs to that end. Unconstrained by technical legislation producing an apparently rigid distinction between direct and indirect discrimination and setting out in detail what has to be proved in order to establish each sub-species of discrimination, the Court of Justice usually approaches cases in a far-sighted and teleological spirit.

In relation to direct discrimination, it has in the majority of cases adopted an objective test for causation, ensuring that semantic distinctions do not obstruct claims. It has also operated that test in an intelligent and sensitive way, not allowing itself to become misled by misconceived arguments about culpability and not becoming confused about the tort-based nature of the equality legislation. Its attitude towards the component of adverse impact is arguably less satisfactory, as a consequence of its abandoning a requirement of comparability; it is perhaps significant that it has hitherto approached this matter in the context of pregnancy, obviously the truly exceptional situation from this point of view. It may be that, faced with a different factual background, it will perceive the danger inherent in a court making its own subjective assessment of whether treatment is adverse and will reconsider the need for comparison with the treatment received or receivable by a member of the opposite sex.

Its contribution in the field of indirect discrimination has been extremely important. Finding itself much freer than the United Kingdom courts to recognise adverse impact in this context, it has demonstrated real practical understanding of the difficulties which confront a complainant who is trying to construct a case and is faced with a complex organisation whose workings are not disclosed to many of its employees. There can also be no doubt that the Court's distinctly robust attitude to claims of justification have forced national courts, in particular those of the United Kingdom, to reject their former uncritical stance and to subject the argument to far closer and more demanding scrutiny than hitherto.

3

LEGAL CONCEPTS OF JUSTIFYING DISCRIMINATION

Pauline Matthews

Cases which raise the question of justification reflect debate as to what kinds of discrimination are tolerable in our society. Thus, although ostensibly, justification provides an objective test, insofar as it reflects that level of toleration, it does not, in fact, provide such a test.

I would like, first, to consider justification in the context of direct discrimination before moving on to consider the extent of jurisprudence in the field of indirect discrimination.

GENUINE OCCUPATIONAL QUALIFICATIONS UNDER THE SEX DISCRIMINATION ACT 1975 AND THE RACE RELATIONS ACT 1976

(1) Genuine Occupational Qualifications allow single sex recruitment where the nature of the job requires a certain sex, although the test is not, in some circumstances, a very rigorous one. One of the most popular GOQs is 7(2)(e) where 'the holder of the job provides individuals with personal services providing their welfare or education, and those services can most effectively be provided by a man ...'. The statutory language does not require that it is necessary or essential that the individual be of a certain sex, only that 'the services can be most effectively provided by one sex'. This was confirmed in *Tottenham Under Fives Centre v Marshall EAT*[1] where the EAT said the question was 'would the personal services be less effective if provided by others'?

The Equal Treatment Directive allows this derogation from the principle of equality but does it allow it to this extent?

Also, the increasing publicity given to child sex abuse and the increasing interest of men in what were traditionally women's jobs has led to employers being placed in difficulties where men apply for jobs in, for example, nurseries and residential homes for children. Parents have fears about the dangers for their children (most sex abuse being perpetrated by men). Should this

[1] [1989] IRLR 147, EAT.

be recognised and accepted or is it a form of sex stereotyping which should remain outlawed by the SDA?

(2) Ministers of religion are exempt where limitation to one sex is a matter of religious doctrine, but is this still the case, for example, with the Church of England? Once it is accepted that women can be priests then the exemption of religious doctrine surely no longer applies and other posts should be as equally open to women as the priesthood.

(3) In the police and prison service the persuasive talents of the EOC and CRE have resulted in, for example, many height requirements being abolished, even though the overarching exemption still exists.

(4) The Armed Services Exemption was successfully challenged using European Law (*R v Secretary of State for Defence ex parte Leale and Lane*), and is now in effect dead, although not removed from the statute book.[2]

The process of challenging these exemptions is a healthy one. Europe expects member states to review any derogations and ensure that they are still necessary.

(5) The provision of services (SDA, s 29 etc): Here there are exemptions for, for example, serious embarrassment, an unlikely concept, we might think, in this day and age but one of some relevance still to some religious cultural groups. It is interesting also to consider in this area exemptions which many women would wish to see but which are not available. For example, women only services have sprung up all over the UK but the legal basis for them is usually shaky. There is no exemption for services such as a women only taxi service. The question of whether one sex is more vulnerable or less 'safe' is not addressed by the SDA. Should it be? Likewise, what about leisure facilities where it is not necessarily a question of serious embarrassment but possibly a reluctance to take part because of the physical dominance of the opposite sex.

UNINTENTIONAL DISCRIMINATION

There have been attempts to, in effect, justify direct discrimination in situations where it is argued the respondent did not *intend* to discriminate.

It was argued in *R v Birmingham City Council*[3] that in order to show less favourable treatment on the grounds of sex it was necessary to establish an intention or motive on the part of the Council to discriminate against the girls. The House of Lords rejected that motive or intention was a necessary condition to liability. If this were correct then 'it would be a good defence for an employer to show that he discriminated against women not because he intended to do so but (for example) because of customer preference, or to save money, or even to avoid controversy'.

---

[2] Since delivering this speech the necessary amendment has been drafted and it should be implemented in 1995.
[3] [1989] IRLR 173, HL.

The Court of Appeal in *James v Eastleigh Borough Council*[4] temporarily threw the situation into confusion by saying that intention or motive may be relevant to discovering the defendant's reason for behaving as he had done – that the *reason why* the defendant treated the plaintiff less favourably was the relevant question. The House of Lords rejected this argument, adopting the 'but for' test proposed in *Birmingham* that 'there is less favourable treatment on the ground of sex if the girls would have received the same treatment as the boys but for their sex'.

So the attempt to introduce a requirement of intentionality into direct discrimination was put to rest but only by a 3 to 2 majority.

PREGNANCY AND MATERNITY

The comparative approach has allowed justification of the adverse treatment of pregnant women in this area. It has been a two-stage process. First, the mainly natural consequences of pregnancy have been separated from the condition itself and isolated as free-standing factors, eg absence, sickness etc, then the treatment of the isolated factors have been compared to how a man in those circumstances would be treated. It is said, of course, that it is not the pregnancy which is objected to, but the consequences of the pregnancy. However, in *Donley v Gallamer*[5] the Northern Ireland Industrial Tribunal said that would be the case also where an employer's customers didn't like a black man serving them and would, therefore, no longer come to his shop. There the employer could say it is not that he objects to the blackness of the employee it is the consequence of his blackness . . . In effect, the consequences to the employer justified the treatment.

That is not to say that this is a matter to be ignored. The practical problem here is that where costs are incurred the burden falls on the employer with little state support, a situation which has been made worse recently by the way in which the government has interpreted the Pregnancy Directive on pay. The answer is that where the recognition and implementation of equality (after all a fundamental human right) necessitates costs being incurred, the costs should be borne by the country as a whole through the tax system or through an insurance scheme and not by individual employers – or, as is more often the case today, by those individual women who are dismissed, never recruited or lose promotion opportunities etc. Without such state support the situation at the moment is that employers are openly stating they will not employ women of childbearing age (although this would be equally unlawful).

The ECJ in *Dekker*[6] and *Hertz*[7] decisively rejected the approach described earlier by characterising the consequences of pregnancy as being so causally

---

4 [1990] IRLR 288, HL.
5 Northern Ireland [1987] 66/86, SD.
6 [1991] IRLR 27, ECJ.
7 [1991] IRLR 31, ECJ.

connected to the pregnancy as to be inseparable. In *Dekker*, the employer refused to appoint a pregnant woman to the post because they would be unable to recoup the maternity pay they were obliged by national law to pay her. As a result they would not be able to employ a substitute while she was on maternity leave. The employer said it was not the pregnancy itself but the financial consequences which motivated his actions.

THE BURDEN OF PROOF DIRECTIVE

As Evelyn Ellis has pointed out[8] the European Court has taken a line on pregnancy which so far has excluded justification of direct discrimination. However, we are told by our sources in Europe that justification of direct discrimination is coming. Indeed, we have seen this concept included in the most recent draft of the Burden of Proof Directive. This says that 'member states may provide that the respondent shall supply the proof referred to when proving that there are objective reasons, not connected with a person's sex, justifying a difference in treatment' and because of this the Commission has felt unable to support this directive. It could be argued that justification here is the process by which the employer proves his actions were *not* based on sex. Even if this is right the use of the word 'justification' is problematic, and if it is to be understood in this way, it does not really add to the purpose of the rest of the directive which already refers (obviously) to the process (the transfer of the burden of proof) by which the employer explains the reasons for the treatment in order to establish that they were not sex based.

Such a development flies in the face of the UK domestic statutes and hard won case law successes and I feel it should be resisted. Maybe this is an issue on which we need to put some 'clear blue water' between ourselves and Brussels. The lack of a formal justification defence in direct discrimination in part reflects the view that no excuses will be tolerated in our society for such discrimination.

INDIRECT DISCRIMINATION

Domestic law

Justification is a clear legal concept in the domestic statute as regards indirect discrimination. There is a question as to whether the genuine material factor also has to be objectively justified which will be discussed in other chapters.

One of the earliest cases of justification under the domestic statute was *Steel v UPW*[9] in 1978. Here the US case of *Griggs v Duke Power Company*[10]

---

[8] See above in Chapter 2.
[9] [1977] IRLR 288.
[10] 1971/401 US 424.

in 1971 was referred to and this case had prompted the inclusion of indirect discrimination in the Sex Discrimination Act. In that case justification had been specifically articulated as only occurring where the employment practice concerned could be shown to be related to job performance. In *Steel*, postal workers were able to choose walks depending on seniority but women workers had, until 1976, not been able to accrue seniority as they were employed as temporary workers and by definition not allowed to acquire seniority no matter how long they had worked for the Post Office. The courts sought to adopt a test requiring that the potentially discriminatory practice had to be *necessary* rather than convenient and stated that 'for this purposes it is relevant to consider whether the employer could find some other non-discriminatory method of achieving his objective.'

This was, to most interested parties, a very acceptable definition of the principle of justification but unfortunately the position was undermined by various cases culminating in 1982 with the Court of Appeal's decision in *Ojutiku v MSC*.[11] In this case, the Court of Appeal decided that the standard should be what was 'acceptable to right thinking people as sound and tolerable reasons for adopting a practice in question'. We cannot begin to unravel the problems of that definition and identify the assumptions behind it, but the decision was very disappointing and extremely subjective. *Bilka-Kaufhaus* to some extent rescued the situation but for a number of years it was not clear how accepted the *Bilka* test was in domestic law.

In *Rainey v Greater Glasgow Health Board*[12] the House of Lords applied this standard to a defence to an equal pay case, pointing out that in their view the same test should be applied in indirect discrimination cases. Another case of interest was *Hampson v DES*[13] where the Court of Appeal decided the test adopted in *Rainey* was the same as that in *Ojutiku* – quite a remarkable achievement!

It was stated that the test should be 'requiring an objective balance to be struck between the discriminatory effect of the condition and the reasonable needs of the party who applies the condition'. However, this is an inadequate test in many ways, first, what is an objective balance? Secondly, the test for reasonableness is not necessarily the same as one of genuine need required by *Bilka*. And thirdly, how was a discriminatory effect to be measured?

Finally, and on a hopeful note, the House of Lords in the EOC's judicial review proceedings (relating to the qualifying period for part-timers under the EP(C)A to claim employment protection rights) applied the *Bilka-Kaufhaus* test most rigorously, finding that the evidence put forward by the government to justify the five-year period required to be worked by part-timers before acquiring protection rights was in no way sufficient. However, the court did accept that the government's aim of increasing the availability of part-time work was a beneficial social policy aim and it could not be said

---

[11] [1982] IRLR 418, CA.
[12] [1987] IRLR 26, HC.
[13] [1989] IRLR 69, CA.

'not to be necessary' – not quite the *Bilka* test! They went on to say that the question was 'whether the threshold provisions of the Act of 1978 have been shown by reference to objective factors, to be suitable and requisite for achieving that aim'

The House of Lords indicated that just as paying part-time workers less than full-time was a gross breach of the principle of equal pay and not a suitable means of achieving an increase in part-time work, likewise keeping indirect labour costs (such as the ability to claim unfair dismissal or a redundancy payment) low where this affected women more than men was unacceptable. Further, in the case taken by Camden Law Centre, *R v Secretary of State for Employment, ex parte Seymour-Smith and Perez*[14] concerning the two-year qualifying period for part-timers, the High Court confirmed that *Bilka-Kaufhaus* will be applied rigorously. Whilst the applicants lost at first instance the Court of Appeal subsequently upheld some of their claims.[15] The Court granted a declaration that the two year qualifying period was indirectly discriminatory against women. The Court held that there was no objective justification for the discrimination.

[14] [1994] IRLR 448, HC.
[15] [1995] IRLR 464, CA.

4

EQUAL TREATMENT AND MANAGERIAL PREROGATIVES

Colin Bourn

In his seminal work 'Taking Rights Seriously', Dworkin draws a distinction between arguments of principle intended to establish individual rights and arguments of policy intended to establish a collective goal.[1] He argues that we may define the weight of a right as its power to withstand the pressure to achieve collective goals.[2] This is a powerful distinction in the context of employment rights, where there is undoubtedly a sharp conflict between conceptions of what is necessary to further the general economic welfare and the rights of existing employees.[3] By legislating for equal treatment, any gains in economic utility which might flow from leaving employers the unfettered power to discriminate on the proscribed grounds are circumscribed. Indeed, employment rights delimit the sphere in which arguments for de-regulation of the labour market on general grounds of allocative efficiency can prevail.

Competition between individual rights and broader collective goals is a common thread in the ongoing debate about the future role of labour law. The aim of this paper is to explore the impact of that distinction as it applies to the array of anti-discrimination rights enjoyed by employees. It will attempt to establish a hierarchy of employee rights in the workplace by reference to the possibility of infractions of those rights being justified by reference to employer interests, or the perceived public good arising from economic development or employment creation.

The conflict between individual rights and managerial prerogatives is central to the debates generated by the policies of the present British Conservative government since 1979, which have been characterised as constituting an ideology of individualism, with policies tending towards the 'deregulation of

---

[1] R Dworkin, *Taking Rights Seriously* (Duckworth, 1977), p 90. Dworkin argues that a right is an 'individual political aim', whereas a goal is a 'non-individuated political aim', ie it does not call for any particular opportunity, resource or liberty for particular individuals.

[2] Above p 92.

[3] SD Anderman, *Labour Law: Management Decisions and Workers Rights* (Butterworths, 1992) p 1.

the labour market' and the enhancement of 'individual economic freedom'.[4] Opposition to the development of the 'social dimension' of the EU by the UK government, resulting in the 'opt-out' from the Social Protocol annexed to the Maastricht Treaty, has largely been justified *ex post facto* by arguments that labour market regulation does not serve the general welfare because such restrictions are likely to destroy jobs and limit employment opportunities.[5] Such arguments are fundamentally utilitarian in character, citing the general economic welfare as ground for policies which may work to the considerable disadvantage of particular groups of workers. In such a utilitarian calculus there is little or no room for the protection of the specific interests of individual workers or groups via employment protection rights. By the 1990s, the terms in which employment issues are generally discussed have become more individualistic and utilitarian and less likely to be cast in terms of workers' rights. Thus 'efficiency and employment creation' talk has tended to supersede 'rights talk' in the discussion of the labour market.

ANTI-DISCRIMINATION RIGHTS

Joseph Raz argues that rights can be said to exist when a person's interest or well-being is a sufficient reason for holding some other person to be under a duty.[6] On this basis, rights to equal treatment may be deduced to be protecting employee interests of sufficient weight and substance to justify placing employers under a duty to respect them. The right not to be dis-

---

[4] 'Politics, Pragmatism and Ideology: the Wellsprings of Conservative Union Legislation (1979–1992)', Fosh, Morris, Martin and Undy, *Industrial Law Journal*, 22, 1, pp 14–31, Lord Wedderburn, 'Freedom of Association and Philosophies of Labour Law', *Industrial Law Journal* 18, 1, (1989).

The UK White Paper Employment for the 1990s, (HMSO 1988, Cmnd 540), sets out the by now familiar case that deregulation of the labour market will further economic progress and thereby stimulate employment. The EC Green Paper on Social Policy placed the debate between the proponents of high social standards and those who argue that present level of employment protection have become unaffordable at the heart of the policy issues facing the Community (COM (93) 551 p 14). While the Green Paper spoke of 'completing the (1989) social action programme and exploiting to the full the possibilities offered by the Social Agreement of the Maastricht Treaty' (at p 60) the White Paper on Growth (Bulletin of the EC Supplement 6/93) sounded a more sceptical note, indicating that lack of labour market flexibility was in large part responsible for Europe's relatively poor record of job creation. The White Paper on Social Policy (COM (94) 333) is notably cautious in its assessment of the prospects for labour law beyond the completion of the 1989 Social Action Programme. Indeed it is clear in hindsight that the 1989 Charter of the Fundamental Rights of Workers represented the zenith of the policy of ensuring a minimum floor of employment rights across Europe, a policy which appears to have given ground to a greater concern about unemployment.

[5] For a recent example, see in particular the terms in which Michael Portillo, as Secretary of State for Employment rejected the draft directive on atypical work, largely concerned with the harmonisation of terms and conditions of part-time workers with those of full-timers, and the terms in which he reluctantly proposed the legislative implementation of the decision of the House of Lords in *R v Secretary of State for Employment ex parte the EOC*, [1994] IRLR 176. ((1994) *The Independent* 20 December).

[6] J Raz, *The Morality of Freedom*, (Clarendon Press, 1986), p 166.

criminated against on grounds of gender implies, for example, an obligation on the employer not to refuse to consider women for certain types of work. This duty will extend to not taking decisions on the proscribed ground, ie discriminating directly, and may extend to arranging one's affairs in such a way that women, for example, are not in fact disadvantaged, so-called indirect discrimination. The range of duties implied by the proscription of some forms of indirect discrimination is much wider than the mere duty not to take decisions on grounds of, say, gender. It implies what might be termed a second order duty to set up objective selection, promotion and other systems, which may have wide effects on business practice and sometimes conflict with other objectives, such as speed or flexibility of operations. It is for this reason that only direct discrimination is proscribed in many instances, such as is currently proposed with respect to disability, and where indirect discrimination is proscribed, there is normally scope for justification.

The concept of justification in equality law goes some way to reconciling the conflict between individual rights and the policy goals of management and the interest of the community in general in economic change and development. The interesting question is whether justification is permitted to the same degree in respect of all types of employee rights against direct and indirect discriminatory treatment.

JUSTIFICATION OF INDIRECT SEX DISCRIMINATION

Hervey distinguishes between three bases of justification in the context of indirect sex discrimination,[7] positing a distinction between job-related, enterprise-related and public interest-related justifications. This typology of justifications is useful in differentiating the immediacy of the considerations involved. Whereas in *Danfoss*[8] weight was given to such job-related factors as seniority, training and flexibility, in the sense of job mobility, the ECJ held that flexibility in the sense of adaptability and general contribution could not be a ground of justification, as any difference in such performance between the sexes was 'inconceivable'. In *Nimz*[9] the court moved towards requiring proof of the contribution of seniority to performance, although in *Rummler v Dato Druck*[10] a requirement of physical strength was admitted as a possible ground of justification.

Under UK law there is no financial compensation available for unintentional indirect discrimination, a limitation which is arguably not consonant with EC law, especially after *Marshall (No 2)*[11] with its principle that to be

---

[7] T Hervey, *Justifications for Sex Discrimination in Employment*, (Butterworths, 1993), pp 62–78.
[8] Case C-109/88, [1989] IRLR 537, ECJ.
[9] *Nimz v Freie und Hansestadt Hamburg* Case C-184/89, [1991] IRLR 222, ECJ.
[10] Case C-237/85, [1987] IRLR 32, ECJ.
[11] Case C-271/91, [1993] IRLR 445, ECJ, *Clifford v Devon County Council* [1994] IRLR 628, EAT.

adequate such compensation must enable the loss and damage actually sustained to be made good in full.[12]

RACE DISCRIMINATION

The law, as regards racial discrimination, has been influenced by the evolution of an objective test in gender cases. There is no provision for direct discrimination to be justified, except in terms of the necessary performance of an express statutory obligation under RRA 1976, s 41(1). This is broader than the corresponding provision of the Sex Discrimination Act 1975, as amended by the Employment Act 1989 in the light of the decision of the ECJ in *Johnson v RUC*.[13] The 1989 Act restricted such statutorily based justification to those provisions which are necessary for the protection of women as regards pregnancy and maternity. Clearly s 3(4), like SDA s 5(3), requires comparisons to be made where the relevant circumstances are not materially different.

In relation to indirect discrimination there has been a long history of uncertainty in the formulation of the test of justifiability. Phillips J in *Steel v PO*,[14] influenced by the seminal US case of *Griggs v Duke Power*[15] in which the Supreme Court had held that 'the touchstone was business necessity', held that to be justifiable a discriminatory practice had to be 'necessary'. Subsequent case law moved towards a subjective test but in *Hampson v DES* Balcombe J held that '"justifiable" requires an objective balance to be stuck between the discriminatory effect of the condition and the reasonable needs of the party who applies the condition'.[16] Such a formulation implies, however, that if an 'objective' balance is to be struck, the needs of the employer have also to be objective and the measures taken proportionate. Thus the test of justification in race cases is undoubtedly an objective one, but allows only the objective needs of the employer, 'the party who applies the condition', to be taken into account.

NATIONALITY

Both direct and indirect[17] discrimination on grounds of nationality is proscribed under EC Art 48 between workers who are EU citizens. These rights are amplified in Regulation 1612/68 and extended to cover eligibility

---

[12] Cf *Macmillan v Edinburgh Voluntary Organisations Council* [1995] IRLR 536, EAT.
[13] Case C-222/84, [1986] IRLR 263, ECJ.
[14] [1978] ICR 1.
[15] (1971) 401 US, 424 (S. Ct. 1971).
[16] For a detailed account of the development of the test of justification in British race cases see Bourn and Whitmore, *Race and Sex Discrimination* (Sweet and Maxwell, 1993), 2.57–2.64.
[17] Ingetraut *Scholtz v Opera Universitaria di Cagliari and Cinzia Porcedda* [1994] ECR (April), noted in White 19 ELR 308.

for employment, equality in terms of treatment and the treatment of workers' families. However, Art 48(3) allows for the justification of discrimination between Community nationals on grounds of public policy, public security and public health. These exceptions are developed in Dir 64/221, which provides that justification based on public policy or public security shall be based exclusively on the personal conduct of the individual concerned. In *Van Duyn v Home Office*[18] which concerned the refusal of entry to a Dutch woman who had secured employment in the Church of Scientology (an organisation considered contrary to the public good but not unlawful in Britain), the ECJ held that Art 48(3) was to be construed restrictively, but allowed that an activity might fall within Art 48(3) if administrative action had been taken against it, even though it was not unlawful. However, in *R v Bouchereau*[19] the ECJ moved to a more restrictive test of justification under Art 48(3) requiring a 'genuine and sufficiently serious threat to the requirements of public policy affecting one of the fundamental interests of society.' Though imprecise, this test is arguably more objective than subjective, requiring more than merely an official view that a person or activity is not conducive to the public good.

RELIGIOUS DISCRIMINATION IN NORTHERN IRELAND

The regulation of religious discrimination in Northern Ireland represents a substantially different case from the issues discussed above. The Fair Employment (Northern Ireland) Act 1989 provides that 'affirmative action' may be required to be taken to bring about 'fair participation' between the religious communities in the Province where an employer is not providing 'equality of opportunity'. The latter is defined as meaning 'equality of opportunity between *persons* of different religious beliefs,'[20] a definition which is cast in terms of individual rights to enjoy 'the same opportunity . . . as that other person would have in those circumstances, due allowance being made for any material difference in their suitability'. Such individual rights to equality of opportunity are made subject to 'anything lawfully done in pursuance of affirmative action'.[21] Affirmative action is in turn defined as 'action designed to secure fair participation in employment'[22] by members of the two religious communities. Thus the right to fair participation[23] is a group interest which to a certain extent prevails over the individual right to equality of opportunity. McCrudden[24] observes that 'It is therefore clearly

---

[18] Case 41/74, [1974] ECR 1337, [1975] 1 CMLR 1.
[19] Case 30/77, [1977] ECR 1999 and *Adoui and Cornuaille v Belgium* Cases 115, 116/81, [1982] ECR 1665.
[20] Fair Employment (NI) Act 1989, s 20(1).
[21] Above s 20(3).
[22] FE(NI)A 1989, s 58.
[23] McCrudden discusses the meaning to be attached to that term extensively in *Affirmative Action and Fair Participation*, ILJ 21, 3, pp 170–198.
[24] Above at p 181.

incorrect to regard fair participation and affirmative action as couched in terms of individual fairness, except that affirmative action is subject to the requirement not to discriminate unlawfully.' Only in relation to indirectly discriminatory redundancy selection procedures, undertaken in pursuance of affirmative action, is there an exception which goes further than these exceptions provided for under the SDA or RRA in respect of training or the encouragement of applications from members of the under-represented community. Thus the group right to fair participation prevails to only a limited extent over the individual right not to be discriminated against on grounds of religious affiliation. This is in spite of the requirement[25] that employers with a workforce of more than 250 shall make an annual return of the composition of their workforce to the Fair Employment Commission[26] and shall from time to time review the balance of their workforce to determine what affirmative action it would be reasonable and appropriate to take to achieve fair participation of the two communities. The scope of lawful affirmative action remains limited and does not go so far as to encompass selection, recruitment or promotion.

DISABILITY

There is an interesting contrast between the terms of the British Civil Rights (Disabled Persons) (No 2) Bill 1993, for which there was extensive cross party support, and the proposals contained in the Disability Discrimination Bill, 1995.[27]

The Disability Discrimination Bill confines itself to dealing with direct discrimination[28] against those who have a physical or mental impairment which has a substantial and long term effect on that person's ability to carry out normal day-to-day activities.[29] Such direct discrimination may be justified if it is reasonable for the employer to be of the opinion that the disabled person is either unsuitable or less suitable than some other person, or his disability would impede the performance of any of his duties, or significantly reduce the value of any training,[30] provided that the employer has taken such steps as are reasonable to prevent any arrangements or physical features of the premises placing the disabled person at a substantial disadvantage.[31] Provision may be made by regulation as to what arrangements and features will fall within the scope of such remedial measures.[32] Thus direct discrimination on

[25] FE(NI)A 1989, s 31.
[26] FE(NI)A 1989, s 27.
[27] At the time of writing both the government Bill and the revived private members' Bill are before the House, on the basis of a Speaker's ruling that the two Bills are incompatible and contain substantially different provisions. ((1995) *The Guardian*, 25 January).
[28] Cl 4.
[29] Cl 1.
[30] Cl 5.
[31] Cl 6.
[32] Cl 6(7).

grounds of disability will be able to be justified on the 'merit' principle,[33] pro- vided that the duty to make prescribed adjustments has been fulfilled.

By contrast the 1993 private members' Bill introduced by Mr Roger Berry includes both direct and indirect discrimination. It defines reasonable accommodation negatively as any level of accommodation short of that which an employer could demonstrate would unduly prejudice the operation of the business.[34] In making that assessment regard was to be had to the nature and cost of making the accommodation, the size and financial resources of the undertaking, the nature of the workforce and the availability of the public funds to help defray the cost of adjustments. While the government Bill explicitly provides for the objective justification on 'merit' grounds of direct discrimination provided that the required adjustments have been made, the Berry Bill provides that a failure to make reasonable accommodation is itself discriminatory, unless this would unduly prejudice the operation of the business.[35] While the Berry Bill allows for the justification of requirements which have an adverse impact on the disabled, the government Bill does not encompass indirect discrimination because, in its view, as expressed in the Consultative Document on the Bill, disabled persons are so diverse a category that it would be difficult to assess disproportionate impact. Only the government Bill provides for the abolition of the quota scheme under the Disabled Persons Act 1944.

Thus, the difference between the two approaches largely concerns the scope of justification allowable under the legislation and the extent to which the right not to be discriminated against on grounds of disability must be accommodated to managerial considerations.

RIGHTS TO FREE ASSOCIATION

The right of free association in the UK has been built out of the building blocks of individual rights, according to Wedderburn.[36] These rights are now contained in Pt III of the Trade Union and Labour Relations (Consolidation) Act 1992, being namely, the right not to be refused employment on grounds of union membership under s 137 *et seq*, the taking of action short of dismissal on grounds of trade union membership or activities under s 146 *et seq* and dismissals on similar grounds under s 152 *et seq*. It is for the employer to establish the purpose for which he took the action in question in each of the three cases set out above. As Townshend-Smith[37] observes these provisions only encompass direct discrimination, in which questions of justification do not arise. In those cases where the employer

[33] Cl 5(4).
[34] Cl 4.(2)(e)
[35] It is this 'undue hardship' standard which was adopted by the Americans with Disability Act 1990, which has tended to act as a model in the minds of campaigners.
[36] (1976) 39 MLR 169.
[37] R Townshend-Smith 'Refusal of Employment on Grounds of Trade Union Membership or Non-Membership: The Employment Act 1990', ILJ (1991) 20, 2, pp 102–112.

institutes a practice which has an indirectly discriminatory effect on trade union membership, there is no call on the employer to justify it.

In relation to action taken under s 137, the employer may not justify his action by reference to trade union pressure and indeed the respondent employer may join the trade union to the proceedings. Thus, neither the employer nor the trade union can justify direct discrimination in recruitment on grounds of trade union membership or non-membership by reference to their separate or joint interests in either industrial peace and/or trade union organisation. The White Paper, 'Removing Barriers to Employment'[38] reveals that the underlying purpose of this section was to remove the legal basis of the pre-entry closed shop. While such a provision might seem conducive to the furtherance of individual autonomy and has an apparent even handedness, it has been argued to be destructive of the right to freedom of association.[39]

The protection of employees against action short of dismissal taken for the purpose of preventing or deterring employees from being, or becoming, members of a trade union or penalising them for doing so under s 146 is again limited to direct discrimination, with the onus on the employer to show the purpose for which the action was taken. Under s 148 there is no account to be taken of trade union pressure on the employer in such cases and the trade union can be joined in the proceedings under s 150. Following the decisions of the Court of Appeal in *Wilson v Associated Newspapers* and *Palmer v ABP*,[40] (in which alleged *douceurs* were offered to employees to enter into personal employment contracts), TURERA 1993 amended s 148 during the course of the Bill's passage to provide that where the employer took action with the purpose of changing his relationship with any or all of his employees and that action also falls within s 146, the former is to be regarded as the purpose for which the action was taken. Thus the employer's purpose in changing his relationship with his employees (typically to derecognise the union and end collective bargaining by instituting a regime of 'personal employment contracts') can now justify anti-trade union discrimination, which would otherwise have fallen within s 146. Subsequently the Lords[41] were divided as to whether an omission to offer an employee a benefit could constitute action taken against an employee under s 23(4), the majority holding that it could not. However, the Lords were agreed that the employer's purpose in acting to bring collective bargaining to an end did not constitute action to deter trade union membership as such. Thus, even without the 1993 Act, managerial freedom to derecognise trade unions and to offer inducements to end collective bargaining would be lawful, even though contrary to a fully-developed right to freedom of association, a right normally seen as being central to 'civil society'[42] and enshrined in ILO conventions.[43]

[38] Cmnd 655, paras 2.1–2.37.
[39] See S Leader, *Freedom of Association*, (Yale University Press, 1992), pp 123–161.
[40] [1993] IRLR 336, CA.
[41] [1995] 2 All ER 100.
[42] Ernest Gellner, *Conditions of Liberty, Civil Society and its Rivals*, (Hamish Hamilton, 1994).
[43] ILO Conventions ESC 87 and 98 etc.

ANALYSIS

Dismissals related to trade union membership, non-membership or activities are rendered unlawful by s 52 and selection for redundancy on such grounds by s 153. The importance of this aspect of the right to freedom of association has been acknowledged in that there is no period of qualifying service in such cases, interim relief can be given under s 161 and a special basic award is available under s 158 where re-instatement or re-engagement are refused. There is no ground of justification comparable to that available under s 146 in respect of action short of dismissal.

ANALYSIS

Anti-discrimination rights run from relatively strong rights in which there is protection against both direct and indirect discrimination, through those situations in which only direct discrimination is protected, to situations in which even the protection against directly discriminatory actions is qualified by considerations of utility. Why should protection from arbitrary treatment on grounds of, say, race, receive more protection than similar treatment on grounds of disability or trade union membership? Waldron counsels that we cannot merely assert or 'intuit' that this or that right is more important than another, but should look for what he terms the 'internal relations' which govern the situation.[44]

It can be argued that the balance struck between civil rights and economic utility will depend upon a trade-off between the strength, substance and political weight of the interest so protected and the degree of interference that the right is likely to cause to the operation of a market-oriented economic logic. The categories of right in which indirect discrimination is proscribed occur where it is not merely the individual interests of individuals which are affected but also their social or personal identity. A black person may identify himself or herself as such, and, therefore, discrimination not merely places him or her at a disadvantage in the labour market but is potentially insulting to the group to which he or she belongs. In all the cases in which indirect discrimination is proscribed there is an important group dimension which can only be protected by the protection of the individuals who compose that group. However, such rights are not necessarily always 'trumps' and a balance has to be struck between the principle of equal treatment and the commercial imperative. It is for this reason that the second order duties implied by indirect discrimination may be balanced by managerial considerations, if these can be objectively justified.

Both direct and indirect discrimination are proscribed as regards race, gender, EC nationality and religion, although objective justification is possible as regards indirect discrimination. All these rights protect individuals as being members of socially significant groups. It would appear, however, that the Race Relations Act has not limited managerial discretion to any signific-

[44] *Ibid* pp 220–224.

ant extent, especially as regards the penetration of senior managerial positions by ethnic minority members. Studies of the impact of the Race Relations Act show that its effects have been limited,[45] perhaps because there has been little reliance on the concept of indirect discrimination to combat established practices, or because the CRE has not been able to make tremendously effective use of its powers of formal investigation.

The Sex Discrimination Act has still not had any great effect in removing or abating the extent of occupational segregation between men and women, or the tendency for women to be concentrated in part-time work within the service industries.[46] Indeed the tremendous growth in part-time and temporary work, often non-unionised, which has taken place in the past decade has enabled managements to increase the flexibility of the labour force. What Rees terms the 'ideology of the family'[47] has often enabled this to be presented as the employer offering a choice women want (although the acceptability of part-time work may be more a question of the reconciliation of the pressures which arise from gender roles in families).[48] Managerial flexibility is little impeded in practice by sex discrimination legislation, especially in view of the limited use made to date of the concept of indirect discrimination. Indeed it has been argued that equal opportunity policies are highly congruent with current managerial ideologies,[49] in view of their inherent individualism, the possibility of decentralised administration via numerical monitoring of targets and the likelihood of being perceived as 'good' employers in tune with the times. It is worth observing that when case law does develop in such a way as to impinge upon managerial prerogatives, as happened, for example, in the EOC judicial review case on eligibility for unfair dismissal and redundancy protection, there is audible protest about the application of indirect discrimination.[50] The UK government was, of course, opposed to the proposed parental leave directive on the ground that it would limit managerial freedom.

Discrimination on grounds of nationality as between EC citizens has been of limited practical consequence to employers, the numbers involved being comparatively small. The Fair Employment Act has had far greater impact upon management prerogatives, but the political necessity of making

---

[45] See Hepple, *Have Twenty Five Years of the Race Relations Act been a Failure* in Hepple and Szyszczak (*ibid*) at p 19 and the sources quoted there. However, T Jones in reporting the results of the most recent PSI survey in *Britains Ethnic Minorities*, 1993 PSI, presents a more differentiated picture, that while certain ethnic minority groups have entered professional work in numbers comparable to that of the indigenous population, the numbers of ethnic minorities in senior management positions in large organisations is much less.

[46] *Women and Men in Britain*, EOC 1993.

[47] T Rees, *Women and the Labour Market* (Routledge, 1992), pp 8–9.

[48] S Newell, 'Superwoman Syndrome: Gender Differences in Attitudes Towards Equal Opportunities at work and Towards Domestic Responsibilities at Home', *Work, Employment and Society*, 7(2), pp 257–9.

[49] N Jewson and D Mason, *Equal Employment Opportunities in the 1990's: A Policy Come of Age?* Discussion Papers in Sociology, Department of Sociology, University of Leicester.

[50] I Chaplin of the Institute of Directors was quoted as saying that 'the decision could have very damaging effects on the job opportunities for part-timers and cause great difficulties for the very people it is intended to assist.' *Personnel Today*, March 1994, p 2.

progress towards equality between the religious communities in Northern Ireland is self-evident.

Where only direct discrimination is proscribed, a narrower range of duties is cast upon employers. The controversy surrounding the Civil Rights (Disability) Bill 1993 and the British government's current proposals turns largely upon the extent of duties placed upon employers by the inclusion of protection from indirect discrimination in the original Bill (cl 2(c)). The disabled have recently become more politicised in the struggle to achieve legislative recognition, which has led to a greater sense of solidarity, the essential component of social identity. It is not surprising therefore that they should have sought the same level of protection as is enjoyed by victims of race or gender discrimination.[51]

Even though anti-trade union discrimination endangers the vital interests of trade unionists[52] only direct discrimination on grounds of trade union membership is proscribed. Here the balance is more tightly drawn because strong trade union organisation could have a major impact on managerial discretion. It could be argued that the refusal of recognition or the offering of inducements to enter personal contracts are forms of indirect discrimination against trade union members, the protection of which might imply a duty on the employer to engage in collective bargaining, at least as far as involves individual representation. Such wide restrictions upon managerial discretion have not hitherto appealed to Parliament. Indeed, it is notable that while trade unions were recognised in 66 per cent of workplaces in 1984, that figure had fallen to 53 per cent by 1990 and the density of trade union membership fallen from 58 per cent to 48 per cent.[53] The removal of the extension, development and reform of collective bargaining from the objects of ACAS in 1993[54] and the imposition of a requirement for a triennial ballot on the 'check-off' seem evidence of a policy which has sought to restrict trade union influence and to expand managerial prerogatives by lessening trade union power, as part of an overall free market philosophy.[55]

CONCLUSIONS

Although the broad trend of government policy has favoured market solutions and endorsed the claims of management to manage, employee rights to freedom from arbitrary or unequal treatment have provided some protection for workers from the abuse of managerial prerogatives. Whether the protec-

[51] The disabled have also climbed up the political agenda of the EC, as is evidenced by the proposals contained in the White Paper on social policy, *European Social Policy; a Way Forward for the Union*, Com (94) 333, Chapter VI, 22–24.

[52] *Anti-Union Discrimination: Practice, Law and Policy*, S Evans and R Lewis, ILJ, 16, 2, pp 88–106.

[53] S Millward *et al*, *Workplace Industrial Relations Survey*, (Blackwell, 1992).

[54] TULR(C)A 1992, s 209 as amended by TURERA 1993.

[55] Davies and Freedland, *Labour Legislation and Public Policy* (Clarendon Press, 1992), pp 425–525.

tion is limited to direct discrimination or extended to indirect discrimination and/or whether justification is permissible, defines the boundary between the discourse of employee rights and the language of economic and managerial efficiency. Where group or wider public interests are advanced through the protection of individual rights against arbitrary or unequal treatment, which do not greatly limit key aspects of the managerial prerogative, protection extends to both direct and indirect discrimination, as with race, sex, nationality and with some qualification, to religion in Northern Ireland. Where significant group interests are protected by rights to non-discriminatory treatment but the impact on managerial prerogatives could be significant, protection is limited to direct discrimination, as with the right to free association and the other species of automatically unfair dismissal. The controversy which has surrounded disability concerns the uncertain status of the disabled as a self-conscious group and the doubts which have arisen about the cost impact of physical changes and their impact on the economic viability of the enterprise. Thus, all forms of anti-discrimination law straddle this barrier between unfettered managerial discretion and the protection of civil rights. The solution to the conflict between these two forms of discourse seems to be a pragmatic adjustment of the scope of protection and the extent of justification.

5

SETTING THE LIMITS OF ANTI-DISCRIMINATION LAW: SOME LEGAL AND SOCIAL CONCEPTS

Nicholas Bamforth

Evelyn Ellis has described the objectives of the Sex Discrimination Act 1975 including those stated in the preceding White Paper.

Little attempt was made in that White Paper, however, to characterise or explain the nature of the social problem which discrimination against women was felt to represent. Instead, the Paper focused on common examples of practices perceived as discriminatory, such as denying women banking or insurance facilities on the same terms as men, and on statistics revealing the manifestly unequal position of women and men in the employment market.[2] The only real clue as to the way in which the White Paper *perceived* gender discrimination as a social practice lay in occasional references to stereotyped attitudes, to the need for equality of opportunity for women, and to the inequalities which had for so long existed.[3] There was no attempt made to explain at any deeper level the conception of equality which the Paper's authors had in mind, or the type of inequality which discrimination against women was felt to represent. This is unfortunate, given the range of well-known ambiguities surrounding the notion of equality.[4] Examples include the question of equality on whose terms, bringing into play the sameness/difference debate; the question of whether equality of opportunity is to be preferred to equality of outcome; and a third issue, which is that, given that inequalities of various sorts are regular and even accepted occurrences in different areas of our social life, what is it about inequalities associated with race or gender which marks them out for legislative intervention? These controversies suggest that the mere incantation of the word 'equality' is not enough on its own to explain anti-discrimination law in a satisfactory fashion.

---

[1] See above in Chapter 2.
[2] Cmnd 5724 (1974), paras 6–15.
[3] Ibid, paras 16–17.
[4] For general discussions of the ambiguous nature of equality, see, for example, Katherine O'Donovan and Erika Szyszczak, *Equality & Sex Discrimination Law* (Oxford, Blackwell, 1988), pp 1–20, 58–62; Didi Herman, *Rights of Passage: Struggles for Lesbian and Gay Legal Equality* (Toronto, University of Toronto Press, 1994), Chapters 4, 5; Nicholas Bamforth, *Sexuality, Morals and Justice: A Theory of Lesbian and Gay Rights and Law* (London, Cassell, 1996).

Debating the meaning of equality is, however, something which lies beyond the remit of this chapter. The White Paper's vagueness about the workings of discriminatory social practices is, instead, a useful introduction to the central task of this chapter, which is to examine some differences between, on the one hand, the scope of the *legal* concepts of direct and indirect discrimination and, on the other, the range of *social* behaviour which we might, in practice, characterise as sexually, or racially, discriminatory. It is these differences between legal concepts and social practices which constitute the limits to anti-discrimination law referred to in the title. Two arguments will be made. First, that the law serves effectively to justify practices which, while fitting within common conceptions of sex and race discrimination as social practices, nevertheless fall outside the scope of the legislation and are, therefore, legally permissible. Secondly, that by manipulating the legal concepts of direct and indirect discrimination, courts and tribunals can alter the range of social behaviour which the law deems to be justifiable in the relevant sense. To be sustainable, these arguments require further discussion of the terms 'justification' and 'discrimination', and it is to this which we will now turn.

CONCEPTS OF JUSTIFICATION

When discussing anti-discrimination law, it is possible to use the term 'justification' in either of two distinct senses. One sense is legalistic, in that it refers to the specific justification provisions contained in the law. Evelyn Ellis employs this sense in drawing a distinction between defences and justifications within the legislation and case law.[5] A defence, Ellis implies, comes into play where all the elements of a discrimination claim have been made out, but there is a relevant saving factor which withdraws the situation from the application of the legislation, immunising the defendant where their conduct would otherwise clearly contravene the law. Relevant saving factors, or defences, are listed in the legislation, and are typified by the genuine occupational qualification defence applicable in direct discrimination claims.[6] A 'justification' in indirect discrimination cases comes into play, by contrast, where, so far as the law is concerned, there is no discrimination at all since an essential element in the legal claim is missing. The requirement or condition which the employer has applied may disproportionately disadvantage the group of which the applicant is a member, but there is no unlawful discrimination because what has happened is referable to a reason other than the difference of sex or race.[7]

---

[5] Evelyn Ellis above in Chapter 2.

[6] Sex Discrimination Act 1975, s 7; Race Relations Act 1976, s 5. For judicial treatment of the defence, see eg *Tottenham Green Under Fives' Centre v Marshall* [1989] IRLR 147; *Tottenham Green Under Fives' Centre v Marshall (No 2)* [1991] ICR 320. (See Pauline Matthews above in Chapter 3.)

[7] Sex Discrimination Act 1975, s 1(1)(*b*)(ii); Race Relations Act 1976, s 1(1)(*b*)(ii). For judicial

The essence of the distinction, Ellis suggests, is that a defence excuses what the law would otherwise categorise as discrimination, whereas a justification suggests that, so far as the law is concerned, there has been no discrimination at all. This parallels a distinction drawn in *The Oxford English Dictionary*, where justification in its legal sense is defined as 'The showing or maintaining in court that one had sufficient reason for doing that which [one] is called to answer; a circumstance affording grounds for such a plea.'[8] The legal sense of 'defence', by contrast, is defined as 'The opposing or denial by the accused party of the truth or validity of the complaint made against him.'[9]

Interesting though Ellis's distinction is, however, it tells us only about concepts in play in the law as it stands: it informs us of the law's characterisation of particular behaviour, but says little about the consequences or propriety of the characterisation adopted. To consider these latter issues, it is necessary to employ a second, linguistic sense of the word 'justification'. To cite *The Oxford English Dictionary* once again, a 'justification' is, in this second sense, 'The action of justifying or showing something to be just, right or proper; vindication of oneself or another; exculpation, verification, proof ... That which justifies; a justifying circumstance; an apology, a defence.'[10] In this linguistic sense, a 'justification' for conduct is a reason, often conclusive, for identifying it as acceptable or supportable. That a particular practice or type of conduct is found not to contravene the requirements of anti-discrimination law represents, therefore, a legitimation or justification of that conduct by the law.

The linguistic sense of 'justification' is broader than the legalistic sense: an action may be seen as 'justified' in the linguistic sense when it falls within a legal *defence* such as general occupational qualification. As *The Oxford English Dictionary* states, the word 'defence' in its general sense means 'The defending, supporting, or maintaining by argument; justification, vindication',[11] and the notion of defending someone in court is equated with 'vindicating' their conduct.[12] This equation of defence (in its general or legal sense) with vindication is significant, since vindication of conduct lies at the heart of the linguistic sense of justification. A practice which falls within the defence or justification provisions of the legislation is, therefore, characterised by the law as justifiable in the linguistic sense.

Apart from defences or justification, courts and tribunals have used at least two other legal techniques to justify conduct in the linguistic sense.

treatment of justifications, see eg *Bilka-Kaufhaus GmbH v Weber von Hartz* [1986] 2 CMLR 701; *Hampson v Department of Education and Science* [1989] IRLR 69 at 75 (revsd by House of Lords on other grounds: [1990] IRLR 302). See also recent controversy about the status of 'justifications' in direct discrimination claims under EC law – Bob Hepple, 'Can direct discrimination be justified?' (1994) 55 EOR 48.

8 *The Oxford English Dictionary* (Oxford, Clarendon Press, 1989, 2nd edn), Vol VIII, p 329.
9 Above n 8, Vol IV, p 376.
10 Above n 8, Vol VIII, p 329.
11 Above n 8, Vol IV, p 376.
12 Above n 8, Vol IV, p 377.

One is the *de minimis* method seen in the *De Souza v AA* case,[13] where a black secretary overheard her manager making a racially offensive remark about her to a colleague at work. The Court of Appeal found that a reasonable coloured secretary, overhearing such a comment, would as a consequence merely feel distressed rather than positively disadvantaged in their employment context. Consequently, it was held that the applicant could not be said to have suffered a detriment, which was necessary under the Race Relations Act, s 2(4)(c) in order to bring a claim.[14] The second technique is to interpret the meanings of legal concepts other than justification and defences – usually direct or indirect discrimination – or the range of situations to which the concepts are said to apply, in order to categorise the respondent's behaviour as falling outside the scope of the legislation, justifying it in the linguistic sense.

An instructive example of this type of justification is to be found in *Amin v Entry Clearance Officer, Bombay*.[15] The appellant, a Commonwealth citizen who held a British passport, was living in Bombay with her husband, and applied to the UK entry clearance officer for what was known as a 'special voucher' which would enable her to settle in the United Kingdom. As a matter of administrative discretion, such vouchers were only issued to heads of households, and the entry clearance officer denied the appellant's request for a voucher on the ground that, being a married woman, she could not qualify as a head of household. The appellant sought judicial review of the clearance officer's decision, invoking the Immigration Act 1971. The second aspect of the proceedings, of concern here, focused on whether the decision to deny her the voucher fell foul of the Sex Discrimination Act 1975. The House of Lords split three-to-two on this issue. Lord Fraser, for the majority, favoured a narrow approach to the scope of the Act and dismissed the appellant's claim. Having categorised as 'erroneous' the Home Office's contention that their guidelines to entry clearance officers – which presumed the head of household to be male – were not discriminatory, he nevertheless went on to say that 'not all sex discrimination is unlawful. Part I of the 1975 Act merely defined discrimination and it contains no provision for making it unlawful. Discrimination is only unlawful if it occurs in one of the fields in which it is prohibited by Parts II, III or IV of the Act.'[16] Since the granting of the special vouchers did not, according to Lord Fraser, amount to the provision of a service under s 29 of the Act, it fell outside the range of situations to which the Act applied.

Lord Scarman, dissenting, reached the opposite conclusion, finding that the provision of special entry vouchers to British passport holders constituted not only the provision of a facility, but the provision of a facility which

---

[13] [1986] IRLR 103.
[14] It is instructive to compare the Court of Appeal's approach in this case with the approach taken in *Gill & Coote v El Vino Co* [1983] IRLR 206; also *Heads v Insitn Cleaning* [1995] IRLR.
[15] [1983] 2 All ER 864.
[16] Above n 15 at 871.

was very valuable to a section of the public, and, therefore, fell within the scope of s 29. However, Lord Scarman's view of the scope of the Act merely involved a difference of degree from Lord Fraser's; for Lord Scarman went on to echo Lord Fraser by asserting that 'not every discrimination against a woman is unlawful',[17] and that Parts II–V of the 1975 Act specified the activities in relation to which a claim could be brought. The differing interpretations of the width of the Act's provisions determined the limits of the protection it could give and the range of conduct which the law would justify in the linguistic sense.

AN EXAMPLE

While courts and tribunals may justify particular practices by finding that they fall outside the scope of the legislation, the legal concepts of discrimination may also be expanded to penalise (or penalise more easily) conduct which was previously justified in the linguistic sense. A striking example is the House of Lords' expansion of direct discrimination in *R v Birmingham City Council, ex parte EOC*[18] and *James v Eastleigh BC*.[19] The key development in these cases was the re-interpretation of the phrase 'on the ground of her sex' in s 1(1)(a) of the 1975 [a]Act. Case law prior to these decisions suggested that the respondent needed to have intended, subjectively, to treat the applicant less favourably on the ground of her sex in order to be liable in direct discrimination,[20] while the respondent's actual motive or reason for treating the applicant less favourably was irrelevant. The *Birmingham City Council* and *James* cases, however, marked a shift to an objective and causal test for liability: Lord Goff stated in *Birmingham City Council* that there was direct discrimination if the applicants would have received the same treatment as comparable members of the opposite gender 'but for their sex. The intention or motive of the defendant to discriminate, though it may be relevant so far as remedies are concerned ... is not a necessary condition of liability; it is perfectly possible to imagine cases where the defendant had no such motive, and yet did in fact discriminate on the ground of sex.'[21] This was taken further in *James* where, according to Lord Goff, an applicant could recover in direct discrimination either where they had been deliberately selected for less favourable treatment because of their sex, or where the less favourable treatment they had suffered resulted from the application to them of a gender-based criterion which favoured the opposite sex.[22]

---

[17] Above n 15 at 877.
[18] [1989] 1 AC 1155.
[19] [1990] 2 AC 751.
[20] For discussion of 'less favourable treatment', see eg *Ministry of Defence v Jeremiah* [1980] 1 QB 87, esp Brightman LJ at 103G–104F; *Gill & Coote v El Vino Co*, above n 14 at 430D–H (Eveleigh LJ), 432A–B (Griffiths LJ), 432D–G (Sir Roger Ormrod); *R v Secretary of State for Education, ex parte Keating* (1985) 84 LGR 469 at 477; *R v Birmingham CC, ex parte Equal Opportunities Commission*, above, n 18 *per* Lord Goff at 1193H–1194A.
[21] Above, n 18, at 1194B–C.
[22] Above, n 19, at 772C–E.

Approving the 'but for' test in the same case, Lord Bridge suggested that 'the purity of the discriminator's subjective motive, intention or reason for discriminating cannot save the criterion applied from the objective taint of discrimination on the ground of sex.'[23]

This re-interpretation has had at least two consequences. The first has been to alter the standard of liability in direct discrimination. On its facts, *James v Eastleigh* concerned the legitimacy of the respondent's reliance on the unequal state retirement age for men and women to determine which of its residents were entitled to use the local authority leisure facilities for free. Relying on the state age meant that men aged between 60 and 65 had to pay, whereas women did not. The House of Lords' re-interpretation of the legal concept of direct discrimination meant, however, that asserting that it had not intended to discriminate and that it had merely desired to help pensioners, however they were officially defined, could no longer assist the local authority in rebutting the applicant's direct discrimination claim. Instead, the effect of the House of Lords' re-interpretation was to destroy the respondent's attempt to justify the differential treatment.

The other consequence of the re-interpretation affected the subject-matter which could form the basis of a direct discrimination claim. Strictly applied, the 'but for' test seemed, for example, capable of creating an easier route than had previously existed for applicants dismissed because of their pregnancy to claim that they had suffered direct discrimination. Since only women can become pregnant, dismissing a woman because she was pregnant would seem, by definition, to involve applying a gender-based criterion which would automatically fail the 'but for' test as defined in *James*, constituting direct discrimination without, as the case law had previously required, the applicant needing to show that an ill male would have been better treated. Instead, the dismissal of the applicant could be seen as resulting from a factor unique to women, ie pregnancy, so a male comparator was unnecessary since it was already implicit that but for her sex, the applicant would not have been so treated.

The treatment of this argument by the English courts in the *Webb v EMO Air Cargo* litigation might be seen as an example of judicial justification of employer action *via* a manipulation of the legal concept of direct discrimination. Giving judgment in the House of Lords, Lord Keith agreed that 'There can be no doubt that in general to dismiss a woman because she is pregnant or to refuse to employ a woman of child-bearing age because she may become pregnant is unlawful direct discrimination. Child-bearing and the capacity for child-bearing are characteristics of the female sex. So to apply these characteristics as the criterion for dismissal or refusal to employ is to apply a gender-based criterion, which the majority of this House in

---

[23] Above, n 19, at 765H–766A.
[24] [1992] 4 All ER 929 at 934a–b; see further Nicholas Bamforth, 'The Changing Concept of Sex Discrimination' (1993) 56 MLR 872.

James v Eastleigh BC . . . held to constitute unlawful direct discrimination.'[24] However, on the facts, it was found that the respondent had not been applying a gender-based criterion.[25] The applicant was not dismissed because she was pregnant, but because her pregnancy meant that she would not be available for work at a critical period,[26] ie to cover for another employee who was to be away on maternity leave, even though the applicant herself was to have been kept on by the company afterwards. In effect, the House of Lords was saying that the employer had a particular economic need for the employee to be present at a certain time, and if the employee could not meet this need, she could be dismissed so long as an absent man would have been similarly treated. The important point here is that the House of Lords was, in effect, establishing a new *ex post facto* justification for the employer's action, taking it outside the scope of the legislation. While the European Court of Justice later rejected this approach – in its judgment in *Webb*[27] – for cases where the pregnant employee's contract of employment was of uncertain duration, the role of the new justification where there is a fixed-term contract was left unclear. As Brian Napier has argued, this might be one area where the European Court of Justice would still give priority to the needs of the employer.[28] This avenue for justification cannot yet be seen as closed.

Another possibility apparently created by the introduction of the 'but for' test is that a strict interpretation of the wording of the test implies that it is unlawful to dismiss an employee because of their sexual orientation. If the key aspect of a person's sexual orientation is the gender (or genders, of those to whom they are sexually attracted or with whom they form sexual relationships,[29] then liability under the 'but for' test should, in logic, arise where a female employee is dismissed for engaging in a sexual relationship with or being attracted to another woman, provided that a male employee would not be dismissed for responding to women in such a fashion. Since the only obvious difference between these two situations is the gender of the employee who is dismissed, it would appear that a gender-based criterion has been used.

This line of argument found support in the advisory opinion of a Scottish Industrial Tribunal in *Wallace & O'Rourke v BG Turnkey Services (Scotland) Ltd*.[30] Here, two women who worked in the same factory claimed to have been dismissed because they were having a lesbian relationship, and argued that if a male employee would not have been dismissed for having a relationship with a female employee, it was direct discrimination for a female

---

[25] Above, n 24, at 934b.

[26] Above, n 24, at 934j.

[27] Case C-32/93, [1994] 3 WLR 941; see further Nicholas Bamforth, 'The Treatment of Pregnancy under European Community Sex Discrimination Law' (1995) 1 European Public Law 59.

[28] '*Webb* in Europe' (1994) New LJ 1020.

[29] *Cf* Robert Wintemute, 'Sexual Orientation Discrimination', in *Individual Rights and the Law in Britain* (Oxford, Clarendon Press, 1994), C McCrudden & G Chambers (eds).

[30] July 1993, unreported; see further Nicholas Bamforth, 'Sexual Orientation and Dismissal' (1994) New LJ 1402. See, however, *R v Ministry of Defence, ex parte Smith*, *The Times* 13 June 1995 (DC).

employee to be dismissed for this reason. The Tribunal dismissed the employer's argument that the applicants could have no case in direct discrimination since they were claiming that they had been dismissed because of their sexual orientation rather than their sex. The parties settled out of court after the Tribunal's preliminary ruling, but the Tribunal found it 'quite impossible' to say that 'there is a rule of law to the effect that the dismissal of a woman, because she is carrying on a lesbian relationship, is never sex discrimination'.

The *dicta* of the Tribunal in *Wallace v BG Turnkey Services* provides no formal precedent, but it is, when taken with the pregnancy cases, a good illustration of how the widening of the legal concept of direct discrimination in the *Birmingham City Council* and *James* cases has been used to support a further expansion of liability. Whatever the eventual fate of the reasoning in the later decisions,[31] it shows how a broadening in the scope of liability reduces the range of dismissals which the law can legitimate or justify in the linguistic sense.

Before leaving these cases, two general points must be made, The first is to acknowledge that courts and tribunals expand and contract legal concepts all the time, and that the anti-discrimination cases are not unique in this. As HLA Hart observed, 'Whichever device, precedent or legislation, is chosen for the communication of standards of behaviour, these, however smoothly they work over the great mass of ordinary cases, will, at some point where their application is in question, prove indeterminate; they will have what has been termed an *open texture* . . . we have presented this, in the case of legislation, as a general feature of human language; uncertainty at the borderline is the price to be paid for the use of general classifying terms in any form of communication covering matters of fact.'[32] The anti-discrimination cases discussed in this chapter clearly fall at Hart's borderline. Nevertheless, the boundary setting and justification exercises in play in the case do have a special significance in sex and race discrimination law, given the overt social goals of the legislation. For the legislation's effectiveness in protecting women and people of colour and in helping to counter sexist and racist behaviour is likely to depend, to some extent, on how widely it is interpreted. The wider the range of situations which are seen to be caught by the legislation, or the narrower the range of justifications in the linguistic sense, the more likely the law is to have a 'chilling' effect – to the extent that it is ever able to have such an effect – on sexually or racially discriminatory social conduct.[33]

---

[31] JM Thomson's article 'Crime, Morality and Unfair Dismissal' (1982) 98 LQR 423 details the types of temptation courts and tribunals may face to contract the concept of direct discrimination, thereby increasing the range of justifiable dismissals.

[32] HLA Hart, *The Concept of Law* (Oxford, Clarendon Press, 1994, 2nd edn), pp 127–128; see also 'Definition and Theory in Jurisprudence', reprinted in HLA Hart, *Essays in Jurisprudence and Philosophy* (Oxford, Clarendon Press, 1983).

[33] On the social effects of law, see Nicholas Bamforth, 'Human Rights, Sexual Orientation, and the Social and Legal Impact of Law and Law Reform' in Conor Gearty and Adam Tomkins (eds), *Understanding Human Rights* (London, Mansell, 1996).

Secondly, the cases are important analytically. Sex and race discrimination have been described as 'statutory torts',[34] civil proceedings under the 1975 and 1976 Acts being treated in the same manner as any other claim in tort.[35] It is possible to suggest of torts in general that each usually contains one, and generally two, sets of reasonably consistent (and usually interconnected) boundaries delimiting their scope – for otherwise, each tort simply blurs into the surrounding law. The first boundary will specify the quality of the act the defendant needs to commit to be made liable under the tort – this is the tort's standard of liability: some torts require intentional conduct for liability;[36] negligence, by contrast, requires conduct which is found to fall below the standard of care expected from the reasonable person, however this is defined.[37] The second boundary could be said to delimit the range of interests the tort exists to protect, or the types of damage for which it will give a remedy – the tort of defamation, for example, can be used where a person's reputation is injured.

Applying this analysis to sex and race discrimination, the move to a standard of strict, or at least stricter liability in the *Birmingham City Council* and *James v Eastleigh* cases can be seen as expanding the first, standard of liability-related boundary for direct discrimination, and as potentially widening the second, subject-matter related boundary to protect pregnant women and lesbians and gays. It was only through introducing a new type of justification, in the linguistic sense, for the applicant's dismissal that the House of Lords was able to rebut the pregnancy-related claim in *Webb v EMO*; and, while the status of this justification is unclear following the decision of the European Court of Justice,[38] it is possible that courts and tribunals might attempt similar justification-creating exercises in order to block future claims concerning sexual orientation.

CONCEPTS OF DISCRIMINATION

This examination of recent cases has shown that courts and tribunals are often willing to re-interpret the legal concepts of discrimination, and that particular practices are, in consequence, either deemed to be justifiable in the linguistic sense or to merit the imposition of a penalty. The boundaries of the legal concepts are, therefore, somewhat fluid. However, this analysis tells us only that the range of conduct deemed justifiable by anti-discrimination law varies over time. We need also to consider a deeper question, which

---

[34] WVH Rogers, *Winfield & Jolowicz on Tort* (London, Sweet & Maxwell, 1994, 15th edn) at p 637; *Alexander v Home Office* [1988] 2 All ER 118.

[35] Sex Discrimination Act 1975, s 66; Race Relations Act 1976, s 57.

[36] Eg *Wilkinson v Downton* [1897] 2 QB 57; *Janvier v Sweeney* [1919] 2 KB 316 (trespass to the person).

[37] Eg *Donoghue v Stevenson* [1932] AC 562. Compare *Anns v Merton LBC* [1978] AC 728; *Caparo Industries plc v Dickman* [1990] 2 AC 605; *Murphy v Brentwood DC* [1991] 1 AC 398. *Spring v Guardian Assurance plc* [1994] 3 All ER 129.

[38] Text to nn 27–28.

is whether the conduct justified or penalised as a result of the boundary alteration exercises can properly be described as 'discrimination'. Should, for example, the House of Lords' approach in *Webb v EMO* be seen as justifying a discriminatory dismissal, or as simply allowing an employer to exercise a legitimate economic choice?

This question goes beyond the legal concepts of direct and indirect discrimination, and can only be answered satisfactorily by employing a notion of discrimination which is independent of the law. Without an extra-legal notion, we are faced – when evaluating cases such as *Webb v EMO Air Cargo* and *Wallace v BG Turnkey Services* – with a choice between wide and narrow interpretations of existing law, with no independent criterion for assessing whether the adoption of a narrow interpretation will result in the justification of discrimination. Unfortunately, lawyers often lose sight of this point, understanding 'discrimination' solely in terms of the legal concepts. A clear example of this tendency is Lord Fraser's assertion, in *Amin v Entry Clearance Officer, Bombay*, that the first section of the 1975 Act *defined* discrimination, which was then made unlawful by the subsequent sections of the Act.[39] In fact, discrimination against women and ethnic minorities had been recognised as a social problem long before the Act. All the Act did was to establish specific legal devices which were to be deployed in tackling some aspects of this problem.

There are other ways in which the adoption of a wholly law-centred view of the word 'discrimination' can blur debate over anti-discrimination law. First, it can obscure the fact that the law exists to serve social goals – ie to counter social behaviour which is seen as sexually or racially discriminatory. Blurring can occur because the law's effectiveness in this task can only meaningfully be measured by comparison with extra-legal notions of 'discrimination'. A wholly law-centred view may, secondly, cause us to forget that the law's social goals can also be served by extra-legal devices such as contract compliance.[40] Again, blurring can occur since a decision whether to use law or extra-legal methods often turns on tactical considerations, and can only be made coherently if an extra-legal notion of 'discrimination' is kept in mind.

To decide whether judicial boundary alteration exercises result in the justification or penalising of conduct which can properly be described as 'discrimination', it is, therefore, necessary to move into the area avoided in the *Equality for Women* White Paper: we must find a justification (in the linguistic sense) for the law's anti-discrimination provisions which will characterise the *nature* of the social problem which discrimination is felt to represent. Such a philosophical justification will reveal the common link between practices penalised under the legal notions of direct and indirect dis-

---

[39] Above n 16.

[40] Although see *Wheeler v Leicester CC* [1985] 1 All ER 1106; Local Government Act 1988, ss 17–19; R v *London Borough of Islington, ex parte Building Employers Confederation* [1989] IRLR 382; R v *London Borough of Lewisham, ex parte Shell UK Ltd* (1988) 18 EOR 43; Christopher McCrudden, 'Codes in a Cold Climate: Administrative Rule-making by the Commission for Racial Equality' (1988) 51 MLR 409.

crimination which merits treating them in this way. If conduct which involves the common element is not currently penalised under the legislation, it will be fair to say that the law is, in the case concerned, justifying discrimination.

Of the philosophical justifications for anti-discrimination law which have been advanced, many distinguish between direct discrimination – seen as a legal remedy which effects corrective justice where a harm has been committed – and indirect discrimination – seen as a vehicle for promoting a specified pattern of distributive justice.[41] As John Gardner has argued, however, this duality may produce incoherence and problems of illegitimacy in factual contexts where the operation of anti-discrimination law invokes a mixture of distributive and corrective justifications.[42] And, while discrimination as a social concern may be seen as continuous, in that situations categorised as invoking the legal concepts of direct or indirect discrimination are simply facets of the same social problem, the use of distinct corrective and distributive justifications for each legal device is discontinuous.[43] As Gardner suggests, 'Given a single [social] practice which could be a harm [invoking corrective justice], or could be an injustice [invoking a pattern of distributive justice], there is no single state response which is a legitimate application of the harm principle *and* a legitimate implementation of distributive justice. So . . . an application of the liberal harm principle will be incoherent and arbitrary from the perspective of liberal distributive justice, because it will look to past behaviour; meanwhile, redistribution will not cohere with the harm principle, because it will look only to the justice of end-states, ignoring how they came about. The two principles are radically discontinuous.'[44]

To avoid these difficulties, it is necessary to find a single, continuous principle which may justify both direct and indirect discrimination as legal devices. I will focus here on two possible justifying principles, going respectively to autonomy and to objectification. Gardner's liberal autonomy theory is based on the writings of Joseph Raz.[45] According to Gardner (citing Raz), 'the right not to suffer [direct] discrimination "is meant to foster a public culture which enables people to take pride in their identity as members of . . . groups." Those who do not enjoy such pride in identity are deprived of a component of valuable autonomy as we understand it, are harmed in the wide sense. Meanwhile, the rules governing indirect discrimination provide another example of a legitimate implementation of our ideal of autonomy: "The government has an obligation to create an environment providing individuals with an adequate range of options *and the opportunities to choose them*."'[46] Gardner's formulation is not intended to provide a litmus test for

---

[41] See, for example, the essays collected in *Equality and Discrimination: Essays in Freedom and Justice* (Stuttgart, Steiner, 1985), S Guest & A Milne (eds).

[42] John Gardner, 'Liberals and Unlawful Discrimination' (1989) 9 OJLS 1 at pp 12–17.

[43] John Gardner, above n 42 at p 15.

[44] John Gardner, above n 42 at p 16. Note that I am not arguing, unlike Gardner, for a liberal interpretation of anti-discrimination legislation.

[45] Principally Raz's *The Morality of Freedom* (Oxford, Clarendon Press, 1986).

[46] John Gardner, above n 42 at pp 18–19.

social situations which should be regarded as examples of discrimination in practice. Rather, the formulation is used to delimit the types of social practice which may properly be penalised using one of the *legal* concepts of discrimination.[47] Nevertheless, the notions of harm to or non-promotion of autonomy may still be invoked as one possible common element in the range of social situations which can be classified as 'discrimination'.

Promising though the Gardner theory sounds, though, its justification for legislation outlawing direct discrimination is problematic. For implicit within this part of the theory is the notion that one's gender or race is an important element of one's personal identity, and for that reason deserves to be protected by anti-discrimination law, identity being a key component of autonomy. Gardner's reliance on identity may prove too much, however. Even assuming that personal identity is a coherent concept, it is difficult to accept that identity as a member of a gender or a racial group is *always* the *specific* aspect of a person's autonomy which is harmed by conduct which the law classifies as direct discrimination. It may be the case, for example, that the victim of such conduct had, prior to the act itself, no sense of identity attaching to their gender or race, and that the hurt inherent in the act was being *made aware* that others ascribed a derogatory identity to them because of their sex or ethnic origins. Unless victims of conduct which the law categorises as direct discrimination are simply to be *assumed* to possess identities of which their gender or ethnic origins are important components – an assumption which is both artificial and illiberal – Gardner's theory cannot adequately justify direct discrimination as a legal device.

The objectification theory avoids the unreliable notion of personal identity.[48] Instead, it views sex and race discrimination as social practices which treat people as unworthy of full consideration as human beings due to a characteristic (or characteristics) which they are assumed to possess by virtue of their actual or perceived membership of a group to which social sensitivity attaches. People are the victims of discrimination where they are treated as objects rather than subjects,[49] the objectification relating to their actual or perceived membership of the group in question and to characteristics which are assumed to attach to that group. Human beings, under this theory, should always be worthy of consideration as subjects, and it is this which justifies the use of anti-discrimination law. Direct discrimination provides the legal basis for a remedy where people are objectified overtly by conduct; indirect discrimination remedies hidden practices which have the effect of denying people the chance of consideration as subjects.

Objectification can, therefore, operate actively, where an individual is singled out for open abuse or attack because of a perceived gender- or race-related

---

[47] John Gardner, above n 42 at pp 17–22.

[48] See further Nicholas Bamforth, *Sexuality, Morals and Justice: A Theory of Lesbian and Gay Rights and Law*, above n 4.

[49] See Richard Mohr, *Gays/Justice: A Study of Ethics, Society and Law* (New York, Columbia University Press, 1988), p 58; note, however, that Mohr's comments are made in the context of US constitutional law, and are therefore coupled with notions of privacy.

attribute; or passively, where they are denied a benefit because of a traditional assumption, for example, about appropriate gender roles. The social sensitivity surrounding gender and race means that adverse treatment on either ground may be seen as objectification, whereas adverse treatment because of a non-sensitive characteristic may not. As such, the objectification theory is capable of defining what can, in broad terms, be identified as practical examples of sex and race discrimination.

It is important, at this stage, to stress two points. The first is that the autonomy and objectification theories are merely examples of philosophical justifications for anti-discrimination law; as different justifications suggest different boundaries for the law, one's personal choice of justification will determine what types of conduct one regards as 'discrimination' in the extra-legal sense. Secondly, even if the law is seen, under whichever theory, as justifying discrimination in the linguistic sense in a particular situation, this provides only a *prima facie* reason for penalising the relevant conduct under one of the legal concepts of discrimination. The reason is *prima facie* rather than conclusive since, as Joseph Raz has observed, 'It seems to be a common philosophical mistake to think that the core justification of a right or any other normative institution is sufficient for fixing its boundaries. The boundaries of a right are greatly affected by existing local conventions and practices . . .'[50]

The practical role of 'local conventions and practices' in fixing the boundaries of a 'right' has been powerfully demonstrated in the *Mossop* litigation in Canada.[51] In issue was the refusal of the plaintiff's employer to grant him bereavement leave to attend the funeral of the father of his longstanding male partner. Assuming that an employee with a partner of the opposite gender would have been granted leave, the plaintiff argued that the employer's refusal in his case was discrimination on the basis of 'family status', contrary to the provisions of the Canadian Human Rights Act. As such, the case turned on whether a same-sex relationship could constitute a 'family', thereby gaining the Act's protection and rendering the refusal of bereavement leave unlawful. The majority judgments in the Federal Court of Appeal and Supreme Court of Canada invoked the notion of parliamentary intent to rebuf the plaintiff's claim: if Parliament had intended to protect same-sex relationships under the 'family status' provisions of the Canadian Human Rights Act, it would have done so explicitly; as this had not happened, the courts could not amend the Act on a *de facto* basis by reading such relationships into it.[52] A conservative view of the appropriate judicial

---

[50] Joseph Raz, *Ethics in the Public Domain: Essays in the Morality of Law and Politics* (Oxford, Clarendon Press, 1994), p 133.

[51] *Canada (AG) v Mossop* (1990) 71 DLR (4th) 661 (Federal Court of Appeal); [1993] 1 SCR 554 (Supreme Court of Canada). For comment, see Robert Wintemute, 'Sexual Orientation Discrimination as Sex Discrimination: Same-Sex Couples and the *Charter* in *Mossop*, *Egan* and *Layland*' (1994) 39 McGill LJ 429 at pp 432–441; Didi Herman, above n 4 at pp 133–139, 147.

[52] In the Federal Court of Appeal, see Marceau JA, above n 51 at pp 675–678; in the Supreme Court of Canada, see Lamer CJ, above n 51 at pp 580, 582 and La Forest J, above n 52 at pp 586–587.

function in human rights litigation – in Raz's terms, a 'local convention' or practice – was, therefore, used to justify a restrictive interpretation of the legal right to protection on the basis of 'family status', leaving lesbian and gay couples outside the boundary of this right.[53]

A more fundamental difficulty, what Raz would describe as the 'core justification' for the legal right to protection from sex discrimination, arises in cases – like *Wallace v BG Turnkey Services* – where claimants argue that adverse treatment due to sexuality should be classified as *sex* discrimination. For, while discrimination due to sex, race or sexual orientation may all involve a similar *type* of moral wrongdoing, legal systems tend to employ distinct *provisions* for dealing with sex and race discrimination cases – for race and gender are seen as separate grounds on which victims can be adversely treated. In similar vein, it could be argued that sexual orientation and gender are, conceptually, distinct grounds for discrimination, so that rules designed to penalise sex discrimination would be artificially stretched if used to penalise sexual orientation discrimination. In the absence of a general anti-discrimination provision which placed no limits on the range of impermissible grounds for discrimination, sexual orientation discrimination could not, unless shown conceptually to be a form of sex discrimination, be penalised under sex discrimination provisions. Consequently, Canadian courts have, to date, been generally unfavourable to such an argument.[54]

CONCLUSION

This chapter has concentrated on cases concerning gender rather than race discrimination provisions, and direct rather than indirect discrimination. Judicial justification exercises of the type analysed here can, however, be found throughout anti-discrimination law – one obvious example is in the dispute over the meaning of a requirement or condition in indirect discrimination cases such as *Perera v Civil Service Commission*.[55] If one general theme emerges from this chapter, it is that meaningful analysis of anti-discrimination law requires us to move beyond the legal concepts of justification and discrimination. For, while the chapter has highlighted the judicial habit of justifying actions or practices in the linguistic sense by reinterpreting the legal concepts of discrimination, it is according to our personal theories of what discrimination is, and of the philosophical justifications for using law to penalise it as a social practice, that we have to decide whether such reinterpretations act to justify discrimination.

[53] Cases where the Canadian judiciary has adopted a wider view of its function are discussed by Robert Wintemute, above n 52.

[54] See Robert Wintemute, above n 52 at pp 459–478; the Supreme Court of Hawaii was, by contrast, happy to accept that discrimination due to sexual orientation was a form of sex discrimination in *Baehr v Lewin* 852 P 2d 44 (1993).

[55] [1983] IRLR 166.

6

GENDER AND COMMERCIAL DISCRIMINATION

Catherine Barnard

The principle of non-discrimination – on the grounds of nationality or sex – is a central tenet of Community jurisprudence. This chapter will show that the principle of non-discrimination underpins the fundamental freedoms in the Community. It will suggest that the principle of non-discrimination outlaws both direct and indirect discrimination, by whatever name they are described, and will argue that, while there is – and should be – no defences to direct discrimination (except those expressly provided for by the Treaty) by contrast, indirect discrimination is unlawful unless it can be objectively justified. Finally it will be suggested that the distinction between these two concepts should be maintained.

THE PRINCIPLE OF NON-DISCRIMINATION

The significance of non-discrimination is clearly stated in Part One of the Treaty entitled 'Principles'. Article 7 EEC/6 EC provides that:

'Within the scope of application of this Treaty, and without prejudice to any special provisions contained therein, any discrimination on the grounds of nationality shall be prohibited'.

Thus in the context of nationality the principle of non-discrimination applies, unless there are any express derogations to the contrary. Specific reference to the principle of non-discrimination on the grounds of nationality can be found in Art 48(2) on the free movement of persons and Art 67 on capital. It also underpins Art 95 on internal taxation.[1] In the context of services, Art 65 provides that:

'As long as restrictions on freedom to provide services have not been abolished, each member state shall apply such restrictions without distinction on the grounds of nationality or residence to all persons providing services within the meaning of the first paragraph of Art 59'.

[1] No member state shall impose directly or indirectly on the products of other member states any internal taxation of any kind in excess of that imposed directly or indirectly on similar domestic products'.

[2] Case 33/74 [1974] ECR 1299.

In the early case of *Van Binsbergen*[2] Advocate-General Mayras made clear that Art 59 and Art 60(3) were intended to bring about '*equality of treatment* between the nationals of one member state and the nationals of the other states of the Common Market ... These provisions thereby ensure the implementation of the general rules laid down in Art 7 of the Treaty [which prohibits] any discrimination on the grounds of nationality' (emphasis added).[3] The Advocate-General argued that the requirement of discrimination dominates the application of Art 48 on the freedom of movement for employed persons and that it lies behind the provisions of Art 52 on the freedom of establishment.[4] The European Court of Justice agreed. In both *Debauve*[5] and *Van Wesemael*[6] the Court talked of the requirement imposed by Art 59 of abolishing 'all discrimination against the person providing the service by reason of his nationality or the fact that he is established in a member state other than that in which the service is to be provided'.[7]

The drafting of Art 30 is quite different. It states that:

'Quantitative restrictions on imports and all measures having equivalent effect shall without prejudice to the following provisions, be prohibited between member states.'

The Court has developed such a simple statement into a complex and extensive jurisprudence on the free movement of goods.[8] Yet Art 30 differs from the other fundamental Treaty provisions in that it makes no express reference to the principle of non-discrimination on the grounds of nationality. Consequently, some commentators have argued that discrimination is not an essential component of Art 30.[9] However, legislation and the jurisprudence of the Court seem to disagree. For example, Art 2 of Dir 70/50[10] apparently envisages an element of discrimination. It provides that the Directive covers measures, other than those applicable equally to domestic and imported products (which hinder imports which could otherwise take place) 'including measures which make the importation more difficult or costly than the disposal of domestic production'. In *Commission v Ireland*[11]

---

[3] P 1316.
[4] Case 2/74 *Reyners v Belgium* [1974] ECR 631. Art 52(3) provides that 'Freedom of establishment shall include the right to take up and pursue activities as self-employed persons ... under the same conditions laid down by its own nationals by the law of the country where such establishment is effected'.
[5] Case 52/79 *Procureur du Roi v Debauve* [1986] ECR 2375, para 11.
[6] Case 110 and 111/78 [1979] ECR 35, para 27.
[7] Paragraphs 11 and 27 respectively.
[8] This jurisprudence is discussed at length in, for example, Green Hartley and Usher, *The Legal Foundations of the Single European Market* (OUP, 1991), Chapters 5–7; Wyatt and Dashwood, *European Community Law* (Sweet and Maxwell, 1993), Chapter 8; Weatherill and Beaumont, *EC Law* (Penguin, 1993), Chapters 15–17.
[9] The German authors have insisted that discrimination is an essential element of Art 30 while others, such as Verloren Van Themaat, have argued that the emphasis is on the effect of trade between member states – see the discussion by Gormley, L, *Prohibiting Restrictions on Trade within the EEC*, TMC Asser Instituut, The Hague, 1985, pp 8–19.
[10] 1970 OJ SE/I, p 17.
[11] Case 113/80 [1981] ECR 1625.

the Court of Justice also used the language of discrimination. It ruled that Irish legislation requiring all souvenirs and articles of jewellery imported from other member states to bear an indication of origin or the word 'foreign' 'indisputably constitutes a discriminatory measure'.[12] More recently, in the important case of *Keck and Mithouard*,[13] the Court seemed to exclude from the scope of Art 30 certain measures which do not have a discriminatory effect – that is those national provisions restricting or prohibiting certain selling arrangements whose purpose is not to regulate the trade in goods between the member states,[14] which 'apply to all affected traders operating within the national territory and ... affect in the same manner, *in law and in fact*, the marketing of domestic products and of those from other Member States'.[15]

The application of the principle of non-discrimination is not confined to nationality. As we have seen,[16] in Art 119 it applies to another fundamental principle[17] – equal treatment between the sexes on the grounds of pay which, as the court observed in *Roberts v Birds Eye Walls*,[18] '*like the general principle of non-discrimination which it embodies in a specific form*, presupposes that men and women to whom it applies are in identical situations' (emphasis added). Additionally, Art 40(3) excludes any discrimination between producers or consumers in the Community. On the strength of these constitutional precedents the Court has ruled that there is a general principle of non-discrimination[19] or 'equality which is one of the fundamental principles of Community Law'.[20] This chapter, however, will focus more specifically on conduct which has some sort of adverse impact on its victims and a prohibited classification (such as nationality or sex) underlying that impact.

DIRECT DISCRIMINATION

Although a directly discriminatory national measure *prima facie* contravenes the Treaty, it can be saved by reference to one of the express derogations

---

[12] Paragraph 16.

[13] Joined Cases C-267 and C-268/91 [1993] ECR I-6097.

[14] It is unusual in the context of discrimination law to look at the intention behind a measure, although given the nature of the defences available (see below) it is implicit that as a rule of thumb while direct discrimination is considered intentional, indirect discrimination is usually unintentional, since regard is had to the effect of the measure.

[15] An interesting parallel exists between the wording in *Keck* and Art 2 of Dir 70/50. See further Chalmers, D, 'Repackaging the Internal Market – The Ramifications of the *Keck* Judgment' (1994) 19 EL Rev 385, Reich, 'The November Revolution of the European Court of Justice: *Keck, Meng* and *Audi* revisited' (1994) 31 CML Rev 459, Gormley, 'Reasoning Renounced? The Remarkable Judgment in *Keck and Mithouard*' (1994) European Business Law Review 63 and the note by Roth (1994) 31 CML Rev 845.

[16] See above in Chapter 2.

[17] Case 149/77 *Defrenne v Sabena* (no 3) [1978] ECR 1365.

[18] Case No C-132/92 [1993] IRLR 29.

[19] Case 1/72 *Frilli v Belgium* [1972] EWCR 457, para 19; Case 152/73 *Sotgiu v Deutsche Bundespost* [1974] ECR 153, para 11; Case 162/82 *ECSC v Ferrier Sant'Anna* [1983] ECR 1681.

[20] Joined Cases 117/76 *Albert Rucksdeschel and another v HZA Hamburg-St Annen* and 16/77

provided by the Treaty. This was made clear in *Gouda*,[21] where the Court said that national rules which are not applicable to services without discrimination as regards their origin are compatible with Community law only if they can be brought within the scope of an express exception, such as that contained in Art 56 of the Treaty.[22] Similar express exceptions are provided in the context of Art 48(3) on workers, while a wider range of exceptions is provided in Art 36 on goods. However, there is no defence specified to some Treaty provisions – most notably to Art 119 on equal pay, Art 95 on internal taxation and Art 12[23] on custom duties. It would seem, therefore, that member states have no defence when faced with a claim of direct discrimination under one of these Articles.

INDIRECT DISCRIMINATION

In addition to the more common disparate adverse impact situations described by Evelyn Ellis,[24] it could be said that indirect discrimination arises where the national system applies the same criteria to different circumstances which then has the effect of disadvantaging the protected group.[25] Art 52 on establishment provides a good illustration of this. Art 52(2) envisages that the host member state applies the same conditions to its own nationals as to those foreign nationals who wish to establish themselves. This would mean that a person fully qualified in state A would have to requalify in state B, imposing a particular burden on those wishing to exercise their right of free movement and, as a result, representing a significant disincentive to movement. This point was recognised by the Court in *Vlassopoulou*.[26] Consequently, by applying the principle of mutual recognition, the court ruled that national authorities were obliged to take the qualifications the person had gained in state A into account and to compare them

---

[21] Case C-288/89 [1991] ECR I-4007.

[22] It has been suggested (Craig and De Burca, *EC Law, Text, Cases and Materials* (OUP, 1995), p 735) that in the earlier Case 352/85 *Bond van Adverteerders v Netherlands* [1988] ECR 2085 the court seemed to go one stage further, drawing a distinction between rules which were intended to discriminate and those which were genuinely equally applicable but which happened to impose an unequal burden (indirectly discriminatory measures). In the case of intentionally discriminatory restrictions, overt or covert, member states could rely only on the express derogations.

[23] In Case 24/68 *Commission v Italy* [1969] ECR 193 the Court confirmed that Art 12 constitutes a fundamental rule which does not permit of any exceptions.

[24] See above in Chapter 2.

[25] Some of the earlier case law also recognised this type of discrimination – see, for example, Case 13/63 *Italy v Commission* [1963] ECR 165. See Herdegen, *op cit*, p 684.

[26] Case 340/89 *Vlassopoulou v Ministerium fur Justiz* [1991] ECR 2347. See also Case 221/85 *Commission v Belgium* [1987] ECR 719 and Case 182/83 *Robert Fearon v Irish Land Commission* [1984] ECR 3677 and the cases on single practice restrictions – Case 107/83 *Ordre des Avocats v Klopp* [1984] ECR 2971; Case 96/85 *Commission v France* [1986] ECR 1475; Case C-351/90 *Commission v Luxembourg* [1992] ECR I-3945 and Case C-106/91 *Ramrath v Ministre de la Justice* [1992] ECR I-3351.

with those required in state B. A similar approach was also adopted in the two Directives on Mutual Recognition of Diplomas.[27]

The Court has also been ready to recognise, and strike down, indirectly discriminatory measures in the context of Art 48. For example, in *Sotgiu*[28] the Court said that 'the rules regarding equality of treatment, both in the Treaty and in Art 7 of Reg 1612/68, forbid not only overt discrimination by reason of nationality but also all covert forms of discrimination, which, by the application of other criteria of differentiation, lead in fact to the same result'.

In the context of Art 30 on the free movement of goods and Art 59 on the freedom to provide services, it is suggested that the Court also recognises indirect discrimination, although it has been less specific in its identification. In the early case of *Seco*[29] it was recognised that the provisions contained in Arts 59 and 60 'prohibit not only overt discrimination based on the nationality of the person providing a service but also cover all forms of discrimination which, although based on criteria which appear to be neutral, in practice lead to the same result'.[30] Advocate-General Slynn in *Cinéthèque* also considered that Art 30 applied not only to national measures which discriminate against imports but also to those rules which, 'although not directed at importation as such but covering both national goods and imports' require 'a producer or distributor to take steps additional to those which he would normally and lawfully take in the marketing of goods, which thereby render importation more difficult so that imports may be restricted and national producers be given more protection in practice.'[31] He continued that such national measures would not be in breach of Art 30 if it could be shown that the measure was justified by mandatory requirements of the kind contemplated in *Cassis de Dijon*.[32] In that case, as subsequently interpreted by the Court in *Keck*, it was said that Art 30 precluded the application of 'rules that lay down requirements to be met by such goods (such as requirements as to designation, form, size, weight, composition, presentation, labelling, packaging) to goods from other member states where they are lawfully manufactured and marketed, even if those rules apply without

---

27 Dir 89/48/EEC (OJ 1989 L19/16) and Dir 92/51/EEC (OJ 1992 L209/25).
28 Case 152/73 *Sotgiu v Deutsche Bundespost* [1974] ECR 153. See also Case 15/69 *Wurtemmbergische Milchverwertung-Sudmilch AG v Ugliola* [1970] ECR 363.
29 Cases 62 and 63/8 [1982] ECR 223.
30 Paragraph 8. Similar views were expressed by the Court in Case 152/73 *Sotgiu* [1974] ECR 153 a case concerning the equality of treatment in the context of the free movement of workers.
31 Case 60 and 61/84 *Cinéthèque SA v Federation Nationale des Cinemas Francais* [1985] ECR 2605. Advocate-General Slynn believed that the facts of *Cinéthèque* did not fall into this category because the national measure was not specifically directed at imports, did not discriminate against imports, did not make it any more difficult for an importer to sell his products than it was for a domestic producer and gave no protection to domestic producers. In his view, the measure did not fall within Art 30, even if it did lead to a restriction or reduction of imports. The Court, however, took a different approach. It said that the measure fell within Art 30, although it was capable of being justified. The Advocate-General's approach seemed to have gained subsequent support from the Court in the case of *Keck and Mithouard*.
32 Case 4/75 *Rewe Zentralfinanz GmbH v Landwirtschaftskammer* [1975] ECR 843.

distinction to all products, unless their application can be justified by a public interest objective taking precedence over the free movement of goods'.[33]

While the statements in *Seco* and *Cinéthèque* closely reflect the definition of indirect discrimination outlined above, confusion has arisen as a result of the use of diverse terminology to describe what is, in essence, indirect discrimination. For example, some authors talk in terms of 'distinctly' and 'indistinctly applicable' measures,[34] while others speak of 'equally applicable' measures.[35] The Advocates-General have also muddied the water by taking a restrictive view of the meaning of 'discrimination', equating it with direct, and possibly intentional indirect,[36] discrimination. Advocate-General Slynn in *Webb*[37] referred to the fact that:

> '... The abolition of the restrictions on the freedom to supply services within the Community entails *more than the abolition of discrimination* on the grounds of nationality or place of establishment and extends to the removal of all obstacles to the freedom to supply services across the Community's internal borders'[38] (emphasis added).

Similarly, Advocate-General Van Gerven in *SPUC v Grogan*[39] said that the European Court of Justice had not yet expressly ruled that Art 59 was applicable to '*non-discriminatory*[40] measures which impede intra-Community trade in services' (emphasis added), but he said that the court had not expressly

[33] Joined Cases C-267 and 268/91 *Keck and Mithouard* [1993] ECR I-6097, para 15. The list of production requirements found in para 15 parallels the list found in Art 3 of Dir 70/50.

[34] For example, Weatherill and Beaumont, *op cit*, pp 275–376 and Chapter 17.

[35] Green, Hartley and Usher, *op cit*, Chapter 6.

[36] See above, n 22. Imposing a residence requirement on a foreign provider of services might constitute an example of intentional indirect discrimination.

[37] Case 279/80 [1981] ECR 3305. Advocate-General Slynn also said in *Cinéthèque* that 'discrimination ... although it may be sufficient or even conclusive, to bring a measure within Art 30, is not a necessary precondition for Art 30 to apply'. However, it does seem that in this context he meant that direct discrimination was not a necessary precondition, because he continues in the same paragraph that 'Measures applied equally to imports and domestically produced goods may in practice require importers to take steps which otherwise they would not take and which indirectly discourage them from importing or, by creating additional problems hinder them from doing so ... These measures may ... amount to a restriction within Art 30'.

[38] These pronouncements by the Advocates-General are based on a careful textual analysis of the Treaty. Art 65, it is argued, prohibits discrimination on the grounds of nationality or residence prior to the abolition of restrictions on the freedom to provide services. Thus, for example, in *Debauve*, the Court found that in the absence of any harmonisation of the rules relating to the transmission of adverts by cable television the matter falls within the residual power of each member state to regulate. But any rules enacted by the member states must be applied 'without distinction as regards the origin ... the nationality of the person providing the service, or the place where he is established' (paras 15 and 16). This is a good example of the transitional or residual role played by the Art 7 notion of non-discrimination. If Art 65 prohibits discrimination on the grounds of nationality or residence, it is difficult to argue that Art 59 is concerned only with the abolition of discrimination, 'For there would be little, if anything, left to be abolished under its provisions that had not already been abolished by Article 65'.

[39] Case C-159/90 [1991] ECR I-4685.

[40] Advocate-General Jacobs in Case C-76/90 [1991] ECR I-4221 has also said that to allow measures which are non-discriminatory but detrimental to intra-Community trade in services to fall *a priori* outside the scope of Art 59 of the EEC Treaty would detract substantially from the effectiveness of the principle of the free movement of services.

restricted the scope of Art 59 to 'overt or covert discriminatory measures'. This led him to conclude that '. . . national rules which, albeit not discriminatory, may, overtly or covertly, actually or potentially, impede intra-Community trade in services fall in principle within the scope of Arts 59 and 60 of the EEC Treaty'.

In *Torfaen*[41] Advocate-General Van Gerven tried to rationalise the Court's jurisprudence in respect of these so-called non-discriminatory measures. He suggested that in its early case law the Court recognised that Art 30 caught measures which applied to national and imported products without distinction where the 'measures are not discriminatory in their aims but which are *de facto* more burdensome for imported products than for domestic products, in other words they place imported products in a disadvantageous position in relation to domestic products'. He then explained that the disparities between national laws may result in 'serious obstacles to intra-Community trade since they may necessitate extra expense or additional efforts in order to make the manufacture or the marketing of the product comply with laws differing from one member state to another'. However, in more recent case law Advocate-General Van Gerven suggested that the Court's approach has been 'not to examine whether imported products were put at a disadvantage but whether the Community market was partitioned into separate national markets'.[42] A combination of these approaches seems to have been adopted by the Court in the context of services. In *Säger*,[43] for example, the Court recognised that 'Art 59 of the Treaty requires not only the elimination of all discrimination on the ground of nationality but also the abolition of any restriction, even if it applies without distinction to national providers of services and to those of other member states, *when it is liable to impede the activities of a provider of services established in another Member State* where he lawfully provides similar services' (emphasis added).[44]

---

[41] Case C-145/88 [1989] ECR I-3851, citing Case 120/78 *Cassis de Dijon* [1979] ECR 649, 662.

[42] Joined Cases 60 and 61/84 *Cinéthèque* [1985] ECR 2605, Case 216/84 *Commission v Germany* [1988] ECR 793, Case 158/86 *Commission v Germany* [1989] ECR 1021, Case 158/86 *Warner Brothers* [1988] ECR 2605, Case 382/87 *Buet* [1989] ECR 1235 and Joined Cases 266 and 267/87 *The Queen v Pharmaceutical Society of Great Britain and Others* [1989] ECR 1295. See also Steiner, 'Drawing the Line: Uses and Abuses of Article 30' (1992) 29 CML Rev 749, 758 'But spreading the net of Art 30 to embrace distinctly applicable measures which cannot be said seriously to *hinder* imports, even if they *affect* trade between member states or bring about some alteration to the pattern or in some cases the volume of trade, and requiring that such measures be justified, creates problems'.

[43] Case C-76/90 [1991] ECR I-4221.

[44] In Case C-384/93 *Alpine Investments BV v Minister van Financien* [1995] All ER (EC) 543, a decision concerning cold calling in the financial sector, the Court rejected the application of the *Keck* approach to the facts of the case. It said that 'Although a prohibition such as the one at issue in the main proceedings is general and non-discriminatory and neither its object nor effect is to put the national market at an advantage over providers of services in other member states, it can nevertheless . . . constitute a restriction on the freedom to provide cross-border services'. Nevertheless, distinguishing *Keck*, it then continued that the national measure prohibiting cold calling 'directly affects access to the market in services in the other member states and is thus capable of hindering intra-Community trade in services'. This would suggest that the measure actually has an indirectly discriminatory effect – it makes access for the service provider to other markets more difficult.

If Advocate-General Van Gerven's arguments are accepted then it seems that the emphasis has moved away from examining specific notions of discrimination to looking at the effects of a particular measure on market integration and Community trade.[45] However, it could be argued that in reality the 'different' approaches are merely two sides of the same indirectly discriminatory coin – the earlier approach examines the effect from a subjective perspective (the effect of the national measure on the individual concerned), the later approach an objective perspective (the effect of the national measure on the Community market).

Two cases illustrate this point. In *Rau*[46] a challenge was made to Belgian rules requiring all margarine to be packaged in cube-shaped containers. In *Webb*[47] a British employment agency, holding a licence in the UK provided temporary workers to Dutch businesses. The manager, Mr Webb, was prosecuted for supplying workers without possessing a Dutch licence. In both cases the national measure applied to all producers/service providers (both foreign and national) but placed a particular burden on the foreigner who had to bear the additional costs and inconvenience of repackaging the goods or obtaining an additional licence. Alternatively it could be said that the national measure represented a particular disincentive for the foreigner from providing the goods/services, which affected Community trade in goods and services.

OBJECTIVE JUSTIFICATION

It has been argued that a directly discriminatory measure breaches the relevant Treaty provision and can be saved only by reference to an express exception, where one is provided. In contrast, indirectly discriminatory measures may be justified by reference to a much wider range of objectives. If one such justification is proved, the measure is not caught by the Treaty provisions at all.

The Court seems to have adopted this approach in the context of free movement of workers. Indirectly discriminatory measures can be saved not only by reference to one of the express exceptions,[48] but also by being objectively justified. For example, in *Maria Chiara Spotti v Freistaat Bayern*[49]

[45] The need to look at the effect of a particular measure was identified at an early stage in Case 8/74 *Dassonville* [1974] ECR 837 where the court emphasised that 'all trading rules which are capable of hindering directly or indirectly, actually or potentially intra-Community trade are to be considered as measures having an effect equivalent to quantitative restrictions'. In the context of Art 85 the Treaty talks of 'agreements between undertakings ... which have as their object *or effect* the prevention, restriction or distortion of competition ...' (emphasis added).

[46] Case 261/81 *Walter Rau Lebensmittelwerke v de Smedt Pvba* [1982] ECR 3961.

[47] Case 279/80 *Criminal Proceedings against Webb* [1982] ECR 3305.

[48] For example, Case 379/87 *Groener v Minister for Education* [1989] ECR 3967 where the requirement of having knowledge of the Irish language, although indirectly discriminatory, was compatible with the exception in Art 3(1) of Reg 1612/68.

[49] Case C-272/92, decision of the Full Court of 20 October 1993.

a German law required contacts with foreign language assistants to be for a limited duration. The Court ruled that since the great majority of language assistants were foreign nationals, the German law placed them at a disadvantage in respect of German nationals. Consequently the Court said that the national rule constituted indirect discrimination prohibited by Art 48(2) unless it could be justified for objective reasons.[50] In the related area of social security the Court ruled in *CRAM v Toia*[51] that indirectly discriminatory measures must be objectively justified. On the facts of the case the Court found that there were no objective grounds to justify the discrimination.[52] Similarly, in the context of Art 52, the Court ruled in *Gullung*[53] that an indirectly discriminatory measure (all practising lawyers must register at the Bar of the host state) which might breach the rules on freedom of establishment could be justified, on the grounds of ensuring the observance of moral and ethical principles and the disciplinary control of the activity of lawyers.

The court also seems to be moving towards establishing this pattern in respect of Art 95(1) on internal taxation. In *Chemical Farmaceutici v DAF*[54] the court said that Community law did not restrict the freedom of each member state to lay down tax arrangements which differentiated between certain products on the basis of objective criteria, such as the nature of the raw materials used or the production processes employed. It added 'such differentiation is compatible with Community law if it pursues economic policy objectives which are themselves compatible with the requirements of the Treaty and its secondary law and if the detailed rules are such as to avoid any discrimination, direct or indirect, in regard to imports from other member states or any other form of protection of competing domestic products'. However, it does seem possible, according to this reasoning, to justify both direct and indirect discrimination on objective grounds. On the facts of the case the national rule hit importers harder than it did firms based in Italy.[55] Subsequent case law tends to suggest that only indirectly discriminatory measures can be justified.[56]

Given the model established in the context of Arts 119, 48 and 52 it would seem logical that indirectly discriminatory measures contrary to Arts 30 and 59 would follow the same pattern. However, the Court currently uses a different terminology. It talks of mandatory requirements or public interest requirements, and not objective justification. In *Rau*,[57] for example, the Court, citing its earlier jurisprudence in *Cassis de Dijon*,[58] ruled that:

[50] See also Cases C-300/90 *Commission v Belgium* [1992] ECR I-305 and C-204/90 *Bachmann v Belgium* [1992] ECR I-249 where the Court of Justice talked of justification in order to safeguard the cohesion of the tax system.
[51] Case 237/78 [1979] ECR 2645.
[52] See also Case 33/88 *Allue and Coonan* [1989] ECR 1591.
[53] Case 292/86 *Gullung v Conseil de l'Ordre des Avocats* [1988] ECR 111.
[54] Case 140/79 [1981] ECR 1. See also Case 48/80 *Vinal v Orbat* [1981] ECR 77.
[55] See Craig and de Burca, *op cit*, p 566.
[56] Case 196/85 *Commission v France* [1987] ECR 1597 Case C-132/88 [1991] 3 CMLR 1.
[57] Case 261/81 [1982] ECR 3961.
[58] Case 120/78 *Rewe-Zentrale AG v Bundesmonopolverwaltung fur Branntwein* [1979] ECR 649, para 8.

'in the absence of common rules relating to the marketing of products, obstacles to free movement within the Community resulting from the disparities between the national laws must be accepted in so far as such rules, applicable to domestic and imported products without distinction, may be recognised as being necessary in order to satisfy the mandatory requirements relating to [the effectiveness of fiscal supervision, the protection of pubic health, the fairness of commercial transactions and the defence of the consumer].[59] It is also necessary for such rules to be proportionate to the aim in view'.

Similarly in *Gouda*[60] the Court ruled that the application of national rules which affect any person established in the national territory to persons providing services established in the territory of another member state, fall within the scope of Art 59 'if the national rules are not justified by overriding reasons relating to the public interest ... and that the national rules must be such as to guarantee the achievement of the intended aim and must not go beyond that which is necessary to achieve that objective'.[61] The overriding reasons relating to the public interest recognised by the court include professional rules intended to protect the recipients of the service,[62] protection of intellectual property,[63] the protection of workers,[64] consumer protection,[65] the conservation of national historic and artistic heritage,[66] turning to account the archaeological, historical and artistic heritage of a country and the widest possible dissemination of knowledge of the artistic and cultural heritage of a country.[67]

These 'overriding interests' relating to the public interest in Art 59 closely resemble the mandatory requirements laid down in *Cassis de Dijon*[68] and

[59] Case 120/78 *Rewe-Zentrale* [1979] ECR 649.

[60] Case C-288/89 *Stichting Collectieve Antennevoorsienin Gouda v Commissariat voor Media* [1991] ECR I-4007.

[61] The court has also made clear that not only must the measure be proportionate but any requirement must be 'imposed on all persons or undertakings operating in the said state in so far as that interest is not safeguarded by the provisions to which the provider of the service is subject in the member state of establishment'. Case 279/80 *Webb*, para 17, citing Cases 110 and 111/78 *Van Wesemael* [1979] ECR 35. See also Case C-154/89 *Commission v France* [1991] ECR I-659, paras 14 and 15, Case C-180/89 *Commission v Italy* [1991] ECR I-709, paras 17 and 18 and Case C-198/89 *Commission v Greece* [1991] ECR I-727, paras 18 and 19.

[62] Joined Cases 110/78 and 111/78 *Van Wesemael* [1979] ECR 35, para 28. See also the earlier Case 33/74 *Van Binsbergen v Bestuur van de Bedrijfsvereniging voor de Metallnijverheid* [1974] ECR 1299 where the court talked about 'professional rules justified by the general good – in particular rules relating to the organisation, qualifications, professional ethics, supervision and liability'.

[63] Case 62/79 *Coditel* [1980] ECR 881.

[64] Case 279/80 *Webb* [1981] ECR 3305, para 19, Joined Case 62/81 and 63/81 *Seco v EVI* [1982] ECR 223, para 14, Case C-113/89 *Rush Portuguesa* [1990] ECR I-1417, para 18.

[65] Case 220/83 *Commission v France* [1986] ECR 3663, para 210, Case 252/83 *Commission v Denmark* [1986] ECR 3713, para 20, Case 205/84 *Commission v Germany* [1986] ECR 3755, para 30, Case 206/84 *Commission v Ireland* [1986] ECR 3817, Case C-180/89 *Commission v Italy* [1991] ECR I-709, para 20, Case C-198/89 *Commission v Greece* [1991] ECR I-727, para 21.

[66] Case C-180/89 *Commission v Italy* [1991] ECR I-709, para 20.

[67] Case C-154/89 *Commission v France* [1991] ECR I-659, para 17 and Case C-198/89 *Commission v Greece* [1991] ECR I-727, para 21.

[68] Case 120/78 *Rewe-Zentrale AG v Bundesmonopolverwaltung fur Branntwein* [1979] ECR 649, para 8.

could fall under the broader umbrella of objective justification. Certainly, the Court hinted at the parallels in the *German Insurance*[69] case, referring to the fact that the freedom to provide services 'may be restricted only by provisions which are justified by the general good' and later that such requirements must be 'objectively justified'. In other words, it could be argued that the existing headings of mandatory requirements and public interest requirements are merely examples of what might constitute acceptable objective justification.

The foregoing chapters and these examples suggest that the structure of the definitions of indirectly discriminatory measures in the contexts of goods, persons, services and sex discrimination contain a common core – the requirement that a measure which applies equally to domestic and imported goods, but which has a particular burden on the protected group, breaches the prohibition contained in the Treaty provision unless the defendant can prove certain 'objectively justified' reasons which must also be proportionate. If so, the measures do not infringe the Treaty provision concerned. However, there are limits on the extent to which parallels can be drawn between the jurisprudence on sex discrimination and that on free movement. While Arts 30, 48, 52 and 59 seek to ensure market integration in order to achieve a unified internal market, Art 119 aspires to realise the more limited objective of achieving equality of opportunity in the workplace. Consequently, the Court is prepared to allow economic efficiency arguments to justify discrimination in the context of sex, but not in the context of goods, persons and services. Therefore, while employers can pay certain groups of workers more on the grounds that, for example, due to market forces their skills are much in demand, albeit that such a pay structure indirectly discriminates against women, member states cannot invoke equivalent economic arguments in order to protect the domestic market in goods, persons, and services.

This distinction between discrimination on the grounds of nationality and discrimination on the ground of sex may be acceptable on the basis that the member states voluntarily committed themselves to the completion of the internal market in which the free movement of goods, persons, services and capital[70] constituted the fundamental pillars, while employers found themselves forced to comply with obligations in respect of equal pay which risked challenging practices which had made sound business sense. However, as Weiler and Dehousse point out, free movement is not an end in itself, but a way to promote a more efficient use of resources at Community level, *inter alia* through economies of scale.[71] Any indirectly discriminatory national law restrictions which are allowed to take precedence over the principles of free movement are liable to jeopardise the attainment of this objective. Similarly,

---

[69] Case 205/84 *Commission v Germany* [1986] ECR 3755.
[70] EEC, Art 89/EC, Art 79.
[71] 'The Legal Dimension' in *The Dynamics of European Integration*, Wallace, W (ed) (The Royal Institute of International Affairs, Pinter 1990).

it could be argued that giving women the same pay as men for equal work has both moral and economic benefits, allowing full recognition of women's contribution to the workplace, fostering a commitment to the enterprise by women, and potentially increasing their productivity.[72] Legally justifiable discrimination may interfere with achieving this objective

CONCLUSION

The argument has been made that Arts 119, 30, 48, 52, 59 and 95 are underpinned by notions of non-discrimination, and that these Treaty provisions outlaw both direct and indirect discrimination. It has been suggested that direct discrimination (and possibly intentional indirect or covert discrimination) is *per se* unlawful; it breaches the relevant Treaty provision and it can be saved only by reference to an express exception. By contrast, a measure which appears indirectly discriminatory is unlawful only if it cannot be objectively justified. If this argument is accepted then it would seem logical for the court to recognise the parallels between the provisions in order to draw links between the different sectors in order to develop a coherent jurisprudence. These Treaty provisions are fundamental freedoms, forming the foundations of the Community, and they are also directly effective – they can be raised before national judges who must be able to understand the terminology and the jurisprudence in order to apply them correctly. The need for a clear and comprehensible jurisprudence was brought into sharp focus by the litigation in the Sunday trading cases[73] where complex and opaque jurisprudence of the Court of Justice defeated national courts which had the duty to apply it.[74]

An ability to see the broader picture might also help the Court resolve some of the existing tensions in the jurisprudence. For example, if the Court is committed to using the Treaty provisions to combat discrimination then, as it indicated in *Keck*, a measure which is genuinely non-discriminatory, ie it places no greater burden in law and in fact on the foreign trader and is not intended to impede trade, falls outside the scope of the Treaty. Consequently, it could be argued that a Constitutional provision banning abortion[75] and a national law banning large-scale lotteries[76] do not

---

[72] See generally Deakin and Wilkinson, *The Economics of Employment Rights*, Institute of Employment Rights, 1991, pp 32–33.

[73] See, for example, Case 145/88 *Torfaen Borough Council v B&Q plc* [1989] ECR 3851 and Case C-306/88, C-304/90, C-169/91 *Stoke-on-Trent City Council v B&Q plc* [1993] 1 CMLR 426; Diamond, 'Dishonourable Defences: the Use of Injunctions and the EEC Treaty' (1991) 54 MLR 72; Arnull, 'What shall we do on Sunday?' (1991) 16 EL Rev 112; Rawlings 'The Euro-law Game: Some Deductions from a saga' (1993) 20 Journal of Law and Society 309, Barnard, 'Sunday Trading: A Drama in Five Acts' (1994) 57 MLR 449.

[74] See, for example, *Wellingborough BC v Payless DIY Ltd* [1990] 1 CMLR 773, *Shrewsbury and Atcham BC v B&Q plc* [1990] 3 CMLR 535.

[75] Case C-159/90 *SPUC v Grogan* [1991] ECR I-4685.

[76] Case C-275/92 *Customs and Excise v Schindler* [1994] ECR I-1039.

have any discriminatory effect and should fall wholly outside the scope of the Treaty.

However, the question remains whether it is right to make such a distinction between direct and indirect discrimination and the availability of justification. This problem was illustrated by submissions made by the Commission and the Advocate-General in the recent pensions cases.[77] In *Birds Eye Walls v Roberts* the employer paid a bridging pension to its male employees but not to its female employees, to compensate the men for the fact that they did not receive a state pension until they were 65, while female employees were paid a state pension from 60. Male employees, therefore, received more 'pay' from the employer than female employees. While this appeared at face value to be direct discrimination, equality was achieved overall.

The absence of any derogation from Art 119 prompted the Commission to argue that direct discrimination could be objectively justified 'since the very concept of discrimination, whether direct or indirect involves a difference in treatment which is not justified'. The Advocate-General also suggested that the Court had not stated that direct discrimination could never be justified by objective factors[78] and pointed out that direct and indirect discrimination could not always be distinguished with clarity,[79] making it arbitrary to permit the possibility of justifying a clear inequality of treatment dependent on whether that discrimination is direct or indirect. The Court did not, however, rule on this point, considering that the difference in the objective premise – that men receive their pension at 65, women at 60 – which necessarily entails that the amount of the bridging pension is not the same for men and women could not be considered discriminatory.[80]

The points made by the Advocate-General necessarily raises the question why a distinction exists between direct and indirect discrimination. The explanation may be attributed in part to historical factors: direct discrimination, often fuelled by prejudice, represented the most obvious form of discrimination which had to be eliminated. A simple rule which maintained that direct discrimination was unlawful had the merit of being easy to apply. However, particularly in the Community context, it became apparent that

---

[77] Case C-132/92 *Birds Eye Walls v Roberts* [1994] IRLR 29; Case C-152/91 *Neath* [1994] IRLR 91.

[78] See, for example, Case C-217/91 *Spain v Commission*, judgment of 7 July 1993, 'The principle of equal treatment, viewed as a general principle of Community law requires that similar situations shall not be treated differently and that different situations shall not be treated in the same manner unless such differentiation is objectively justified'.

[79] For example, while *Birds Eye Walls v Roberts* looked like a case of direct discrimination, if emphasis were laid on the fact that the employer calculated the bridging pension in the same way but the result of such calculation was that for five years women received a lower bridging pension, this would constitute indirect discrimination.

[80] In Case C-32/93 *Webb v EMO Air Cargo* [1994] ECR I-3567 the Court ruled in the context of the Equal Treatment Directive that the termination of a contract of indefinite duration on grounds of the woman's pregnancy, which constitutes direct discrimination, 'cannot be justified by the fact that she is prevented, purely on a temporary basis, from performing the work for which she has been engaged'.

other barriers to free movement, although not directly discriminatory, had the effect of either burdening the importer or interfering with the pattern of trade. However, these measures were introduced for a variety of reasons often unrelated to trade – consumer protection, health and safety, worker protection – and, it could be argued, their impact on trade was unintentional.[81] For these very pragmatic reasons it was inevitable that the court had to permit a wider range of justifications to take precedence over the principles of free trade. Has the time now come for this distinction to be abolished? The answer should be no. Direct discrimination in the context of sex or race is morally abhorrent; direct discrimination on the ground of nationality in the context of the fundamental freedoms of the Community is politically and constitutionally abhorrent. Consequently, this principle should not be weakened by reference to a broader category of objective justification. This distinction has served the public interest well. Its abolition would mix the concepts of direct and indirect discrimination into an unstable cocktail. The resulting brew might prove better than the two separated, but the unknown risks are as yet too dangerous to allow such an experiment with fundamental rights to be undertaken.

[81] See, Case 145/88 *Torfaen Borough Council v B&Q plc* [1989] ECR 3851 and Cases C-306/88, C-304/90, C-169/91 *Stoke-on-Trent City Council v B&Q plc* [1993] 1 CMLR 426.

7

WHAT ARE THE PURPOSES OF EC DISCRIMINATION LAW?

Nicolas Bernard

Few would doubt the benefits of comparative law. Even in the context of a single legal system, comparison between different areas of the law can enhance our understanding of legal principles and institutions. The EC Treaty contains several Articles which impose, explicitly or implicitly, some obligations of non-discrimination.[1] It may not seem unreasonable to consider that those various provisions are in fact 'merely a specific enunciation of the general principle of equality which is one of the fundamental principles of Community law'[2] and see whether developments of the equality principle in one area of the law can provide useful information for other areas. In internal as well as international comparisons, however, one should bear in mind Otto Kahn-Freund's warning about 'misuses' of comparative approaches.[3] In the same way as national legal institution do not operate in a vacuum, but in a given political, economic and cultural context, tools developed in one area of the law for certain purposes may prove difficult to transplant in other areas where different concerns come into play. If we are to attribute any legal significance to the fact that various aspects of Community anti-discrimination law can be linked to a wider principle of equality, we have to determine the extent to which those various aspects can be seen to fulfil comparable purposes. A review of all the areas of non-discrimination in Community law would be beyond the scope of this chapter. However, it might be worth studying the anti-discrimination principle in three representative areas where it has come to the fore: judicial review of the legality of the economic policy of the Community assumes particular relevance to our study, in that it is primarily in that sphere that the court has developed the principle of equal treatment into a general principle of law binding on the Community institutions, in particular in their legislative function. Secondly, Community sex discrimination law shows the principle of equality at play in a field of positive integration, binding private individuals and firms in the Community, and finally, the principle of non-discrimination

---

[1] See Arts 6, 30–36, 40(3), 48, 52,, 59, 86 and 119.
[2] Anthony Arnull, *The General Principles of EEC Law and the Individual*, (1990), at p 3, citing Case 117/76 *Albert Ruckdeschel* (see below n 5).
[3] Otto Kahn-Freund, 'On Uses and Misuses of Comparative Law', (1974) 37 MLR 1.

on grounds of nationality is an essential element in the removal of barriers between the member states and is, therefore, a central aspect of negative integration. Its principal target her is not so much the Community institutions or private individuals as the member states. This will be our third area of study.

EQUAL TREATMENT AND JUDICIAL REVIEW OF ECONOMIC POLICY

General principles in Community law are legal rules which, although not necessarily made explicit in the Treaties, are nevertheless implicitly present in the Community legal order and, therefore, binding on the Community institutions.[4] The justification for finding a principle to be present in the Community legal order despite the absence of any explicit mention of it in the Treaties is either that the principle forms part of the assumptions which constitute the common legal heritage of the member states and therefore 'goes without saying' or that several legislative provisions in the Community legal order can be seen as specific applications of the principle and, therefore, indicative of the presence of that principle within the legal order. Under both heads, equality is a strong candidate as a general principle of law. Most European countries, and virtually all the member states of the EC, give constitutional recognition to a principle of equality. It would, therefore, seem reasonable to accept that the principle of equality is part of the common legal heritage of the member states of the EC and a general principle of law. If one focuses on the Community legal order, as was noted above, several provisions of the EC Treaty establish prohibitions on discrimination on particular grounds and would seem to provide a sound basis for a general principle of equality.

It is unsurprising then that the court has found equality to be one of the general principles of law binding on the Community institutions. One area in particular where the principle has often been invoked by litigants and applied by the court is that of agriculture. While EC, Art 40(3) explicitly prohibits discrimination between producers and consumers in the context of the CAP, the court has found in the *Ruckdeschel* case that this provision was 'merely a specific enunciation of the general principle of equality which is one of the fundamental principles of Community law.'[5]

In the same case, the court held that the principle required that similar situations should not be treated differently unless differentiation was

---

[4] In the current state of development of Community law, general principles of law do not appear to be *per se* binding on the member states, although they may be used in the interpretation of other Community provisions, which are so binding (see, in particular, the discussion of the issue in Advocate-General Van Gerven's opinion in Case C-159/90 *Society for the Protection of Unborn Children v Grogan* [1991] ECR I-4685; [1991] 3 CMLR 849.

[5] Joined Cases 117/76 *Albert Ruckdeschel and another v HZA Hamburg-St Annen* and 16/77 *Diamalt AG v HZA Itzehoe* [1977] ECR 1753, [1979] 2 CMLR 445, at para 7.

objectively justified.[6] This begs the question of what similar situations, different treatment and objective justifications are, and reflects the vacuity of the equality principle in its raw form.[7] However, the case law of the court indicates that a factor recurs in determining whether situations are similar: as pointed out by Advocate-General Capotorti in *Ruckdeschel*,[8] in the context of economic policy, and in particular in the agricultural context, the comparability of situations has to be assessed against the background of competition. This is neatly illustrated with the *Isoglucose* cases,[9] in which the Court held that the freezing and eventual elimination of a production refund for starch used for the manufacture of isoglucose while maintaining the refund for other uses of starch could not constitute discrimination, as there was no competition between isoglucose and starch or other starch-derived products. On the other hand, having found that competition did exist between isoglucose and sugar, the Court then held that imposing a production levy on isoglucose which was not borne, or only partially borne, by sugar manufacturers constituted a breach of the principle of equality.

Thus, in the first instance, the principle of equality in the case law of the court on economic policy appears to impose a duty on the Community legislator not to distort competition. It is worth noting that it does not extend to imposing a duty to redress 'natural' imbalances between competitors. In *Werhahn*,[10] the applicants, who were German meal producers, argued that a system of aid to production of durum wheat in the Community had resulted in giving an advantage to French meal producers, who would get their supplies from French growers, over their German counterparts, who had to obtain durum wheat from traditional sources outside the Community at a higher price. In the course of argument, the German meal producers asserted that the French market for durum wheat was virtually closed to them and added that, even if it were freed, French mills would still have retained a *de facto* advantage by reason of their proximity to the production centres. The Court considered that this in itself would not constitute discrimination within the meaning of Art 40(3) 'but rather the consequences – that is not contrary to the rules of the Treaty – of a more advantageous location of French undertakings.'[11]

It would be mistaken, however, to see the principle of equality in this field as being exclusively concerned with the maintenance of competitive structure. Not all distortions of competition will necessarily constitute a breach of

---

[6] *Ibid.*
[7] On this see P Westen, 'The Empty Idea of Equality', (1982) 95 Harvard Law Review, p 537.
[8] Cited above n 5, at p 1779.
[9] See, in particular, Joined Cases 103/77 *Royal Scholten-Honig (Holdings) Ltd v Intervention Board for Agricultural Produce* and 145/77 *Tunnel Refineries Ltd v Intervention Board for Agricultural Produce* [1978] ECR 2037, [1979] 1 CMLR 675.
[10] Joined Cases 63 to 69/72 *Wilhelm Werhahn Hansamühle and others v EC Council* [1973] ECR 1229.
[11] *Ibid*, at para 37.

the principle of equality. In the *Durum Wheat* cases,[12] the Court upheld the validity of measures adopted by the Community in relation to the market in durum wheat and the system of aid for the production of that cereal in the Community, notwithstanding the fact that these measures had resulted in a disadvantage for German cereal meal producers as compared to their French competitors. While the court would have been ready to strike down the measures had they been purely arbitrary, insofar as they constituted a rational way to implement the objectives of the CAP as defined in Art 39 of the Treaty, the fact that they brought about a disadvantage for one group of producers would not *per se* render them invalid. The point was forcefully reaffirmed in the *Bozzetti* case, where the court held that 'the fact that the introduction of the co-responsibility levy[13] under the common organisation of the market may affect producers in different ways, depending upon the particular nature of their production or on local conditions, cannot be regarded as discrimination prohibited by Art 40(3) of the Treaty if the levy is determined on the basis of objective rules, formulated to meet the needs of the general common organisation of the market, for all the products concerned by it.'[14]

Similarly, some breaches of the principle of equality are not primarily concerned with competition. Thus, it is clear that competition is not the focus when the court applies the principle of equality not *within* but *between* sectors of the economy: in the *Skimmed-Milk Powder* cases,[15] an obligation on livestock farmers to purchase skimmed-milk powder as a feeding-stuff at a price three times higher than soya oil cakes (which it replaced in order to run down unacceptably high surpluses of milk in the Community) constituted a 'discriminatory distribution of costs between the various agricultural sectors'.[16] The principle of equality tends to merge with the principle of proportionality when applied in this way across sectors of the economy.[17] Without the background of competition, the evaluation of the difference of treatment becomes extremely difficult. The Court will, therefore, need to find a disadvantage going manifestly beyond what is normally imposed on economic operators in whatever sphere of activity they are involved. Insofar as the breach of the principle of equality will, in these situations, require an

---

[12] Joined Cases 63 to 69/72 *Werhahn*, above n 10. See also Joined Cases 56 to 60/74 *Kurt Kampffmeyer Mühlenvereinigung KG and Others v Commission and Council of the EC* [1976] ECR 711.

[13] ie the levy on milk and milk products introduced by Council Regulation 1079/77/EEC (OJ 1977 No L131/6) with the aim of reducing the structural surpluses on the Community milk market.

[14] Case 179/84 *Piercarlo Bozzetti v Spa Invernizzi and Ministero del Tesoro* [1985] ECR 2301, at para 34.

[15] See Case 114/76 *Bela-Mühle Josef Bergmann KG v Grows-Farm GmbH & Co KG* [1977] ECR 1211.

[16] *Ibid*, at para 7.

[17] It is significant in this respect that the parties in *Bela-Mühle* (cited above n 15) had invoked both the principle of equality and the principle of proportionality and that the court considered that, because of the close connection between those grounds of complaints, it would be appropriate to consider them together. See Chapter 8 below.

excessive burden being imposed on certain operators, this excess will be constitutive of a breach of the principle of proportionality.[18] Indeed, according to Herdegen,[19] equality seems to add little to the principle of proportionality in those cases. Perhaps more importantly, it seems that reference to competition does not go further than determining that different products are 'comparable', from which the court infers that the producers of those products are in a comparable situation. It does not, however, require that the producer shows the existence of a comparator with whom the producer is in competition. While there does not appear to be direct authority on the point, it is probable that the Community legislator could not grant a benefit to Danish producers of a given product while refusing the same benefit to Greek producers merely because it could be established that there is in fact no possible competition between Danish and Greek producers of the product in question. They would still have to point to a substantial difference between Danish and Greek producers in order to be able to do that. Despite the background of competition, the principle of equality in the context of judicial review of economic policy remains fairly indeterminate. At that level of generality, the principle of equality turns out to be little more than a requirement of rationality imposed on the legislator.[20] The focus is clearly on the decision-maker and the decision-making process, rather than the persons affected by the measure, as can be observed in the abundant case-law which the introduction of milk quotas[21] has generated. Under the system set up by Council Regulation 857/84/EEC,[22] quotas were allocated on the basis of the quantity of milk delivered by the producer during a reference year to be chosen within the 1981–83 bracket by the member states in which the farm is situated. The Regulation recognised that some farmers, through no

---

[18] The concept of equality which is at play here has some affinity with the concept of equality of citizens in relation to public charges that one finds in some national legal systems. French administrative law, in particular, recognises the principle as a source of non-contractual liability for lawful acts (including legislative acts) of public authorities and also requires a sufficiently grave prejudice to be regarded as 'abnormal' and therefore not normally befalling the individual concerned (see CE Ass 22 Oct 1943, *Société des Etablissements Lacaussade*, Rec 231).

[19] See M Herdegen, 'The Relation between the Principles of Equality and Proportionality', (1985) CML Rev 683.

[20] Incidentally, one may wonder whether requirement of rationality should be imposed on the Community legislator. If one conceives of legislation as a result of a bargaining process, there is no reason why this result should be rational (*cf* Scott Bice, 'Rationality Analysis in Constitutional Law', (1980) 65 Minn L Rev 1). This is particularly true in the Community, where the bargaining aspect of the legislative process is notably more marked than at national level. In effect imposing a requirement of rationality on the Council emphasises its function as a Community institution rather than as a forum for member states to negotiate, In other words, it insists on the supra-national rather than inter-governmental dimensions of the Council.

[21] The scheme, the purpose of which is to curb milk production surpluses in the Community, works by allocating a reference quantity (a quota) to dairy farmers and imposing a levy on quantities of milk produced over the quota. As the levy is normally higher than the price the farmer can obtain for the milk on the market, farmers will avoid producing in excess of their quota.

[22] OJ 1984 No L90/13. This regulation lapsed in 1993 and was replaced by Council Regulation 3950/92, OJ No L405/1 which prolonged the quota system for a further seven years.

fault of their own, might have been unable to produce a representative quantity within the reference year and provided for derogations in case of exceptional events such as a natural disaster or an epizootic affecting the milk herd during the reference year.[23] Those derogations were limited, however, covering only a number of specific circumstances exhaustively listed in the Regulation and, generally allowing for an alternative year within the 1981–83 range. Thus a dairy farmer whose production had been affected throughout the whole of the 1981–83 period, or a farmer whose production had been affected by an event not listed in the Regulation would not have been able to obtain an alternative reference quantity. One such unlucky farmer was Mr Erpelding whose cows had been affected by various illnesses during the 1981–83 period. He argued that his case fell within the spirit of the Regulation and that the Regulation should be interpreted so as to apply to it or that, alternatively, the Regulation was invalid insofar as it discriminated against dairy farmers who had had, through no fault of their own, no representative production during the reference period. The court rejected both contentions. It felt that the list of derogations contained in the Regulation was clearly meant to be exhaustive and also considered that there was no breach of the principle of equality since, although the Regulation would have an adverse effect on a particular category of producers (namely those who were unable to rely on a representative production within the reference period) the limitation of derogations was justified by 'the need to limit the number of years which may be taken as reference years, in the interests of both legal certainty and the effectiveness of the additional levy system'.[24] From Mr Erpelding's point of view, the situation could be perceived as arbitrary, in that his case was as deserving as other cases of derogation covered by the Regulation. Nevertheless, insofar as the Council had adopted a rational attitude to the problem and could not be expected to take into account every conceivable circumstance, the court considered that there was no breach of the principle of equality.

Focused on the decision-making process rather than its results,[25] equality, in the present context, means that the Community legislator should use means which are appropriate to the objective pursued. One can approach this requirement of rationality from a variety of angles. Thus, from what Harlow and Rawlings would call a 'green light' perspective,[26] it can be seen to be concerned with the efficiency of the decision-making process and the

[23] See Art 3 of the Regulation.

[24] Case 84/87 *Marcel Erpelding v Secrétaire d'Etat à l'Agriculture et à la Viticulture* [1988] ECR 2647, at para 30.

[25] Stepping outside the field of economic policy, one can see a patent example of an equality principle focused on process in the finding by the court in *Blomefield* that a Community institution may not depart from a rule of conduct it has imposed on itself through the means of an internal directive 'without specifying the reasons which have led it to do so, since otherwise the principle of equality of treatment would be infringed' (Case 190/82, *Blomefield v Commission* [1983] ECR 3981, at para 20).

[26] ie concerned with the effective running of government rather than the control of power. See C Harlow and R Rawlings, *Law and Administration* (Weidenfeld and Nicolson, London, 1988), Chapters 1 and 2.

realisation of the objectives of the Treaty. It can also be apprehended as an amplification of the principle according to which the Community institutions only have the powers which are expressly granted to them by the Treaty and, therefore, ultimately concerned with the balance of powers in the Community. In the CAP context, its function would thus be to complement Art 39, in which the objectives of the CAP are defined, by requiring the Community legislator to establish that the means it has chosen are rationally related to those objectives. Whatever approach is adopted, equality here has more to do with the structure of decision-making than the protection of individuals and its impact on individual rights is rather limited.

EQUAL TREATMENT AND SEX DISCRIMINATION

If the purpose of equal treatment in sex discrimination cases was the same as in judicial review of economic policy, this would mean that the objective of Art 119 and related secondary legislation would be to ensure the rationality of business decisions relating to employment. Equality between the sexes would, in this perspective, aim at purifying hiring and wage decisions from a factor which is generally irrelevant to the efficient running of a business and the possibility of justifying (indirect) discrimination should be seen as directed at saving those cases where the presumption is rebutted and the discriminatory rule does indeed serve a legitimate purpose and can, therefore, be rationally justified. This, however, is not a very satisfactory justification. While we do entrust public authorities with a certain number of functions and expect them to fulfil their duties in a rational manner, it is unusual in a liberal society to impose legally binding requirements of rationality in the private sphere. Secondly, it is by no means established that sex discrimination is a particularly significant source of irrationality in employment decisions.[27] Thirdly, and more importantly, the origins of sex equality law clearly how that it is directed at a rather different objective. As Evelyn Ellis suggests in Chapter 2, there is plenty of evidence that the British and Community legislators were motivated by a concern about women being treated as an economic underclass and that it is the *effect* on victims [of discrimination] with which the law is concerned, not the precise nature of the conduct of it perpetrators.[28] This is particularly evident in indirect discrimination, the function of which, it is said, is to eradicate 'institutionalised discrimination'.[29] While she does not use that terminology, it is clear that Ellis sees sex discrimination as being concerned with distributive justice, that

---

[27] See RA Posner, 'An Economic Analysis of Sex Discrimination Laws' (1989) 56 University of Chicago Law Review, 1311, at pp 1314–1321.

[28] E Ellis, 'The Definition of Discrimination in European Community Sex Equality Law', above Chapter 2.

[29] On institutionalised discrimination, and the change of meaning of discrimination away from an intent-based approach that indirect discrimination implies, see C McCrudden, 'Institutional Discrimination', (1982) 2 OJLS 303.

is with the correction of existing patterns of disadvantage.[30] If one can agree with her that what sex discrimination legislation should be about is correcting an unsatisfactory state of affairs rather than punishing the guilty, one can entertain some doubts as to whether the case law of the Court of Justice shows a far-sighted approach to 'what sex equality is seeking to achieve and the devices which it employs to that end.'[31]

According to Ellis, indirect discrimination is about identifying practices which are detrimental to one sex and for which there is no alternative explanation than discrimination. This, indeed, is what the Court of Justice seems to do, and in doing so adopts a fairly robust approach to what could constitute an alternative explanation, requiring the employer to justify the *prima facie* discriminatory practice by reference to objective factors showing a genuine need of the business and an adequation between the means chosen and the objective.[32] However, the fact that there is an explanation for a practice which disadvantages one sex does not make the disadvantage disappear. If indirect discrimination is concerned with removing disadvantages, the existence of a justification, even a genuine justification, should not *per se* be conclusive. In other words, justifiable discrimination does not cease to constitute discrimination. What the law should be concerned with is not merely discriminatory practices for which there is no alternative explanation, but discriminatory practices generally. For instance, let us consider the issue of seniority, which the court has recognised in *Danfoss*[33] as, in principle,[34] a valid ground for differential treatment. Seniority has the effect of crystallising, or amplifying, existing patterns of employment and, therefore, of discrimination: if women have been excluded from the labour market as a result of (past) direct discrimination, they will have accumulated less seniority. The use of seniority as a criterion for promotion appears as a classical example of institutionalised or structural discrimination. Holding that this does not constitute discrimination, as opposed to constituting justifiable discrimination, reveals a notion of discrimination which is still based on criminal or tortious principles. All that the existence of an alternative reason shows is that the employer does not intend to discriminate and does not even discriminate negligently. It certainly does not show the absence of discrimination, if discrimination is understood as focusing on whether a particular group suffers a disadvantage. It may be felt that this is more a discussion about semantics than one about the substance of the solutions put forward by the court. Some might feel that it does not matter whether justification in indirect discrimination turns the practice into lawful discrim-

---

[30] *Cf* McCrudden, 'Changing Notions of Discrimination', in Guest and Milne (eds), *Equality and Discrimination: essays in Freedom and Justice* (Stuttgart, 1985).

[31] *Op cit* Ellis.

[32] See Case 170/84 *Bilka-Kaufhaus GmbH v Weber von Hartz* [1986] ECR 1607.

[33] Case C-109/88 *Handels- og Kontorfunktionærernes Forbund i Danmark v Dansk Arbejdsgiverforening* (acting for *Danfoss*) [1989] ECR 3199.

[34] See Case C-184/89 *Nimz v Freie und Hansestadt Hamburg* [1991] ECR I-297, which qualifies *Danfoss* by holding that the circumstances of the case have to be taken into account to determine whether discrimination based on seniority is justifiable.

ination or non-discrimination if, at the end of the day, the prohibited practices are in any case the same. One could object to that as it undervalues the power of language in shaping cultural attitudes.[35] Beyond this (and more significantly for lawyers) adopting one approach rather than the other leads to a difference in the threshold of justifiability, which reflects itself in different notions of proportionality. If justification is meant to establish that there is no alternative explanation for a practice apart from discrimination, the role of the proportionality test is merely to ensure adequation between the objective and the stated objective. This is what Leader would call weak proportionality.[36] If, on the other hand, one accepts that the existence of a justification does not signal the absence of discrimination, the question of justification takes the added dimension of a conflict between discrimination and other values (eg economic efficiency). It may well be that those other values will take priority over non-discrimination. It may also be the case, however, that the gain in terms of economic efficiency is minor whereas the impact on discrimination is significant. In that situation, using a strong proportionality test, which not only questions the means used but also the objective pursued by the employer, one may well want to give priority to non-discrimination over economic efficiency, even though the discrimination can be justified in the weak proportionality sense.

The court thus far does not appear to have once used a strong proportionality test in indirect sex discrimination cases. The judgment of the court in *Enderby*[37] seems to indicate that the court substantially adopts a tortious approach to indirect discrimination and a weak view of justification. It will be recalled that the court decided in that case that, where a difference in pay between a predominantly female profession (*in casu* speech therapists) and a predominantly male profession (pharmacists) is attributable to 'market forces', the need to attract candidates by higher salaries constitutes an objective justification and renders the differential in pay lawful. This makes sense if one places oneself from the point of view of the individual employer, as in a tortious approach. The employer does not intend to discriminate. Indeed, it may even positively not want to discriminate. However, it is forced to do so because of market pressure.[38] If, however, one takes some distance from the individual employer and asks what 'market forces' are, one cannot but conclude that the only justification put forward by an employer invoking market forces is that everybody else does it. 'Market forces are nothing more than the collective behaviour of employers and employees. In traditional economic theory, the attribution by the market of different rates of pay to

---

[35] *Cf* C McCrudden's discussion of the adoption of a 'persuasive definition' of discrimination in 'Institutional Discrimination', *cit* above n 29, at pp 345–346.
[36] See below, Chapter 8.
[37] Case C-127/92, *Enderby v Frenchay Health Authority and the Secretary of State for Health* [1993] ECR I-5535, [1994] 1 CMLR 8.
[38] Even within that framework, it could be counter-argued that market pressure only prevented the employer from paying its male employees as low as its female employees (equalising down) but did not prevent it from raising the pay of its female employees to that of the male ones.

different jobs reflects a difference in value between the jobs. The 'market forces' argument would, therefore, appear *prima facie* as a valid argument to establish not that the discrimination is justified but rather that the jobs are not of equal value and so no issue of discrimination arises. One difficulty, however, is that, non-discrimination has a cost for the employer[39] and that job valuation *via* the market will embody discriminatory elements. One way out of this is to find alternative mechanisms to attribute values to jobs – such as a job evaluation scheme. Thus, a difference in market rates can be either a difference in value between the jobs (sex discrimination being discounted) or evidence of institutionalised discrimination. Whether the jobs at issue in *Enderby* were of equal value was a matter of dispute between the parties at national court level but for the purpose of the reference, the Court of Justice was to proceed on the basis that the jobs were of equal value. This should have led to the conclusion that the difference in rates of pay was attributable to institutionalised discrimination. Paradoxically, however, it is the very demonstration that the differential in pay is attributable to institutionalised discrimination which is treated by the court as justification for the discrimination. In doing so, the court not only undermines the notion of 'work of equal value', the function of which is precisely to get away from market valuation which, since it reflects the collective attitudes of employers and employees, will necessarily incorporate any institutional discrimination; but it also signals a notion of discrimination which is essentially tortious in nature and focuses on the conduct of the discriminator rather than seeking to eradicate discriminatory patterns. Moreover, even within the framework of a tortious approach, it is a fairly restricted one, in that it implies that employers can exploit the weaker position of women on the employment market by paying them less, provided that this practice is sufficiently generalised to be reflected in lower market rates of predominantly female jobs. To this extent, *Enderby* appears difficult to reconcile with *Bilka* since, presumably, employers generally pay part-timers less or treat them less well not so much out of a desire to deliberately harm them, but because they can get away with imposing terms that full-timers would not accept.[40]

It is true though that the court held in *Enderby* that a differential in pay can be justified by the fact that it was the result of a separate collective bargaining process for each group. Even here, however, the court's reasoning seems to betray a focus on the discriminator rather than the victim: the court justified its solution by holding that 'If the employer could rely on the absence of discrimination within each of the collective bargaining processes taken separately as sufficient justification for the difference in pay, he could, as the German government pointed out, easily circumvent the principle of

[39] See R Posner 'An Economic Analysis of Sex Discrimination Laws', (1989) 56 University of Chicago Law Review, 1311.

[40] Assuming that, as in *Bilka*, the difference in treatment results from a choice of the employer rather than the national legislation.

equal pay by using separate bargaining processes.[41] If the test was truly one of effect on the victim, ie of impact, the fact that this situation is arrived at by one way, such as separate bargaining processes, or another is irrelevant. If the justification for the solution is that the employer could adopt a discriminatory conduct, is the court not saying that the real issue is the attitude of the employer rather than the effect on the employee?

By adopting an essentially tortious approach to non-discrimination, the court seems to base the legitimacy of discrimination law on the 'harm principle': an employer cannot discriminate because, in doing so, he/she harms others. John Gardner has pointed out the difficulty from a liberal point of view in legitimating sex discrimination laws on the basis of the 'harm principle'.[42] He has shown that 'the denial of the opportunity to secure a benefit' or mere 'unfairness' are not by themselves enough and that 'our willingness to treat continuing disparate treatment as a harm is a product of its close historical association with distributive injustice'.[43] Even at the more superficial level of legislative intentions, the connection with distributive justice concerns is clear: if we prohibit sex discrimination, it is not only because it is 'wrong' but because we hope that the outlawing of the practice will lead to the disappearance of its outcome. Evelyn Ellis makes this point when she says that 'the statements of the Council and the Commission, and the remarks of the Court of Justice all frequently reveal a perception of women as at least an *economic* underclass; and they, therefore, emphasise the importance of the objective of raising the standard of treatment received by women in the workplace and in vocational training, so as ultimately to give them equality of employment opportunity with men'.[44]

Undoubtedly, therefore, sex discrimination law has a quite different purpose from that of the equality principle in economic policy cases. This begs the question whether it is appropriate to treat them as constituting a single principle and adopt a comparable form of reasoning, focused on the conduct of the decision-maker rather than on the effect on the victims of discrimination. The redistributive function, which is completely foreign in economic policy cases but central in sex discrimination law, may call for a different mode of response. The very structure of the law of indirect discrimination would appear to be designed for coping with institutional discrimination.[45] Yet, what the court seems to be doing is 'aim at catching behaviour which has a detrimental effect on a particular group of people and *for which there is no other explanation than discrimination*'. One would rather expect it to catch those practices which have an adverse impact *even*

---

[41] *Ibid* at para 22.
[42] J Gardner, 'Liberals and Unlawful Discrimination', (1989) 9 OJLS 1, at pp 5–8.
[43] Ibid, at p 7.
[44] See above, Chapter 2.
[45] See Ellis, *op cit*, above, Chapter 2. For a more detailed analysis, primarily in the context of racial discrimination in the UK and the US, see C McCrudden, 'Institutional Discrimination', above n 29.

where there is an alternative explanation for it. This does not necessarily mean that a practice should be unlawful simply because it has an adverse impact. There is still room for justification here. However, the purpose of justification in indirect discrimination would be to establish the existence of a competing interest conflicting with discrimination. The court would then be required to decide which interest should be given priority, using a 'strong proportionality test'.

EQUALITY AND DISCRIMINATION ON GROUNDS OF NATIONALITY

Our third area of enquiry into equality and non-discrimination in EC law is that of discrimination on grounds of nationality. This is somewhat complicated by the fact that we have two categories of cases which the court has tended to treat as applications of the same principle but which, it is submitted, constitute in fact two quite distinct classes: the first category consists of cases where non-discrimination is treated as an adjunct to the right to free movement in the Community and the second category concerns 'stand-alone' applications of the principle of non-discrimination on grounds of nationality, in particular on the basis of Art 6 of the Treaty.

Nationality discrimination and free movement of persons

In this context, discrimination on grounds of nationality is prohibited insofar as it constitutes an obstacle to the free movement of persons.[46] The main relevant Treaty provisions are Art 48 for the free movement of workers, Art 52 for the freedom of establishment and, insofar as relevant to the movement of persons, Art 59 on freedom to provide services. The prohibition covers both direct and indirect discrimination. It is not entirely clear, however, whether the court considers disparate impact as *prima facie* evidence of discriminatory conduct,[47] or whether the court adopts a pure effects-based test. The purpose of the free movement provisions, which is to secure the establishment of an internal market characterised as an 'area without internal frontiers in which the free movement of goods, persons, services and capital

---

[46] Similar principles apply in relation to goods and services that do not involve the movement of persons across borders. In these contexts, it is less a question of nationality than 'origin', in the sense that the goods are imported or the service provided from another state. For the sake of simplicity, the analysis will be confined to the free movement of persons.

[47] The language used sometimes suggests an intention-based approach. In particular, the court often used the phrase 'covert' discrimination rather than indirect discrimination (see, for instance, Case 152/73 *Sotgiu v Deutsche Bundespost* [1974] ECR 153, [1974] CMLR 8257 at para 11). However, insofar as the court will find discriminatory a measure which has an adverse impact and where the justification proposed by the member state is rejected by the court, even if there is nothing to suggest *mala fide* on the part of the state, it would be preferable to treat it as a question of conduct rather than intent (see, for instance, Case C-330/91 *R v Inland Revenue Commissioners, ex parte Commerzbank AG* [1993] ECR I-4017).

is ensured in accordance with the provisions of the [EC] Treaty',[48] would suggest that he proper test should be one based on effect: the provisions are not meant merely as a way to check the protectionist tendencies of the member states, but rather to bring about as much as possible the emergence of a frontier-free Community by removing the obstacles that stand in the way of the movement of people across borders. It is worth noting, in this respect, that the position taken by the court in the free movement of goods and services is clearly focused on the impact of state measures on intra-Community trade in goods and services[49] and there does not seem to be any *prima facie* reason why a different approach should be adopted in relation to the free movement of persons.

Justifying the anti-discrimination principle in the free movement of persons by reference to the need to remove obstacles to such movement is not without some initial difficulties – the link between discrimination and obstacles to free movement is not automatic. One can conceive of non-discriminatory obstacles, and the anti-discrimination principle would appear, therefore, under-inclusive by reference to its objective. Thus, a measure which had a negative impact on the level of employment in a member state could be viewed as an obstacle to the movement of workers between the member states, insofar as it results in fewer job opportunities being available in that member state for workers from other member states. There is no discrimination here, as workers of the member state which has adopted the measure are affected in the same way as workers from other states, but in a non-discriminatory approach to the question, there would still be an obstacle to the free movement of workers. The obvious difficulty with such an approach to the free movement of persons would be that it would imply that Arts 48, 52 and 59 would embody a principle in favour of deregulation and in particular, with regard to Art 48, social deregulation. The approach to social policy adopted by most member states (and in particular the original six founding states) as well as the provisions of the EC Treaty itself, notably Title VIII of Part Three, devoted to 'social policy, education, vocational training and youth', make it quite clear that the free movement provisions cannot be read as incorporating a deregulatory principle. What free movement must mean then is free access for all Community nationals to the labour, goods and services markets of all members states. In some cases, all that will be required will be national treatment, but in some cases equal access may require taking the specific situation of nationals of other member states into account. For instance, on the issue of professional qualifications, equal access for nationals of other member states will usually require not merely national treatment, under which a state could insist on the possession of a national qualification, but mutual recognition of qualifications acquired in other member states. In

---

[48] EC, Art 7A.
[49] See Case 120/78 *Rewe-Zentral AG v Bundesmonopolverwaltung für Branntwein (Cassis de Dijon)*, [1979] ECR 649, [1979] 3 CMLR 494 and Case C-299/89 *Gouda v Commissariaat voor de Media*, [1991] ECR I-4007; [1993] 3 CMLR 659.

discrimination terms, this situation can be dealt with under the concept of indirect discrimination. Insisting on a national diploma will invariably constitute indirect discrimination against nationals of other member states, insofar as most individuals tend to acquire their initial professional qualifications in their state of origin. The real issue is to determine whether such indirect discrimination can be justified. Thus, in the legal profession, it could be justifiable to require a lawyer who qualified in another member state to have some evidence of knowledge of the legal system in which he intends to practice.[50] For other professions, however, indirect discrimination relating to professional qualifications may be harder to justify.[51]

Thus, the anti-discrimination principle appears as an adequate tool to remove obstacles to the free movement of person while at the same time recognising a competence of member states in such fields as social policy or regulation of trade and services.[52] One aspect of the case law of the court, however, still remains puzzling: it is a unclear why the principle of non-discrimination in this area focuses on nationality – what the free movement of persons is concerned with is the free movement of all Community nationals throughout the Community regardless of nationality. A state measure that discriminates against those who exercise their right to free movement does not cease to breach the free movement provisions merely because it is neither directly nor indirectly discriminatory on grounds of nationality. The point was made clearly by the court in the *Stanton* case,[53] in relation to Belgian social security legislation which discriminated against persons who had an activity as a self-employed person in Belgium alongside a salaried activity outside Belgium: insofar as there were no reasons to believe that more non-Belgians than Belgians were in that situation, the legislation could not be regarded as discriminatory on grounds of nationality. The Court nevertheless considered that the legislation in question was incompatible with Art 52. However remarkable the reasoning in *Stanton* was, it has to be said that it remains a fairly isolated case. Even in actions by nationals against the legislation of their own state where the individuals concerned are clearly not discriminated on the ground of their nationality, the court still prefers to follow an analysis based on nationality discrimination. The typical line of reasoning followed by the court is to enquire whether the national in question has exercised his right to free movement and has, therefore, placed himself in a situation which can be assimilated to that of nationals of other member states in the Community. If that is the case, the individual can then invoke the benefit of the provisions on free movement and any right that

[50] See Case C-340/89 *Vlassopoulou* [1991] ECR I-2357, [1993] 2 CMLR 221.
[51] See Case 115/78 *Knoors* [1979] ECR 399, [1979] 2 CMLR 357, for the case of a plumber not possessing the required national qualification, with the additional difference that he could invoke the benefit of a directive.
[52] Despite some hesitations under the *Cassis de Dijon* jurisprudence, the court seems, with *Keck* (Joined Cases C-267 and 268/91, [1993] ECR I-6097) to have adopted this approach in relation to free movement of goods as well. See Catherine Barnard above, Chapter 6.
[53] Case 143/87 *Stanton* [1988] ECR 3877. See also Joined Cases 154 and 155/87 *Wolf and Dorchain* [1988] ECR 3897.

would be available to other Community nationals must be available to him. That is undoubtedly right. However, the Court concludes from this that any legislation which indirectly discriminates against nationals of other member states[54] cannot apply to the individual in question, even though he is not discriminated against on grounds of his nationality. By doing this, the Court seem to be confusing two different issues: the personal scope of the relevant Treaty Article (who can benefit from it?) and its substantive content (what rights are granted under it?). If the right granted by the Treaty is a right not to be discriminated on grounds of nationality, the only right that a national who has placed himself in a situation which is assimilable to that of any other Community national has is also the right not to be discriminated against on grounds of nationality. It is not the right to live in an environment where nationals of other member states are not discriminated on grounds of their nationality. This rather unsatisfactory reasoning of the court is unavoidable as long as it wishes to maintain that what is at stake in free movement is discrimination on grounds of nationality, rather than a more general principle of non-discrimination against Community nationals who wish to exercise their right to free movement. The reason for the court's reluctance is not entirely clear. It is certainly not imposed by the Treaty: Art 48 simply says that 'freedom of movement shall entail the abolition of any discrimination on grounds of nationality'. The use of 'entail' leaves the door open for a wider interpretation of the kind of discrimination prohibited by Art 48.[55] That the founding fathers primarily envisaged the hypothesis of discrimination on grounds of nationality is understandable, as it certainly is the most common form of discrimination against those who wish to exercise their right to free movement. However, they were careful enough to adopt a sufficiently flexible formula which would enable the court to further the objective beyond the initial concerns of 1957. The court seems to have become, to a certain extent, the slave of its own case law, and its own finding that Arts 48, 52 and 59 are specific applications of the principle of non-discrimination on grounds of nationality enunciated in EC, Art 6.[56] It is arguable that Art 6 has a different function in the overall system of the Treaty. Particularly after the express recognition of a concept of European citizenship, Art 6 EC could be seen as an attribute that citizenship, focusing on the person itself rather than the principle of free movement.

Nationality discrimination and European Citizenship[57]

Citizenship evokes the idea of a commonality of rights and duties between the citizens and thus incorporates a notion of equality. In a federal or proto-

[54] And which cannot be justified.
[55] Arts 52 and 59 are also sufficiently wide as to enable a wider interpretation of these articles than a mere prohibition of discrimination on grounds of nationality.
[56] See, for instance, Case 175/78 *R v Saunders* [1979] ECR 1129, [1979] 2 CMLR 216 or Case 2/74 *Jean Reyners v Belgian State* [1974] ECR 631, [1974] 2 SMLR 305.
[57] For further discussion of European citizenship see below, Chapters 10 and 11.

federal structure, there is a close affinity between citizenship of the Union and non-discrimination between the citizens of the states making up the Union. The Supreme Court of the United States has on several occasions stressed this when interpreting the privileges and immunities clause of Art IV, section 2 of the US Constitution, which establishes a principle of equal treatment quite comparable to EC, Art 6.[58] As long ago as 1869, the Supreme Court could say in *Paul v Virginia*[59] that 'it was undoubtedly the object of the clause in question to place the citizens of each state upon the same footing with citizens of other states, so far as the advantages resulting from citizenship in those states are concerned ... It has justly been said that no provision in the Constitution has tended so strongly to constitute the citizens of the United States one people as this'. Similarly, in *Toomer v Witsell*,[60] Mr Chief Justice Vinson held that 'the primary purpose of the clause ... was to help fuse into on nation a collection of independent, sovereign states. It was designed to insure to a citizen of state A who ventures into state B the same privileges which the citizens of state B enjoy. For protection of such equality the citizen of state A was not to be restricted to the uncertain remedies afforded by diplomatic process, and official retaliation. 'Indeed, without some provision of the kind removing from the citizens of each state the disabilities of alienage in the other states, the Republic would have constituted little more than a league of States; it would not have constituted the Union which now exists.'[61] Therefore, it is curious that EC, Arts 8 to 8e introduced by the Maastricht Treaty to establish citizenship of the Union, do not explicitly mention non-discrimination on grounds of nationality as one of the attributes of Union citizenship. It is true that a general prohibition on non-discrimination is contained in EC, Art 6, in the first part of the Treaty. However, the right to free movement is affirmed in several places in the Treaty as well. Yet, it as still felt necessary to reiterate it in Art 8a. It might be felt that non-discrimination is itself a specific aspect of the right to free movement and is, therefore, implicit in Art 8a. It is submitted, however, that certain aspects of the right not to be discriminated against on grounds of nationality bears very little connection with the issue of mobility in Community and needs to be based on an independent principle of non-discrimination.

Long before the Maastricht Treaty, the Court had recognised certain aspects of the prohibition on discrimination on grounds of nationality where the link with free movement was somewhat tenuous. Thus, on the basis of

---

[58] Art IV, section 2 provides that 'The citizens of each State shall be entitled to all privileges and immunities of citizens in the several States'.
[59] 8 Wall (US) 168, 19 L Ed 357.
[60] (1948) 334 US 385, 92 L Ed 1460, 68 S Ct 1156.
[61] *Ibid.* The passage quoted by Vinson CJ refers to the judgment of the Supreme Court in *Paul v Virginia*, cited above n 59.

Art 7(2) of Reg 1612/68,[62] which provides that a national of a member state who works in another member state is entitled to the same tax and social advantages as workers who are nationals of the host state, the court has found that the family of a deceased Italian migrant worker was entitled to the same concessionary fares on French trains as were available under French legislation to French families,[63] or that the right to have criminal proceedings held in the German language in certain areas of Belgium should be available to nationals of other member states working in Belgium on the same terms as for Belgian nationals.[64] The court has thus considered, contrary to what a contextual interpretation of Art 7(2) might have suggested, that the concept of social advantages covered not only advantages granted to individuals primarily by reason of their status as workers but also 'by virtue of the mere fact of their residence on the national territory.'[65] While the Court still formally requires that the advantage must be linked to the movement of workers, D O'Keefe rightly pointed out that 'the causal link between extending a particular benefit to migrants and the consequences for mobility do not seem ever to have been subjected to exhaustive scrutiny.'[66] The fact that the grant of an advantage helps the integration of the worker and/or his or her family in some way seems to be sufficient.[67] Indeed, as the court considers the stigma attached to differential treatment is, in itself, an obstacle to the integration of the worker, the requirement of a link is purely formal.[68]

When the link with employment becomes so weak, it is doubtful whether the right can still be seen as an adjunct to the principle of free movement of workers. In the *migration policy* case,[69] the Court found that the (limited) Community's powers under the EC Treaty over migration from third countries being focused on social matters, the Commission could not adopt measures relating to the integration of third country workers into the cultural life of the member states. In relation to third country workers, the court draws a distinction between integration into the workforce and integration into the community. Similarly, regarding the

---

[62] Council Reg 1612/68/EEC on freedom of movement of workers within the Community, OJ Sp Ed 1968 (II), p 475.
[63] Case 32/75 *Cristini v SNCF* [1975] ECR 1085, [1976] 1 CMLR 573.
[64] Case 137/84 *Mutsch v Ministère Public* [1985] ECR 2681, [1986] 1 CMLR 648.
[65] Case 207/78 *Ministère Public v Even and ONPTS* [1979] ECR 2019, [1980] 2 CMLR 71.
[66] D O'Keeffe, 'Equal Rights for Migrants: the Concept of Social Advantages in Art 7(2), Reg 1612/68', (1985) 5 YEL 93, at p 106.
[67] See the *Mutsch* case (cited above n 64), where the court noted that 'the right to use his own language in proceedings before the courts of the member-State in which he resides, under the same conditions as national workers, plays an important role in the integration of a migrant worker and his family into the host country, and thus in achieving the objective of free movement of workers.'
[68] See also, on the entitlement of the child of a migrant worker to a grant for study abroad, Case C-308/89 *Carmina Di Leo v Land Berlin* [1990] ECR I-4185.
[69] Case 281/85 *Germany and others v Commission* [1987] ECR 3203.

rights of Community nationals, there is more than a quantitative difference between rights of membership of trade unions[70] and language rights in court.[71] Whereas the former is clearly a question of integration of the worker closely linked to Art 48, the latter has more to do with a concept of European citizenship and the general principle of non-discrimination contained in EC, Art 6.

Indeed, it is expressly on the basis of the general non-discrimination clause in EC, Art 6[72] that the court based another judgment where the anti-discrimination principle could be seen as having more to do with European citizenship than free movement. In *Cowan*,[73] the court had to determine the lawfulness of a condition of nationality contained in a French criminal injuries compensation statute. Mr Cowan, a British tourist who had been unfortunate enough to be mugged in the Paris metro, was, as a tourist, a recipient of services and so fell within the scope of Art 59 of the Treaty on freedom to provide services. Despite some ambiguities in the course of reasoning,[74] the court nevertheless chose to base its solution on EEC, Art 7 and considered that the condition of nationality was incompatible with the general prohibition on discrimination on grounds of nationality contained therein. The judgment of the court must be approved. While the risk of mugging may well influence one's choice of destination, it is highly improbable that the availability of compensation when such risk materialises has any effect on one's decision to spend one's holidays in Hull rather than in the French capital. The non-availability of compensation is unlikely then to constitute an obstacle to the freedom to provide services. It is, however, clearly a form of discrimination which is repugnant to the notion of a citizen's Europe and there is no reason why an individual who, as a tourist or otherwise, falls within the scope of the treaty should not be able to invoke the benefit of EEC, Art 7.

Gravier[75] is another remarkable case in the development of a concept of discrimination based on European citizenship: at the time, no provisions of Community law expressly granted any right to nationals of one Member State wishing to follow a course of studies in another Member State.[76] Nevertheless, the Court held, on the rather flimsy basis of Article 128 EEC,[77] that 'access to and participation in courses of instruction and

---

[70] As in Case C-213/90 *ASTI v Chambre des Employés Privés* [1991] ECR I-3507, [1993] 3 CMLR 621.

[71] As in *Mutsch*, cited above note 64.

[72] At the time EEC, Art 7.

[73] Case 186/87 *Cowan v Trésor Public* [1986] ECR 195, [1990] 2 CMLR 613.

[74] Notably in para 17 of the judgment, where the court seemed to consider that the right to compensation on equal terms with nationals was a 'corollary' of free movement.

[75] Case 293/83 *Françoise Gravier v City of Liège* [1985] ECR 593, [1985] 3 CMLR 1.

[76] This situation would now be covered by Dir 93/96/EEC (OJ 1993 No L317/59).

[77] Article 128 EEC merely empowered the Council to develop a common vocational policy, and the Council had only adopted some guidelines and resolutions but no binding act. Indeed, the drafters of the Treaty seemed to have regarded the issue as so minor that Article 128 was one of the rare provisions under which the Council could act by a majority of its members.

apprenticeship, in particular vocational training, are not unconnected with Community law' and that the principle of non-discrimination contained in Article 7 EEC applied to such access. Consequently, nationals of other Member States had to be treated as home students for fee purposes and could not be charged any sum in excess of those demanded from home students. Nothing was said in *Gravier* about rights of entry and residence in the Member State where the individual wishes to pursue a vocational course. This gap was filled in *Raulin*,[78] in which the Court held that 'the principle of non-discrimination with regard to conditions of access to vocational training deriving from Articles 7 and 128 of the EEC Treaty implies that a national of a Member State who has been admitted to a vocational training course in another Member State enjoys, in this respect, a right of residence for the duration of the course', since 'it is clear that a student admitted to a course of vocational training might be unable to attend the course if he did not have a right of residence in the Member State where the course takes place.' Thus, while an analysis based on Article 48 would make the principle of non-discrimination an adjunct of the right to free movement, *Raulin* shows that, under Article 6 EC, the analysis is completely reversed and it is the right of free movement which is the corollary of the principle of non-discrimination.

It is clear, therefore, that one can distinguish between two distinct principles of non-discrimination in relation to migrants: a right of non-discrimination which buttresses the right to free movement, and which is based on the specific provisions of the Treaty relating to free movement, and an independent principle of non-discrimination, based primarily on Art 6 but which can also be found in secondary legislation, and notably in certain aspects of the court's interpretation of Art 7(2) of Reg 1612/68.[79]

This distinction is not simply a purely intellectual nicety, as it has consequences to the test of discrimination being applied. In free movement-based discrimination, the key question if whether access to the labour or services market is made more difficult for nationals or residents of other member states.[80] It is clearly an effects-based test. In citizenship-oriented non-discrimination, the focus shifts onto the *treatment* by a member state of nationals of other member states. It might be tempting to try to analyse that in terms of effect as well, by saying that the issue is whether the integration of the national of another member state is hindered. Two remarks

---

[78] Case C-357/89 *VJM Raulin v Minister van Onderwijs en Wetenschappen* [1992] ECR I-1027. See also Case C-295/90 *Re students' right of residence: European Parliament v Council* [1992] ECR I-4193, [1992] 3 CMLR 281.

[79] Incidentally, this would suggest that Reg 1612/68 should have been based not only on Art 49 but also on EEC, Art 7. However, the Community legislator could not have guessed that the court would interpret the Regulation beyond what was probably the legislator's intention.

[80] Or more accurately, as it has been argued above, those who exercise their right to free movement.

need to be made. First, not all cases of citizenship-discrimination can be analysed in terms of integration. This would be particularly true as regards providers or recipients of services, who will not seek integration in the host state. *Cowan* would be a good example of that. More importantly, when one seeks to analyse what 'integration' means in this context, one is forced to recognise that what one is interested in is the treatment received by the national of another member state: the issue is whether the member state excludes the foreign national by making him feel that she or he is not 'one of ours'. It is striking that, whereas cases on free-movement-based discrimination tend to be cases of indirect discrimination, citizenship-oriented cases are virtually all direct discrimination cases. It is submitted that the relevant test is ultimately one of intention. What is meant by 'intention', however, needs to be clarified. First, the existence of other motives or purposes does not *per se* preclude the existence of an intention to discriminate. This is so even if the ulterior purpose is the primary purpose, or indeed the only objective which is actively sought. Intention, therefore, covers what is sometimes referred to in criminal law as 'oblique intention'. Thus, the fact that a member state restricts the availability of certain benefits to its own nationals in order to reduce costs to the taxpayers rather than out of a deliberate will to harm non-nationals will not make the discrimination any less intentional, as long as the state adopts mean which the state can be taken to know will result in discrimination against foreign nationals. Secondly, the test of intention is an objectified test. A concept of subjective intention for an abstract entity such as a state would often have to be purely fictional, It cannot but be an attributed intention, based on inferences from the objective consequences of the measure.

Accepting that citizenship-discrimination is based on intention does not necessarily rule out indirect discrimination. However, indirect discrimination in an intent-based approach tends to merge with the notion of 'covert' discrimination used by the court in the early cases. Thus, the *Sotgiu* formula, according to which the prohibition on non-discrimination covers not only overt discrimination but also 'all covert forms of discrimination which, by the application of other criteria of differentiation, lead in fact to the same result',[81] would remain applicable in this context. On the other hand, a pure disparate impact analysis seems to be ruled out, although it is still possible to use disparate impact as *prima facie* evidence of intentional discrimination, leaving the burden of establishing the absence of such intent on the member states. In practical terms, what would probably constitute the most frequent application of the notion of indirect discrimination would be classifications based on residence within the host state, which without doubt are bound to often work to the detriment of nationals of other member states.

---

[81] Case 152/73 *Sotgiu v Deutsche Bundespost* [1974] ECR 153, at para 11.

A measure may, however, still be lawful, even if a discriminatory intent can be established. In particular, discrimination against non-nationals will most certainly be lawful where a 'special relationship of allegiance with the state[82] is at issue. Thus, it is virtually certain that benefits awarded to war veterans could legitimately exclude non-nationals[83] and that the principle of non-discrimination on its own would not be enough to justify the grant of political rights, such as voting. A rather more difficult question concerns the extent to which a state's taxpayers should bear the burden of providing benefits to nationals of other member states who have no substantial connection with that state. While this is not a factor which it expressly acknowledges, the court is undoubtedly influenced by it. Thus, while the Court found that equal access to vocational training meant that a state had to extend to other Community nationals, the financial assistance it gives to its own nationals as regards registration and tuition fees, it nevertheless considered that 'at the present stage of development of Community law assistance given to students for maintenance and training falls in principle outside the scope of the EEC Treaty for the purposes of Art 7'.[84] The reasons put forward by the Court for excluding maintenance grants form the ambit of EEC, Art 7[85] are unconvincing, in that they would apply equally to tuition fees. Clearly, the Court is drawing an artificial distinction in order to avoid placing an undue burden on the finances of some member states. In principle there is no reason why this should not be a factor to be taken into account, subject to two qualifications. First, it should be noted that, if the underlying rationale is that certain benefits or advantages should be reserved to those who contribute to the welfare of the community, it may well justify in appropriate cases indirect discrimination based on residence but it is hard to see how it could provide legitimacy for direct discrimination explicitly based on nationality. The second qualification is that there may be a case for requiring a member state invoking that argument to back discriminatory practice up with sufficient evidence that not discriminating against non-residents would in fact create a serious difficulty for that member state.

---

[82] The issues raised here are comparable to those raised by the pubic service exception to the free movement of workers under Art 48(4). See Weatherill & Beaumont, *EC Law*, London, Penguin Books, 1993, at p 500 (from whom the phrase quoted in the text is borrowed).

[83] See Case 207/78 *Even*, *cit* above n 64. *Even* is not, strictly speaking, conclusive of the issue, as the court simply held that a war pension scheme fell neither within the scope (as opposed to falling within the scope but being nevertheless permissible) of Reg 1408/71 on social security for migrants nor within the scope of Art 7(2) of Reg 1612/68 on social advantages. This still leaves the theoretical possibility that it might fall within EC, Art 6. There is, however, little doubt as to what the answer to that question would be.

[84] Case 39/86 *Sylvie Lair v Universität Hannover* [1988] ECR 3161, at para 15.

[85] Namely that 'It is, on the one hand, a matter of educational policy, which is not as such included in the spheres entrusted to the Community institutions and, on the other, a matter of social policy, which falls within the competence of the member states insofar as it is not covered by specific provisions of the EEC Treaty'. *Ibid*.

This approach has been adopted by the US Supreme Court when dealing with breaches of the privileges and immunities clause in Art 4, section 2 of the US Constitution. Thus, in *Hicklin v Orbeck*,[86] in which the Supreme Court was asked to rule on the compatibility with the privileges and immunities clause of an Alaskan statute requiring certain employers to give priority to Alaskan residents in preference to non-residents, the Supreme Court held that, 'even assuming that a state may validly attempt to alleviate its unemployment problem by requiring private employers within the state to discriminate against non-residents', the state would still have to show that out-of-state job seekers constituted 'a peculiar source of the evil at which the statute is aimed' and that the statute was an adequate way to solve the problem.[87] This candid and pragmatic approach, which openly admits clear discrimination when there is a substantial reason for it, might be culturally more difficult to accept for European minds. However, given that, 'in the current state of development of Community law', the court is unwilling, as the *Lair* case shows, to eradicate all forms of discrimination on grounds of nationality at whatever cost, it might be preferable to let the member states argue their case where there is a genuine problem rather than relying on dubious distinctions and, in the process, risk letting slip through cases of discrimination which could easily be eliminated without great consequences. Moreover, this approach would also give the court a more flexible test, capable of adjustment to the development of European integration than the approach in terms of scope adopted in *Lair*, which makes the evolution of the court's case law dependent on changes to the Treaty.

CONCLUSION

What our enquiry seems to indicate is that analysing different non-discrimination provisions in the EC Treaty as being merely specific applications of a single equality principle may be misleading. There is very little in common between the concerns about powers, processes and institutional balance that are behind the equality principle when it comes to judicial review of Community legislation and the desire to correct an unacceptable state of affairs in relation to sex discrimination. Even when the non-discrimination principle apparently focuses on the same 'evil', as in cases on discrimination on grounds of nationality, it may in fact cover very different purposes, each with their own internal logic. Treating them as falling within a single principle without clearly ascertaining their different purposes may be a

---

[86] (1978) 437 US 518, 57 L Ed 2d 397.
[87] In other cases, the Supreme Court has also clarified this last point by considering that it embodied what would be called in the European context a 'proportionality test', ie that no less restrictive means exist to eliminate the problem. See, for instance, *Supreme Court of New Hampshire v Piper* 84 L Ed 2d 205.

source of confusion and hamper a coherent development of the law. Perhaps what we have most to learn from internal comparisons of the equality principle in EC law is the differences more than the similarities between its various applications.

8

CONSTITUTIONAL LAW AND LABOUR LAW DIMENSIONS OF ARTICLE 119: THE CASE OF JUSTIFICATION FOR INDIRECT DISCRIMINATION[1]

Steve Anderman

INTRODUCTION

Article 119 requires member states to ensure, and maintain, the principle that men and women should receive equal pay for equal work. It is the only substantive Article of Social Policy in the original Treaty of Rome. Its prohibition on discrimination has been held to be sufficiently precise and unconditional to apply with direct effect both horizontally and vertically, ie not only to member states as employers and as a source of social legislation, but also to collective agreements and contracts between individual workers and private employers.[2] Moreover, its prohibition has been held to apply to a wide range of employment issues, partly because the concept of 'pay'[3] has been given a wide interpretation, partly because 'equal work' has been interpreted to mean 'work of equal value',[4] and partly because discrimination has been interpreted to include indirect as well as direct discrimination.[5]

The Scope of Art 119

On first impression, the case law on Art 119 appears to be quite fiercely assertive on the substantive rights of equal pay for employees. We can see this quite dramatically in the case of *Defrenne (No 2)*,[6] in which the prohibition in Art 119 was held to be directly applicable to private employers and also in *Barber*,[7] which confirmed earlier definitions of pay not merely

---

[1] My thanks to colleagues Nick Bernard, Janet Dine and Sheldon Leader for their help and sharing of ideas on the contents of this chapter.

[2] *Defrenne v Sabena* (Case 43/75) [1976] ECR 455.

[3] See eg *Barber v Guardian Royal Exchange Assurance Group* [1990] IRLR 240.

[4] See *Jenkins v Kingsgate (Clothing) Productions Ltd* [1981] IRLR 333, in which the ECJ stated that Art 1 of the Equal Pay Directive stated the principle of Art 119 and 'in no way alters the content or scope of the principle as defined in the Treaty.'

[5] See eg *Bilka-Kaufhaus GmbH v Weber Von Hartz* [1986] IRLR 317.

[6] *Defrenne v Sabena* above n 2.

[7] *Barber v Guardian Royal Exchange* above n 3.

as the wage or salary but also any other consideration whether in cash or kind, immediate or future, provided that the worker receives it, albeit indirectly in respect of his employment. On closer inspection, however, these decisions suggest that another factor was involved. The Court of Justice was driven by 'constitutional' concerns to establish a wide scope for Art 119 in order to ensure uniformity of treatment of employees in respect of pay throughout the Community. In *Defrenne (No 2)* the decision to give Art 119 direct effect both horizontally and vertically was part of a wider constitutional effort by the Court of Justice to establish the new legal order.[8] In *Barber*, the court was acutely aware that their compromised decision in *Marshall (No 1)*[9] had the effect of producing different rules for public and private employees, and they were not impervious to the arguments that a wider scope for Art 119 would help to reduce the situations in which there would be one rule for public employees an another for private employees. This concern to strike the right balance between Community and national law was so strong in both cases that the financial consequences to employers (normally a factor in striking a balance in labour law issues) was viewed to be of minor importance. Even where the resolution of the constitutional issue produced a highly unusual result in terms of costs to employers, the court was not deflected from its statement of principle; its sole concession was to attempt to limit the effect in time of the application of that principle.[10]

This willingness to give a wide reach to Art 119 may also have been prompted by the court's awareness of the original purpose of the Article. Although firmly lodged in the Social Policy Title of the Treaty, and characterised as 'part of the fundamental rights' of the Treaty,[11] the principle of equal pay was initially motivated as much by the economic imperative of avoiding 'social dumping' as by the social value of equal pay.[12] The French government, prompted by a strong commitment to equal pay in its national constitution, insisted on the inclusion of a similar principle in the Treaty.[13] The objective was clearly to ensure uniformity of labour standards throughout the Community, presumably levelling up to the French standard. In this sense the historical economic function of Art 119 has been a contributing factor to its robust interpretation by the Court of Justice.

[8] See Preschal and Burrows, *Gender Discrimination Law of the European Community* (Dartmouth, 1990) pp 27–31.

[9] *Marshall v Southampton and South West Hampshire Health Authority (Teaching)* [1986] ECR 723.

[10] The *Barber* judgment left the precise limits unclear as to its retrospective effects. An 'entitlement to a pension, with effect from a date prior to this judgment' was excluded. The ambiguities led to a special protocol (No 2) in the Treaty on European Union and a large number of legal actions. Finally, in *Ten Oever v Stichting Bedrijfspensioenfonds voor het Glazenwassers- en Schoonmaakbedrijf* [1993] IRLR 601 the court explained what it meant by its attempts to limit the effect in time of the *Barber* judgment.

[11] See *Razzouk and Beydoun v Commission* [1984] ECR 1509.

[12] See Fredman, 'European Community Discrimination Law: a Critique' (1992) 21 ILJ pp 119, 130.

[13] See eg Neilson and Szyszczak, *The Social Dimension of the EC* (Handelshøjsholens Forlag, 1991) Chapter 3, p 109.

The standard of protection established by Art 119

When one moves from issues of scope to cases which have contributed to the standards established in the application of the equal pay principle, one can see the uniformity factor continuing to influence the court to give a robust interpretation on certain issues. The application of the prohibition against indirect discrimination to 'any practice' of the employer which has a disproportionate adverse impact on employees of one sex,[14] and the shift of the burden of proof to the employer once the employee has shown that the employer's pay practice, has an adverse impact on one sex.[15] These add to the impression of a court prepared in the interests of uniformity to interpret Art 119 so as to give a high standard of legislative protection against pay discrimination.

However, in the case of the interpretation given to the employer's defence of justification for indirect discrimination, one encounters a more complex set of factors influencing judicial interpretation. The judges' concerns with preserving the integrity of Art 119 do not extend to maximising the protective aims of the treaty provision in the labour law sense of using the legislative rights to make inroads into the encrusted managerial practices, collective arrangements and labour market practices which have for decades combined to produce unequal pay and discrimination in the treatment of women in the market. Nor is the value of uniform application given as high a priority in examining the potential discriminatory effects of the social legislation of the member states. Instead, the policy of achieving equal pay is balanced with other values, some not mentioned explicitly in the Treaty but read in to the interpretation of Art 119 as if they were written there: the values of providing an appropriate role for the national courts in the application of an Art 119 with direct effect, the values of respecting subsidiarity in applying Art 119 to the legislative provision of the member states and last, but not least, the values of cost efficiency and managerial discretion in the case of the pay practices of private employers.

It is perhaps not a coincidence that the issue of justification is the one on which the compromises have been made. Though technical in appearance, it is in fact one of the more important elements of discretion in establishing the standard of the statutory protection. The treaty provision can place great pressure on management and legislators to deal with the historical patterns of institutionalised discrimination if it is given a strict interpretation. If it is given a liberal interpretation, it will mean that despite the treaty provision managers and legislators will be allowed to preserve existing patterns of institutionalised discrimination. In the event, it is interesting to examine precisely how the constitutional concerns have been married to ensure uniform standards of enforcement of Art 119 with these other influences to establish the test of justification.

---

[14] See *Enderby v Frenchay Health Authority and the Secretary of State for Health* [1993] ECR I-5535.

[15] See eg *Handels-Og Kontorfunktionaerernes Forbund i Danmark v Dansk Arbejdsgiverforening (acting for Danfoss)* [1989] ECR 3199.

JUSTIFICATION FOR INDIRECT DISCRIMINATION

The defence of justification applies only after an employee has shown that an employer's pay practice, which on its face is gender neutral, ie not applying solely to men or women directly, has in its application a greater detrimental effect or 'adverse impact' on one sex than the other. For example, in *Jenkins* where the employer adopted a practice of paying different hourly rates of pay for full-time and part-time employees, the practice could not be said to be directly discriminatory in the sense of openly stipulating one rate of pay for women and another for men. Nevertheless, since most of the part-timers were women and most of the full-timers were men, the practice was discriminatory because of its clear adverse impact on one sex.[16]

In such cases, employers are allowed a defence of 'justification' under EC law if they can show that such a practice can be explained by factors unrelated to any discrimination on grounds of sex. The foundations for this defence were laid down in *Bilka-Kaufhaus*[17] a case in which the employer refused to pay retirement pensions to part-time employees while paying them to full-timers, in a situation where there were many more women than men working as part-time employees. The Court of Justice held that the employer could establish that Art 119 was not infringed if he could show that the pay practice was 'objectively justified' on economic grounds. The court added that if:

> 'the measures correspond to a real need on the part of the undertaking, are appropriate with a view to achieving the objectives pursued, and are necessary to that end, the fact that the measures affect a greater number of men than women is not sufficient to show that they constitute an infringement of Art 119.'[18]

In *Bilka*, the Court of Justice in fact established four major propositions about the defence of justification for indirect discrimination:

(i) The first was that the defence of justification for indirect discrimination must be based on an objective factor on economic grounds. This required the employer to prove *prima facie* that the reason for the practice was that it met a real need of the business. In *Bilka*, for example, the employer had argued that its policies were prompted by the business goal of reducing the numbers of part-time workers to as small a number as possible because of the benefit to the business of full-timers. The court said that this could be an objectively justifiable factor in the sense that one couldn't exclude all possibilities of it being acceptable.

(ii) The second proposition of the court was that the employer had to meet the further test of 'proportionality'. This test, deriving from the general community law principle,[19] is defined as requiring the employer to show first that its measures were appropriate to achieve the objectives pursued. Then the employer had to show that those measures were necessary to achieve those objectives. The principle of proportionality introduces a restriction upon the

---

[16] See eg Ellis, *European Community Sex Discrimination Law* (OUP, 1991) pp 68–76.
[17] See n 5 above.
[18] *Ibid* at p 1628.
[19] See eg Weatherill, *Cases and Materials on EEC Law* (Blackstone, 1992) pp 27–31.

employer's exercise of business discretion. The tests which are applied once the employer has shown a genuine business reason for the practice require that the means chosen by the employer to achieve its business objective must be proportional. If the employee's advocate can produce a less discriminatory variant of the employer's practice, then the justification defence would fail. Depending on its interpretation, the test of proportionality provides a more or less clear legal limitation on the capacity of managers to perpetuate institutionalised discriminatory practices.[20]

(iii) The third proposition was that the burden of proving justification falls upon the employer as the one best placed to divulge the reason. Since there was no legislative definition of the burden of proof it was necessary to spell out in the case law that once the employee had made out a *prima facie* case of adverse impact, it was incumbent upon the employer as the one with a virtual monopoly of information, to carry the burden of providing evidence that the pay practice could be regarded as objectively justified on economic grounds.

(iv) The fourth proposition was that the issue of deciding whether the employer had met that burden of proof was an issue for national courts to decide because they had sole jurisdiction to make findings of fact. In other words, it was left to national courts to make specific findings of fact on the issues of objective justifying factor and proportionality based on the division of the burden of proof suggested by the Court of Justice.

Although the *Bilka* test allocated a major fact finding role to national courts, it also ensured that their discretion to find the fact of justification was carefully circumscribed by Community law. Moreover, it prompted the Court of Justice to deal with Art 177 references in such a way as to promote a uniform application of the Community law requirement of the employer's burden of proof and the test of objective justification, with its components of 'real business need' and 'proportionality'.

On the whole, the Court of Justice has been fairly consistent in its monitoring of the Community law requirements of the allocation of burden of proof of justification between the employer and the employee,[21] and the test of proportionality as a limit to the discretion of employers to adopt discriminatory pay practices on the basis of business necessity.[22] However, the court has allowed greater variability in shaping the Community law standard on the issue of which factors employers may put forward as objective justifications on economic grounds.

OBJECTIVE JUSTIFYING FACTORS

The *Bilka* case made it plain that the EC test of justification contained within it the age-old labour law principle of deference to management discretion to pursue business objectives. Although the test of whether the employer has a genuine business need is subject to the standard that it must provide an

[20] See Chapter 9 by Sheldon Leader.
[21] See eg *Danfoss* n 15 above.
[22] See eg *Nimz* C-184/34 (1992] 3 CMLR 245.

objective justification, the Court of Justice did not take the further step of setting acceptable limits to the employer's view of business necessity in the light of the objectives of the Treaty provisions. It did not, for example, require that the employer's need must be shown to be 'essential' to the firm in the sense of being necessary to remain in business or to stave off a business deficit; it apparently only required the employer to show that its need was genuine, ie that it was occasioned by a tangible benefit to the business.[23] In the *Jenkins* case, for example, where the differential rate of pay between full-timers and part-timers was found to be indirectly discriminatory against women, the ECJ suggested that if the employer had the commercial objective of wanting to integrate full-timers in the undertaking he could have justified different rates of pay for full- and part-timers. Similarly in *Danfoss*, the ECJ said that the employer's assessment of employee adaptability and vocational training could provide justification for different earnings between men and women, if they could be shown objectively to enhance job performance.

In such cases, it seemed that all the Court of Justice was, until recently,[24] prepared to do was to assure itself that there is a *prima facie* objectively justifying factor and then apply a second stage test of proportionality. It was not prepared to give guidance on the ground rules which the national courts should take into account in deciding when certain factors which are *prima facie* objectively justifying should be ruled out on any other grounds. For example, the court has never indicated that the national courts should, when making their finding that there is a possibly justifying factor, strike a balance between the importance of the need of the business and the extent of the discriminatory effect. The UK courts do insist, however, that there must be an 'objective balance between the discriminatory effect of the condition and the reasonable needs of the party who applies the condition,'[25] even though there are cases where the balance has not always been struck with great care.[26] These cases offer an example of how the issue of justification could include a reference to the trade-off between the relative importance of the business practice and its discriminatory effects. The importance of the court giving more precise guidance on these issues is underlined by the fact that if the national court finds that the objective justification test is met in all respects, then 'the fact that the measures affect a far greater number of women than men is not sufficient to show that they infringe Art 119.'[27] Finally, *Bilka* also made it plain that the issue of family circumstances could not figure in the justification test. In its third holding, it stated that, 'Art 119 does not have the effect of requiring an employer to organise its occupational pension scheme in such a manner as to take into account the particular

---

[23] See chapter 9 by Sheldon Leader.

[24] See discussion of *Enderby* below.

[25] See *Hampson v Department of Education and Science* [1989] IRLR 69 at p 75.

[26] Compare eg *Jones v University of Manchester* [1993] IRLR 218 where discriminatory effect was taken seriously by the EAT with *Bullock v Alice Ottley School* [1992] IRLR 564 where the Court of Appeal virtually ignored it.

[27] See *Bilka* n 5 above.

difficulties faced by persons with family responsibilities in meeting the conditions for entitlement to such a pension.'[28]

In later cases, the court proceeded to extend the main elements of the *Bilka* test from employer practices to the social security legislation of member states. In *Rinner-Kuhn*,[29] the Court of Justice held that the *Bilka-Kaufhaus* test for justifying indirect discrimination would apply to German sick pay legislation which restricted sick pay entitlement to employees who worked for more than ten hours per week or 45 hours per month. Instead of a first step test of genuine business need, the test imposed was whether the state could show that the restriction was a necessary aim of state social policy. This was presumably in deference to the principle of subsidiarity, now explicitly mentioned in the Treaty on European Union. The proportionality test was retained as a second step, as indeed was the concept that the national court was the competent judicial forum to make the finding of fact whether, and to what extent, the indirectly discriminatory legislative provision was justified 'on objective grounds unrelated to any discrimination on grounds of sex.'[30]

In *Rinner-Kuhn* and subsequent cases we can see the court's determination to monitor the national court's exercise of discretion in making a finding of objective justification. Thus, in *Rinner-Kuhn*,[31] the German government's argument that legislation for not providing sick pay for part-time workers working a small number of hours was justified because such workers were not as integrated in, or dependent upon, their employer as employees working longer hours was dismissed by the ECJ as 'only generalisations ... [which] do not enable criteria which are both objective and unrelated to any discrimination on the grounds of sex to be identified.'[32] And, in *Botel*,[33] the court, at the invitation of the Advocate-General, made it a point to demolish the German government's attempted justification for a law which limited part-time employees attending full-time training courses to smaller amounts of paid leave for training purposes than full-time employees. It left the possibility open for the German government to establish a justification on objective grounds before the national court, but made it clear that all arguments advanced thus far were outside the range of the national court's discretion to make a finding of fact. This requirement of a legitimate basis for assertion of necessity has been carried over into the application of Art 119 claims to private employers as a matter of European law. In *Nimz*,[34] for example, the City of Hamburg chose to give credit for full seniority to full-time employees and three-quarter part-timers for the purposes of reclassifying their pay grades while allowing credit for only half seniority to part-timers with shorter working weeks. It put forward that

---

[28] See *Bilka-Kaufhaus GmbH v Weber von Hartz* [1986] IRLR 317 at p 103.
[29] *Rinner-Kuhn FWW Spezial-Gebaudereinigung GmbH* [1989] IRLR 493. See n 5 above.
[30] *Ibid* at p 496.
[31] *Rinner-Kuhn v FWW Spezial-Gebaudereinigung GmbH & Co KG* [1989] IRLR 493.
[32] *Ibid.*
[33] *Arbeiterwohlfahrt der Stadt Berlin e V v Botel* [1992] IRLR 423.
[34] *Nimz v Freie und Hansestadt Hamburg* [1991] IRLR 222.

full-time or three-quarter part-timers acquire the skills necessary for their employment more quickly than other employees as a justification of their argument. The English and German governments invited the ECJ, not to pronounce upon the merits of the employer's justification defence but, to leave the issue to the national court to decide. The Advocate-General suggested that while it was not for the court to assess the facts, nothing prevented the court from specifying in an appropriate case that arguments which are too general cannot be considered objective criteria. The Court of Justice agreed, stating that 'such considerations, in so far as they are simply generalisations, cannot amount to objective criteria unrelated to any discrimination based on sex'.[35]

These cases provide further examples of how the Court of Justice has been exercising a supervisory jurisdiction over national courts on the issue of what may or may not be an objective factor unrelated to any discrimination on grounds of sex in its constitutional concern to ensure that national courts produce harmonised results. This helps to maintain high standards as to what may be acceptable as a *prima facie* objective factor, ruling out generalisations as well a other spurious grounds.[36] In these cases, the interpretation of objective justification by the court has remained essentially a preliminary vetting process providing little guidance to national courts about the way they should deal with the issues raised once a factor is found to be *prima facie* an objective justification, apart from insisting upon a second stage test of proportionality. The court has provided little guidance to national courts on the issue of the need to balance the importance of the business need with its perpetuation of discriminatory effect. It is true that in defining what is a generalisation the court has occasionally hinted at the need for national courts to be careful to be rigorous in its assessment of what is both objective and unrelated to any discrimination on grounds of sex. In *Nimz*,[37] for example, the court pointed out that length of service by itself could not be assumed to equate with better performance and was, therefore, not sufficient by itself to provide an objective justification. It gave guidance to the national court about the type of further investigation that was needed to establish objectivity the effect of experience on the performance on the particular work in question.[38] On the whole however, the court has confined its monitoring function to the exclusion of certain factors as objective as a matter of EC law because it considered they were either too general or so spurious that they could in no circumstances be objective justifying factors.

In its more recent decision in *Enderby v Frenchay Health Authority*,[39] the court engaged in a more intrusive examination of the issues setting the

[35] *Ibid* at p 225.
[36] See eg *Ruzius-Wilbrink* [1989] ECR 4311 in which the court found that the Dutch government's sole argument justifying its restriction of disability allowances for part-timers was not consistent with its practices in other spheres of social legislation.
[37] See above n 19.
[38] See Ellis, *Discrimination in European Community Sex Equality Law* p 579.
[39] See n 14 above.

standard of protection offered by Art 119. In *Enderby*, the court held first of all that the fact that the different rates of pay for the speech therapists and the clinical psychologists were decided by distinct collective bargaining processes (conducted separately for each of the professional groups and without any discriminatory effect within each group) was not a sufficient objective justification for the difference in pay between these two jobs. The court reasoned that to allow such a factor to preclude a finding of *prima facie* discrimination would open the door to the use of separate collective bargaining processes as a device to circumvent the principle of equal pay. To introduce, as *Enderby* does, a categorical exclusion of certain factors as capable of providing a justification is to make the vetting process into something rather different than the exclusion of generalisations and non-objective arguments. In *Enderby*, the court stated that separate collective agreements without more could not as a matter of Community law, be a ground sufficient to offset a *prima facie* finding of adverse impact, where it contains the potential to undermine the principle of equal pay. In other words, as in the case of the seniority issue in *Nimz*, the court was not prepared to leave the discretion to national courts to determine that a particular factor, taken by itself, could be sufficient justification for a difference in pay.

The court's reason in *Enderby* may have been that it considered that the justification test had to apply to the discriminatory result of the practice, not the process that produced that result. As Advocate-General Lenz had pointed out:

> 'Since justification of the discriminatory result is called for, it cannot be sufficient [merely] to explain the causes leading to the discrimination ... The historical and social context of a "purely female profession" is most probably sex related. If an explanatory approach were accepted as sufficient justification, that would lead to the perpetuation of sexual roles in working life. Instead of the equality of treatment which is sought, there would be afforded a legal argument for maintaining the *status quo*.

Nevertheless, by ruling that agreements between an employer and trade unions by themselves could not be an objective ground in itself and that something more was required by way of justification, the court was entering into the realm of providing guidance to national courts about the trade-off which must be made between historical practices which have a potential to maintain the *status quo* and the need to promote equality. In contrast, the Court of Justice then held that the fact that part of the difference in pay was attributable to a shortage of candidates for one job and the need to attract them by higher salaries could be an objective ground to justify that pay differential. Indeed, the court stated that if the national court found that the state of the employment market had led the employer to increase the pay of a particular job in order to attract candidates, this must necessarily constitute an objectively justified economic ground. The court went on to require the national court to assess whether the role of market forces in determining the rate of pay was sufficiently significant to provide objective justification for part, or all, of the difference. It also insisted on the application of the principle of proportionality before a finding of objective justification could be made. Nevertheless, by its holding, the court had ruled that the principle of equal pay was limited by market forces despite the capacity of market forces to undermine that principle. It avoided the thornier option of leaving the possibility open of national courts attempting an accommodation between the two values in appropriate cases, particularly where the market forces themselves were a product of historical patterns of institutionalised discrimination. As in the case of other potential objective factors already suggested, such as those in *Bilka*, (reducing part-timers) and *Danfoss* (the worker's flexibility, or adaptability to hours and places of work, training or length of service), the court made no attempt to require national courts to attempt to strike a balance between commercial necessity and discriminatory effect but left it to them to apply the test of proportionality as the sole balancing factor with commercial necessity. By limiting the factor of commercial necessity solely to the principle of proportionality in this way, the court's interpretation will have the effect of limiting the principle of equal pay. A wide interpretation of the proportionality principle might have included a reasonable balance between business necessity and discriminatory effect but that is not how the Court of Justice has interpreted it.[40] One explanation for the court's interpretation of this issue is that at this level it is fearful of the potentially disruptive effects of equal pay decisions if legislation were to be used to maximise equality of pay between men and women.[41] If so, it is simply reverting to the traditional stance of judges interpreting labour legislation in which the promotion of employee rights is compromised because of reluctance to interfere with managerial discretion or to impose heavy costs on businesses.

It has also been suggested that the real factor explaining the court's judgment on this issue is that the judges have viewed market forces as providing an example of non-discrimination because the difference in treatment is not attributable to gender.[42] This may be what the judges themselves are convinced of, but that is not of course the actual effect of their decision. In fact, such an interpretation of the standard of equalisation established by Art 119 itself may be 'indirectly discriminatory' in the sense that while on its face it is gender neutral, in its operation by diminishing the protective thrust of the legislation it maintains the institutionalised patterns of discrimination in pay between men and women in equal work.

If the Court of Justice continues to be hesitant to provide a more stringent test of the sufficiency of *prima facie* factors justifying indirect discrimination other than the proportionality test, then the only remedy can be more precise legislative guidance, possibly by amending the Equal Pay Directive. As long as historically produced patterns of indirect discrimination are allowed to be perpetuated, there is little hope for equality of pay between men and women who perform work of equal value.

---

[40] See Chapter 9 by Sheldon Leader.
[41] See eg Hepple 'Social Values in European Law' (1995) 48 CLP Vol II.
[42] See Watson, 'Equality of Treatment: A Viable Concept?' [1995] 24 ILJ 33 at p 45.

9

PROPORTIONALITY AND THE JUSTIFICATION OF DISCRIMINATION[1]

Sheldon Leader

INTRODUCTION

To speak of *justified* discrimination sounds strange. It is understandable to say that behaviour that looks discriminatory at first glance really is not after all, as when we realise that women were not as badly affected by a particular measure that excludes them as we first thought. But the law invites us to do something else as well: to take a complaint about discrimination that is in all other respects valid, and to allow it to be overridden in the name of some competing objective. It is an objective that is not even clearly spelt out in advance, but simply fits into the general category of being 'justifiable irrespective of the sex of the person to whom it is applied';[2] or a '. . . material factor which is not the difference of sex . . .'.[3]

The ligament that is often proposed as a way of holding together the commitment to resisting discrimination and the commitment to permitting activity that could actually have discriminatory effects as its by-product, is the famous proportionality test. This chapter will briefly investigate the place of that test in the overall structure of discrimination law.

The first thing to establish is the point of entry for the principle of proportionality into this domain. We have in the legal system, and in the social principles it expresses, two possible and legitimate ways of treating people unequally. One is the mirror image of the way they are to be treated equally. For example, if women and men are to receive equal pay for work of equal value, then they may certainly be paid different amounts, but the differences should only emerge from variations in, say, their skills and responsibilities within the job. The legitimate demands of the job generate an understanding both of what is relevant and of what is irrelevant in giving rewards, and the two are reflections of one another.

On the other hand, we may find that even though there is nothing in the character of the work that would justify unequal rewards between a man and

---

[1] My thanks to Nick Barnard, Bob Watt, Janet Dine and Steve Anderman for their help.
[2] Sex Discrimination Act 1975 s 1(1)(b)(ii), describing a condition under which a claim of 'indirect' discrimination may be overridden.
[3] Equal Pay Act 1970 s 1(3), describing a factor which will permit an employer not to respect an equality clause in contract of employment.

a woman, a difference nevertheless emerges because of a consideration that falls across the concern to avoid unequal treatment altogether. It is here, for example, that we can locate the claim by a hospital that if it can hire a man at a discriminatory wage it will be able to open a new department for artificial limbs;[4] or the claim by the state that if it excludes part-timers, who are largely female, from protection against unfair dismissal, then it will encourage their being taken on by businesses.[5] In the first class of cases, the differences in reward for, or access to, a job are considered in common parlance (if not in legal jargon) not to be discriminatory differences; while in the second class of case they are, only we have compromised the objection to discrimination by introducing another, competing objective altogether.

The distinction between these two kinds of reasons for unequal treatment, mirror image and cross-cutting justifications, should help us to locate the proper role for a principle of proportionality for the principle seems to have its proper place as a way of evaluating cross-cutting reasons for discrimination. This gives it a role that is not simply different in degree, but different in kind from the principle of reasonableness, the latter being at home in evaluating mirror image justifications.

In order to see what use, if any, these points might be, it will help to define the notions of proportionality and reasonableness more closely.

DEFINING THE PROPORTIONAL AND THE REASONABLE USES OF POWER

The definition here will not correspond to the full range of usage that we find in the law, since any single definition which has tried to capture that variety would be hopelessly vague. Instead, what will be offered is a stipulation of the meaning of the terms that aim to be of use in our concern about discrimination, and hope that the usage matches the bulk of what lawyers would be willing to include, and that they be understanding about what is left out.

A principle of proportionality states the conditions under which the state, or a private entity subject to public law standards, is entitled to override the exercise of a fundamental right. The principle puts the following requirements:

(a) that the means chosen are suitable for achieving an objective which competes with the requirement that one respect the fundamental right in question;
(b) that the object be a legitimate one; and
(c) if (a) and (b) are satisfied, that the means chosen, and/or the objective as interpreted, impinge on the exercise of a fundamental right no more than is necessary.

An example of these three elements in case law is to be found in one of the classic recent formulations of the principle as applied in discrimination law, *Bilka-Kaufhaus GmbH v Weber von Hartz*.[6] The European Court of

[4] *Rainey v Greater Glasgow Health Board* [1987] IRLR 26.
[5] *R v Secretary of State for Employment, ex parte EOC* [1993] IRLR 176.
[6] [1986] IRLR 317.

Justice in this case said that in order for an employer to defeat a claim of sex discrimination, the measures adopted 'must correspond to a real need on the part of the undertaking, are appropriate with a view to achieving the object-ive in question, and are necessary to that end.'[7]

If a court with supervisory jurisdiction requires (a) and (b) only, then it can be called a reasonableness requirement. This means that the objective pursued must not be independently illegal, and the means chosen must plausibly further the ends chosen. Objects and means which are themselves either criminal or tortious, or which fall outside any plausible authority given by statute, or by other rules which structure the relevant entity subject to control will be excluded here.

While a principle of proportionality tightens the requirements placed on (a) and (b) by introducing (c), note that this difference is not one of degree, but rather in kind: the demand of reasonableness is one that is put on any use of substantial power that is to be regulated by public law standards, however inoffensive the use of that power might otherwise be. It is a con-cern that the power emerges from a legitimate source; that it be furthered by plausible means; and that it be motivated by a legitimate purpose. Thus, if a local authority awards promotion to its employees on the basis of productiv-ity, then this may well introduce unequal pay between a woman and a man doing the same work, but the only relevant basis on which that might be challenged as an unjustifiable difference would be that for some reason pro-ductivity was not a legitimate concern of the particular body in question, or was a cover for another, malicious motive, etc.

The demand that an exercise of power be proportional points in a different direction altogether. Whereas the principle of reasonableness focuses on a set of complementary concerns, proportionality is a way of relating two dis-tinct concerns: that a fundamental right against discrimination be respected and that a competing objective, which clearly compromises that right, also be permitted.[8] Indeed, the principle goes further: someone who relies on it has already made the implicit concession that the competing objective can take precedence over the fundamental right under the appropriate condi-tions, exacting in exchange the requirement that the damage done to the right be no greater than is necessary. If the right needs stronger protection than that in a particular situation, then the solution is to avoid the propor-

---

[7] *Ibid* p 320, para 36.

[8] See, for example, the opinion of the Advocate-General in *Stoke-on-Trent CC v B&Q plc* 1992 ECR I-6457, who says that the proportionality principle contrasts two contradictory values, the maximum degree of free exchange of goods within the community and the aims pursued by national Sunday trading legislation. (para 31). Outside of the domain of discrim-ination law, we see this feature of the conflict picked out in *Wheeler v Leicester City Council* [1985] AC 1054. In considering the withdrawal of a licence from a rugby club that had refused to pressure its members not to travel to South Africa for a match, Browne-Wilkinson LJ saw the conflict as one between two basic principles of a democratic society: the one allowing a democratically elected body to conduct its affairs in accordance with its own views, and the other the right to freedom of speech and conscience enjoyed by each individual. *Ibid* at 1064–65 cited by J Jowell and A Lester 'Beyond Wednesbury' 1987 *Public Law* p 368 at 373.

tionality principle altogether. Therefore, alongside the assessments of proportionality, it is important to identify those points at which a court must take a firmer line, refusing to justify a competing objective at all because of the damage to the right it will do.

In the light of these general points we can explore some of the tensions within the proportionality principle as we watch it provide a justification for discrimination. It will then go on to examine those situations in which it seems right to refuse to apply the principle in favour of a stronger guarantee.

TWO VERSIONS OF THE PROPORTIONALITY PRINCIPLE

Within the definition of proportionality provided, there is a weak and a strong version of the principle to consider. The weak version results from tightening element (a), but not (b), that is the constraint is placed on means adopted to achieve an end, but not on the end itself. The latter is left to the free choice of the body or organ whose power is being scrutinised. The strong version, on the other hand, emerges as a result of tightening both (a) and (b): objectives must also impinge on a fundamental right no more than is necessary for their successful attainment. What this second version of the principle implies in practice is not that the choice of an objective *per se* is totally prohibited because of its effect on a fundamental right (that is a matter to be treated below), but rather that if there are alternative interpretations of that objective which can be given, one must choose the one with the least impact on the right, on pain of having to compensate a victim for violation of it.

An example of the weak version of the proportionality requirement would be found in one way of interpreting the *Bilka* decision mentioned earlier. Bilka-Kaufhaus GmbH had made it more difficult for part-time workers than for full-time ones to obtain a supplementary occupational pension, requiring the former to have worked full time for at least 15 years over a total period of 20 years. It advanced as its reason the fact that 'employment of full-time workers entails lower ancillary costs and permits the use of staff throughout opening hours.'[9] In making the latter point, Bilka was pointing to its worry that, in general, part-time workers refuse to work in the late afternoon and on Saturdays.[10]

Now, one way of understanding the requirement that emerged from the decision of the European Court would be that a company such as Bilka was free to pursue the objective it wished to (a more efficient and less expensive workforce) subject only to the constraints that this purpose corresponded to a 'real need' which the company had. This need would then be understood as 'real' if the company's objective had been genuinely and responsibly formulated rather than the fruit of an employer's whim or bad faith. Once satisfied on that score, the national court asks whether the means chosen are

[9] *Ibid* p 319, para 7.
[10] *Ibid* para 33.

necessary to achieve the end that has been fixed. Mrs Weber von Hartz had directed her attack here, claiming that there were other ways of achieving the objective of recomposing the workforce. Bilka simply could refuse to hire part-timers. Therefore, they did not, she claimed, need to exclude those that were hired from the pension scheme in order to reach their overall objective.[11]

But there is a different possible reading of this decision, putting forward a different principle of proportionality. Recall the question that had been put by the German court in its *Bilka* reference: 'Can the undertaking justify that disadvantage on the ground that its objective is to employ as few part-time workers as possible *even though in the department store sector there are no reasons of commercial expediency which necessitate such a staff policy?*'[12] In other words, the doubt might be cast not simply on Bilka's chosen method of achieving its staffing objectives, but on those objectives themselves. It might be that, on the evidence provided by the sector in which Bilka is a major participant, it is not necessary to pursue such a policy of reducing part-time employment. If so, the German court could be taken to be asking, may Bilka nevertheless go ahead with its own agenda and still escape the need to compensate those largely female part-timers who are excluded as a result?

With this part of the question that formed the reference thrown into relief, the answer actually given by the European Court might be interpreted differently. When it said that the measures chosen had to correspond to a 'real need' of the undertaking, it may be taken to have pointed in the same direction as had the German court making the reference: testing the objective sought by Bilka against the background of what employers in the sector as a whole have identified as commercially necessary. On this approach, the policy of reducing part-time employment may emerge as discriminatory, quite apart from anything objectionable about exclusions from pension funds. For, if exclusion of part-timers from the fund turns out on the facts of the case to be discriminatory, then the very same factors are present which would make it discriminatory to exclude them from the jobs to which these pension rights are attached. Therefore, in both cases the exclusions would properly be subjected to the test of whether the company faced such commercial pressure that it needed to impose them, the general practice of the department store sector providing evidence about such commercial needs and a reasonable response to them.

Naturally, since this second approach places a restriction on both the choice of objectives and methods of attaining them, it has a more fundamental impact on administrative and commercial policy. Some might think that, for this reason, the strong version of proportionality goes too far. On the other hand, there are reasons for being wary of the weak version.

[11] *Ibid* para 34.
[12] *Ibid* para 8.

CHOOSING BETWEEN THE WEAK AND THE STRONG VERSIONS

The basic reason for having a proportionality principle is, as we have seen, that the legal system wants to pursue two aims at once: it wants to minimise the damage done to fundamental rights while still allowing other distinct objectives, including commercial ones, to be pursued. But if we take this rationale seriously it is submitted, it requires adoption of the strong versions of the principle: it requires supervision of the objectives of those who discriminate as well as the means chosen to pursue those objectives. If we do not do this, but concentrate instead only on the latter, then what the proportionality principle introduces through one door can be effectively removed by another. If companies or public authorities are forced to use non-discriminatory means to achieve their ends, while having a wide discretion over the selection of those ends themselves, then gains in the former area can be removed in the latter. For example, even if they were granted equal access to the pension fund in a case such as *Bilka*, people *like* Mrs Weber von Hartz could still find themselves excluded from part-time work *per se* at Bilka because of its desire to increase the number of full-timers. Yet, as already argued, if it is discriminatory for an employer to exclude a woman from a benefit attached to a job, the same elements in the situation should make it discriminatory to exclude her from the job *per se*. The only difference between the two cases is that we are naturally tempted to allocate greater freedom of choice to the employer over the type of job on offer in comparison with the benefits attached to the job itself. On a closer inspection, this looks arbitrary: the damage wrought by exclusion from work is, if anything, more severe than the damage wrought by exclusion from benefits attached to work.

Of course, the impact of this employment policy on women may well be justified in terms of the employers' needs, but that is a second stage in the analysis of the problem. The employer would only be able to justify this policy by showing a commercial need to compose his workforce in that particular way: if he does not carry out the policy, his business will suffer significantly. We already find this kind of impact on the business used by some judges as the test for deciding on the justifiability of a dismissal.[13]

---

[13] *Ellis v Brighton Cooperative Society* [1976] IRLR 419, where the EAT pointed out that if a re-organisation of the workforce was not carried out, the business would face real difficulty. This element of real pressure on the business was also held to be relevant in *Evans v Elementa Holdings Ltd* [1982] IRLR 143, and despite its difference from *Evans* on other grounds, in *Chubb Fire Security Ltd v Harper* [1983] IRLR 311. The authorities have been most recently surveyed in Scotland in *McGibbin et al v OIL Ltd* No EAT/537/94 (Unreported). There the EAT held that 'where it is sought to justify a dismissal as due to some other substantial reason, there must be some situation of pressure on the employer. It is not enough for an employer simply to say that it is convenient or helpful to him to carry out a re-organisation, or that to do so would reduce his employment costs.' Were dismissals to be allowed on such grounds, said the EAT, then that '... would seriously impair the effectiveness of the employment protection legislation.' (p 14). I am grateful to Professor Steve Anderman for referring me to this case.

A case which vividly illustrates the difference between what we have labelled the weak and strong versions of proportionality is *Board of Governors of St Matthias C of E School v Crizzle*[14] The Board of Governors of a voluntary-aided school had stipulated that the vacant post of head-teacher was to be occupied by a committed, practising Christian. Ms Crizzle, of Asian origin, was a non-practising Roman Catholic, and for this reason was refused the post. An Industrial Tribunal had found this require-ment to amount to indirect discrimination because of the disproportionately fewer number of Asians able to comply with it, and also to be without suffi-cient justification since the objectives as defined by the Governors had given too little weight to the primary need to provide an efficient education within the framework of the Education Act, 1944. The EAT reversed on the issue of justification. It found that the Governors were entitled to pursue a mix of objectives with greater freedom than that given them by the Industrial Tribunal, and in particular to decide that the school should place great emphasis on the place of religious worship. Satisfied that the objectives were themselves reasonable, the EAT focused on the means used to attain them by way of insisting that the headteacher be a practising Christian, and here the proportionality principle was used to balance the discriminatory effect of the exclusion of Ms Crizzle against the reasonable needs of the school as defined by the Governors. The Governors passed the test.[15]

Commenting on the case, Michael Rubenstein argues that if a condition attached to access to a job operates to the disadvantage of a racial group, then the employer must show more than a reasonable objective in order to justify the discriminatory impact.[16] Instead, the objective itself must be justi-fied as corresponding to a real need the employer has, and subjected to the test of seeing if it can be pursued in a less discriminatory way.[17] If, rather than do that, the court defers to the employer's own characterisation of his objectives, then, says Rubenstein:

> 'it is difficult to see why the governors could not require all of a school's teachers to be committed Christians (or Jews or Muslims as the case may be). If that is what Parliament intended, it would have provided a special exemption from the Race Relations Act covering teachers in voluntary-aided religious schools.'[18]

Rubenstein is surely right here. If the management of an institution is at liberty to characterise its objectives without regard to their discriminatory impact, then the real exclusions from it happen at that point, and little is left to remedy by focusing on the means the employer uses. It is tempting to

---

[14] [1993] IRLR 472.

[15] *Ibid* at 476 para 39.

[16] *Ibid* at 467.

[17] Someone else than the headteacher, for example, would have been able to conduct the school's religious service.

[18] Idem. Using reasoning much like this, the French courts have refused to allow the Catholic church to require all of its employees to subscribe to its doctrine, and for this reason refused to accept as legitimate the Church's dismissal of a homosexual sacristan. See *P c Association Fraternité Sait Pie* Cass Soc, 17 Avril 1991. Case No 21724, *La Semaine Juridique* (Ed G n 38) p 303.

respond to this point by arguing that this interferes too much with management's rights to manage as it sees fit. However, if that claim to institutional autonomy were to carry the day, one cuts across the assumption of more than a century of labour law: that the meeting ground between employee and employer is not so free that as to be left unregulated by standards of fundamental rights.

It would force one to consider the profile of types of employee in any institution. The result of adopting this second version of the proportionality principle is that it would push the law towards a requirement similar to the one we find in the UK Disabled Persons (Employment) Act 1944, which requires that employers with 'substantial numbers' of employees to hire a prescribed quota of persons registered as disabled.[19] In other words, whatever the objectives of, and character of, the institution, there would be a presumption, albeit rebuttable, against structuring the workforce in such a way that it excluded a disproportionate number of a group that the law aims to protect. The presumption could be overcome on demonstration of the employer's need.

By subjecting the employers' objectives as well as his methods to the proportionality requirements, one does not prevent management from innovating and changing, but it does push higher their need to compensate those suffering discrimination in the process. It also allows the employer to avoid compensation if it can be shown that the objective he is pursuing is one which is essential to the viability of his business, assessed either in terms of his own balance sheet, or – as in *Bilka* – in terms of evidence provided by the sector concerned.

REFUSING PROPORTIONALITY

It is also important to see when a court rightly refuses to apply the proportionality principle at all, giving instead complete priority to the fundamental right that is being threatened. Recall that the principle *assumes* that it is appropriate to override the right in question, and then sets about searching for ways of minimising the damage being done, paring it down to that which is 'proportionate'. However, it is quite conceivable that a court refuses to take the first step – refusing even a *prima facie* claim to be able to override the fundamental right in question.

A good example of such a line being drawn, with one issue allocated to the proportionality principle and another kept away from it, would be the decision given by the European Court of Justice in *Enderby v Frenchay Health Authority*.[20] Mrs Enderby had claimed that in the National Health Service 'members of her profession, which is overwhelmingly female, are appreciably less well paid than members of comparable professions in

[19] Sections 9 and 10.
[20] [1994] 1 CMLR 8.

which, at an equivalent professional level, there are more men than women.'[21] This disparity arose in part out of the fact that the professions were grouped into different collective bargaining structures with which the employer carried out distinct rounds of collective bargaining. While there was no discrimination within each bargaining structure, when one compared professions across the different groups involved in bargaining, discrimination did emerge. The difference in pay could also be attributed to the fact that there were serious shortages on the market for members of the other profession with which the comparison was drawn which did not exist for Mrs Enderby's own.

The Court of Justice was asked if the advantages flowing from the maintenance of separate collective bargaining structures, as well as the scarcity due to market forces, could justify the discrimination. The court replied that the latter could do so, subject to the demands of proportionality,[22] but the former could not provide a justification at all. On the latter point, the court reasoned that 'if the employer could rely on the absence of discrimination within each of the collective bargaining processes taken separately as a sufficient justification for the difference in pay, he could . . . easily circumvent the principle of equal pay by using separate bargaining processes.'[23] In other words, with sufficient advance planning, the employer would be in a position to resist a claim against discrimination in collective bargaining practically every time it was raised.

So, while the court was prepared to listen to the claim that labour was scarce, and filtered that claim through the demand for proportionality, it was not prepared to do the same for the employer's argument that it would be highly disruptive to important and well-established bargaining relations if it were forced away from dealing with separate groups of employees in separate bargaining rounds. It is not, at first glance, easy to see a justification for the line being drawn here. It surely cannot be that the one activity, recruiting scarce labour, is intrinsically more important than is the other, that of maintaining efficient bargaining. How are we to understand, for use in other cases, when the court will and will not be willing to resort to the proportionality principle?

While the decision does not give us any general criterion, the facts coupled with the solutions provided do suggest a guideline. We might say that there are those measures an employer can take that partially limit an employee's exercise of the right against discrimination; and there are those, on the other hand, which could totally defeat that right. The principle of proportionality is appropriate in the former situation but not in the latter. 'Defeat' of a right, including a right against discrimination, is a notion that highlights a way of impinging on it which is not conveyed by the broader idea of violating the right. Violations cover a broad spectrum of situations in

---

[21] *Ibid*, at p 31.

[22] Though the particular portion of the wage attributable to scarcity would have to be identified. *Ibid*, at 35, para 27.

[23] *Ibid*, at 34, para 22.

which the right is wrongly interfered with, ranging from intentional violations on a particular occasion to unintentional ones arising from structures or practices. To defeat a right, on the other hand, is to violate it in a particular way: it results from adopting a general policy which prevents the right from being exercised on practically every occasion of use to a claimant, and over a wide variety of situations. This is what the court had in mind when it objected to a justification rooted in separate bargaining structures, which would have allowed employers to redraw at will the boundaries around the relevant profession in a single bargaining arrangement, and so escape any demand for parity. The employer would be able to block the exercise of a right on most important occasions that a claim arises.

We can say that the exercise of a fundamental right is limited, but not defeated, when there remain real possibilities for it still to be satisfied on other occasions even though a particular restriction is in place. Thus, in most organisations, an employee is able to make a range of claims to equal pay by pointing to a range of potential comparators. If market forces block her ability to demand strict parity with those who are demonstrably scarce, in an organisation such as the Health Service this still leaves open the real possibility of making other comparisons. In that case, the complainant's right to equal pay survives within the enterprise, while still being limited at certain points. Therefore, any such limitation must respect the requirements of proportionality, such as the employer demonstrating that it is not within his own capacity or resources to level up the pay of relevant employees.

Where else can we see the threat to defeat, rather than simply to limit, an employee's right against discrimination? It might arise were one to justify discrimination by the employer's need to increase his marginal profitability. This ground for justifying action taken against employees has always played a troublesome role in jurisprudence.[24] On the one hand, it seems eminently natural that gains in profitability, however small, be an objective pursued by a competitive commercial company: it is after all what it is there for. It therefore seems, on this view, unnatural to force an employer to compromise this objective in order to avoid unequal pay or other forms of discrimination. On the other hand, it is precisely such an objective that can open the way to resist most claims for equal pay. This is simply because a demand for equal pay will cost something to satisfy. Higher costs will mean less profit, at least in the same accounting year. If the employer can justify the inequality every time his profit level is affected, then he will be able to block claims to equality practically every time they arise. So, if we ask the question that the proportionality principle directs us to ask: whether allocating unequal pay for equal work is necessary to meet the employer's need to reduce his marginal costs, and so increase his profit, the answer is highly

---

[24] Contrast *Kidd v DRG (UK) Ltd* [1985] IRLR 192 which holds that marginal advantages in cost and efficiency can provide justification for discrimination, with the rejection of such marginal gain as sufficient to justify a dismissal in *McGibbin* (above n 54) and the authorities cited therein.

likely to come out that it is. We would then have left the right to equal pay as an empty shell.[25]

For this reason, it seems wrong to always allow the proportionality principle to accompany any fundamental right. To do so is to invite that special kind of impact on the right that the notion of its defeat used here tries to capture. If that result is to be avoided, then we must limit the principle to those domains in which the right can properly compete with other interests, while also having some chance to survive in a world of unequal power between institution and individual. Without that constraint, invoking proportionality as a reason for overriding the right against discrimination could swallow the protection that the right promises.

CONCLUSION

Discrimination law presents a deceptive face. It is not aiming totally to eliminate the practice, as it would do if we had only what we have called mirror image justifications of inequalities to contend with. Instead, the appearance of cross-cutting justifications for unequal treatment places the reduction of discrimination alongside other objectives, working towards the simultaneous satisfaction of all of them. But simultaneous satisfaction is partial satisfaction, and an invitation to frustration for those who take seriously the promise behind the law. This chapter has investigated two ways in which we might minimise such frustrations: by adopting the strong rather than the weak version of the proportionality principle; and by recognising those domains where the principle should not be allowed to penetrate, on pain of seeing the guarantees against discrimination become worthless. The proportionality principle provides a way of strengthening, but also of tailoring, our ambition to be fair.

[25] This is why the Scottish EAT seems correct in *McGibbin et al v OIL Ltd* (above n 54).

Part II

DISCRIMINATION AND GROUPS IN SOCIETY

I O

FREE MOVEMENT OF WORKERS:
NATIONALITY, DISCRIMINATION
AND EUROPEAN CITIZENSHIP

Brian Wilkinson

INTRODUCTION

The focus of this chapter is the extent to which member states may legally discriminate against nationals of other member states in the context of the provisions on the free movement of workers. It is suggested that the development of the law in this area reflects a progressive diminution of the legal ability of the member states to justify such discriminatory treatment. It is suggested furthermore that this has been a particularly deliberate interpretation of the exceptions of Art 48 from two perspectives: that of the sovereign member state seeking to preserve its traditional ability to determine its immigration and labour market policies and, secondly, that of the Court, whose integrationist approach may be said to be directed at ultimate elimination of the ability of the member states to exercise such powers (at least in relation to European Union (EU) nationals).

As the case law in this area is familiar to most people with an interest in EU law, it will not be discussed in great detail. However, it is important to highlight the impact which the Court's decisions have had on the traditional ability of the member states to decide who may enter their territory, have access to employment, and the grounds on which such persons may be excluded or deported.

PROVISIONS OF EC LAW DESIGNED TO ACHIEVE LABOUR MOBILITY

An initial attempt to achieve labour mobility was made in Art 3(c) of the EEC Treaty, which requires 'the abolition, as between member states, of obstacles to freedom of movement for persons.' This was supplemented by Art 7 of the Treaty (EC, Art 6) which provided for a general prohibition of discrimination based on nationality. Finally, Art 48 provided greater detail as to the extent of the obligation to achieve free movement of workers by requiring member states to remove any national legislation which discriminated in terms of employment against other EC nationals. According to

Art 48:

(1) Freedom of movement for workers shall be secured within the Community.
(2) Such freedom of movement shall entail the abolition of any discrimination based on nationality between workers of the member states as regards employment, remuneration and other conditions of work and employment.
(3) It shall entail the right, subject to limitations justified on grounds of public policy, public security or public health:

    (a) to accept offers of employment actually made;
    (b) to move freely within the territory of member states for this purpose;
    (c) to stay in a member state for the purpose of employment in accordance with the provisions governing the employment of nationals of that state laid down by law, regulation or administrative action;
    (d) to remain in the territory of a member state after having been employed in that state, subject to conditions which shall be embodied in implementing Regulations.

If one looks at the provisions of the EEC Treaty from the perspective of the 1950s, it becomes clear that while those who originally drafted the Treaty intended that free movement of labour should occur for economic purpose, the member states were still to retain significant control over their immigration policies. Thus while Art 48 established that free movement of workers would be allowed, and that discrimination on grounds of nationality would no longer be justified, the member states explicitly retained the ability to exclude or deport such EC non-nationals on grounds of public policy, public security or public health. From the perspective of national governments, such concepts were for their determination. Thus, it is suggested, despite the express wish in the Preamble of the Treaty of Rome (EEC) to achieve closer union between the peoples of Europe, Art 48 and its exceptions were premised on a view of the European Community which saw the Community as 'at most, a compact among states.'[1] In such an inter-governmental co-operative framework, the provisions on free movement were designed to overcome obstacles posed by traditional immigration policies and practices, rather than creating a unified area in which workers of any EC nationality could freely move. In other words, while the member states removed certain obstacles to labour migration, they intended to retain ultimate control on immigration policy.

It is suggested, this is borne out by an examination of the early implementing and supporting legislation designed to achieve free movement of workers, as well as the Treaty provisions themselves. Article 48 allowed rights of entry and residence for those accepting an offer of a job already made. It is suggested too that the requirement that the job offer already existed before the migrant worker entered the territory of the host member state reflected the fears of member state governments that general free movement rights would (or at least could) result in an influx of the unem-

[1] Koen Lenaerts, 'Some Thoughts About the Interaction Between Judges and Politicians in the European Community' (1992) 12 YEL 1, at p 1.

ployed into wealthier member states.[2] This desire to maintain state control of labour migration was further shown in 1968 when the Council of Ministers agreed to allow rights of entry for up to three months for job seekers, as long as they did not draw on the public funds of the host member state. The desire to insulate the host member state against social security or other welfare claims by migrant workers was further reflected in Reg 1408/71. This Regulation provided in Art 69(1) that individuals could draw unemployment benefit from their own member state for up to three months while seeking work in another member state. Furthermore, Dir 68/360[3] provided for limited renewal of a first residence permit in circumstances where the migrant worker had been involuntarily unemployed for 12 consecutive months. Cumulatively, it is suggested, these measures support an analysis of the free movement of labour provisions under which the member states saw themselves as surrendering minimal powers over their immigration and labour market policies.

It is clear from the fate of a 1979 Commission proposal that the member states were not prepared to go further and create a unified area in which all EC nationals could move freely. The Commission had proposed a directive under Art 235[4] allowing for a right of entry for all Community nationals,[5] a right of residence for all who could support themselves economically,[6] with a restriction on the ability of national authorities to require a greater ability on the part of the Community national to support him or herself than that required of their own nationals.[7] The proposed directive did not allow member states to withhold non-contributory or non-means-tested benefits from such migrant Community nationals. While the European Parliament was to describe the proposed directive as the first step towards the creation of European citizenship,[8] the member states were not so enthusiastic, particularly with regard to access to non-contributory and non-means-tested benefits by other EC nationals which seems to have been a major obstacle to acceptance of the proposed directive.

Thus, while Art 2(2) of Dir 64/221 established that national economic circumstances could not be relied on under the public policy exception in Art 48(3) as a basis for discriminatory treatment of other EC nationals, the preponderance of the measures introduced in the 1960s and 70s were concerned with ensuring that only the economically active should be allowed to take advantage of the free movement provisions. To summarise, workers who had an offer of employment were the first to benefit from the free movement provisions, followed by those seeking work. Here too, however,

---

2 See 'Comité Intergovernmental Crée par la Conférènce de Messine', *Rapport des Chefs de Delegation aux Ministres des Affaires Etrangeres* (1956) at pp 89–91.
3 JO 1968, L257/13.
4 See OJ 1979, C207/14, as amended by OJ 1980. C188/7 and OJ 1980, C292/3.
5 Art 3(10).
6 Art 4.
7 Art 5.
8 Resolution of the EP, April 1980, (OJ 1980, C117/48). See also the European Parliament's *Thirteenth General Report* (1979) at p 84.

job-seekers were restricted to a three-month period of residence in another member state for the purposes of seeking work. Moreover, concerns that such migration might lead to a drain on the social welfare of the recipient state led to the passage of a Directive on rights to draw unemployment benefit from the job-seeker's own state while seeking work in the host state.

The related case law on these issues, it is suggested, reflects the view on the part of the member states that control of their immigration and labour market policies remained their prerogative, albeit slightly qualified by the provisions of Art 48. In particular, this viewpoint is demonstrated in the case law which established that the concept of 'worker' is one of Community law rather than of national law[9] and that the attribution of nationality by one member state is not open to question by another.[10] As such, we see in these cases a clear battle between the 'sovereign state' approach of the member states and the integrationist approach of the Court of Justice. This becomes all the more clear when one examines the restrictive interpretation which the Court of Justice has placed on the exceptions to free movement of workers contained in Art 48. In each of these – public policy, public security and public health – and with particular emphasis in the later cases on public policy, the Court has refused to allow the member states to unilaterally determine whether exclusion of an EC national may be justified on such grounds. Rather than leaving the contents of such concepts for the member state to decide, the Court has been adamant that Community law will determine their content and has emphasised that the exercise of these exceptions by the members states is open to review by the Court of Justice. A brief examination of the case law on the public policy exception illustrates this point.

In *Van Duyn v Home Office*, the first of the public policy cases to be considered by the Court, the Court seemed disposed to allow a degree of state autonomy which it has since restricted.[11] *Van Duyn* concerned a Dutch national who was refused entry into Britain to take up employment with the Church of Scientology. While the practice of scientology was not illegal in Britain, the Home Office viewed it as undesirable. Article 3(1) of Dir 64/221 requires that a refusal of entry on public policy grounds must be based on the personal conduct of the individual. The question which the Court of Justice had to decide was whether membership of an organisation which is not illegal counted as 'personal conduct' for the purposes of the public policy ground. The Court's response was that the conduct of the individual did not have to be illegal in order to justify the exclusion as long as the state

---

[9] See the following cases on part-time workers *DM Levin v Secretary of State of Justice* Case 53/81 [1982] ECR 1035; *Kempf v Staatssecretaris van Justitie* Case 139/85 [1986] ECR 1741; *Steymann v Staatssecretaris van Justitie* Case 196/87 [1988] ECR 6159. In *Lawrie Blum v Land Baden Wurtemberg* Case 66/85 [1986] ECR 2121 the court ruled that the essential feature under Community law was that for a certain time a person performed services for and under the direction of another, in return for which remuneration was received.

[10] *Micheletti and others v Delegacion del Gobierno en Cantabria* Case C-369/90 nyr. Case note by Jessurun d'Oliveira, (1993) 30 Common Market Law Review p 623.

[11] Case 42/74 [1975] 1 CMLR 1.

had made it clear that it viewed the activity as socially harmful. This decision has been criticised as it clearly allowed a member state to discriminate in relation to how it viewed the same activity depending on the nationality of the person involved. A possible explanation is that the decision can be explained on political grounds: it arose soon after United Kingdom accession to the Community and shortly before the 1975 referendum on continued membership.[12]

The Court of Justice tightened its approach to the issue in subsequent cases. Thus in *R v Bouchereau*[13] it decided that the activities must be sufficiently socially harmful to pose a genuine and sufficiently serious threat to the requirements of public policy affecting one of the fundamental interests of society. The case involved a French national in Britain who was found in possession of drugs on a number of occasions. The fact that he had previous convictions for drug possession would not justify deportation as Art 3(2) of the Directive expressly provides that previous criminal convictions do not constitute grounds for measures taken on public policy ground. However, the Court of Justice stated that such previous convictions could be used to demonstrate a propensity to act in the same way again. This decision raised the question as to what type of evidence would be required to prove that a member state considered a particular activity to be sufficiently harmful so as to justify the exclusion of an EC national. In *Adoui and Cornuaille v Belgian State*[14] two prostitutes appealed against a decision to refuse them a residence permit. The Court decided that it was not open to a member state to refuse a residence permit to non-nationals on the grounds that they engaged in an activity – ie prostitution – which, when practised by a national of the member state, did not give rise to repressive measures or other genuine and effective measures to combat such activity. The reversal of the Court's position in the earlier case of *Van Duyn* is clear.

In describing these developments as some sort of clash of ideologies (state's rights on the one hand and European integration on the other) it is not intended to imply that the Court has been thoroughly consistent in its approach to the use of Art 48(3) by the member states. With reference to the public policy provision in particular, it is clear that the Court began in *Van Duyn's* case by allowing the member state a large margin of discretion. In fact, the Court seemed to accept a double standard under which discriminatory treatment could be based on grounds of nationality. However, in its subsequent jurisprudence it has insisted that the member states are not entitled to apply a different standard to the activities of their own nationals and those of other EC nationals when seeking to apply these exceptions.

In the context of the public health exceptions, it should be noted that while Dir 221 of 1964 establishes that member states may use public health

---

12 See R Dallen, 'An Overview of European Community Protection of Human Rights, with some Special References to the UK' (1990) 27 CML Rev 761, at p 776.
13 Case 30/77 [1977] 2 CMLR 800.
14 Cases 115 and 116/81 [1982] 3 CMLR 631.

as a ground for exclusion, the public health exception is not open to use by the member states unilaterally. The only diseases or disabilities which can be used as the basis for a refusal of entry are those listed in the annex to Dir 221. Moreover, where an EC national becomes subjected to a disease or disability after entry or the issue of a first residence permit, the member state may not rely on the disease or disability so as to refuse a renewal of a residence permit nor to justify an expulsion. Thus, while the mid-to-late 1980s saw a considerable degree of hysteria concerning HIV/AIDS in the media, with some consideration being given to the possibility of excluding those infected by the virus or those thought likely to be, such action would have been illegal under Community law if applied to Community nationals.[15]

Having gradually eroded the ability of member states to apply Art 48(3) solely in accordance with their own perception of what was required in order to protect public policy, public security or public health, the question which arose was whether Art 48(4) provided member states with a refuge against the Court's integrationist approach. Article 48(4) states that the provisions of Art 48(1) to (3) do not apply to employment in the public service. Consequently, it seems, at least from an initial reading of the Treaty, as if the member state is able to prevent EC nationals from obtaining employment in this area. Moreover, looking at this provision from the perspective of independent states, it becomes clear that the provision reflects concerns that the interests of the individual states may be compromised if non-nationals are allowed access to such employment.

However, the Court has limited such refuge provided by Art 48(4). The Court of Justice has been loathe to accept an interpretation of the public service exception which allows the member states significant discretion. The reasons for this become clear when one examines the concept and range of public service employment across the member states. Whereas in countries such as the United Kingdom and Ireland public service employment is readily recognised as applying largely to the Civil Service and certain local government positions, in other member states the concept of public service covers virtually all persons employed by the state. Moreover, given this context, it became clear that while Dir 221 of 1964 prevented member states from relying on economic necessity as a ground for excluding other EC nationals from their labour markets, a unilateral change in the definition of public service employment by any member state could achieve a similar effect. Consequently, when the issue arose for detailed discussion before the Court in *Commission v Belgium*,[16] there were a number of aspects to the

[15] See P.M. van Overbeek (1990) 27 CMLRev 791 A. Hendriks (1990) Nordic J. Intnl Law 186, M Shrimpton in Harris and Haigh *Aids: A Guide to the Law* (London: Routledge/Terence Higgins Trust, 1990) 111, *Nicola Conte v Stadt Wurzber* (decision 16 May 1989).

[16] Case 149/79 [1980] ECR 3881 and [1982] ECR 1845. Article 48(4) had previously arisen in the case of *Sotgiu v Deutsche Bundespost* Case 152/73 [1974] ECR 153, but only in the context of discrimination in the conditions of employment applying to an EC national employed in the German public service, not in terms of access to such employment.

case. Not only was there an argument as to the need for restrictions based on the security requirements of the individual member states, but there was also a second theme of possible circumvention of the provisions in Art 48(1).

It is particularly interesting to examine this case from the two points of view outlined earlier, because it is one of those cases where we have a clear conflict between the state's rights approach to Community law and the Court of Justice's integrationist approach. It is also interesting to examine the type of argument put forward by each party in the case, and to note also those areas which were not addressed. Turning first to the argument advanced by the Commission, it rapidly became clear that the Commission viewed Art 48(4) as a means of circumventing the free movement provisions. Indeed, the Commission was explicit as to the need for public service employment to be seen as a Community law concept. According to the Commission, if public service employment was not given a Community law content '. . . the Member states could by means of a unilateral definition of that concept thwart the application of the principle of free movement of workers whenever they chose.'[17] Consequently, the Commission argued for a functional analysis of each position from which an EC national was being excluded. Was it necessary in terms of the security interests of the host state to so exclude the individual?

The intervention by Germany, France and the United Kingdom in support of the Belgian position indicate a strong desire on the part of these countries to isolate their public services from the free movement provisions. All four governments argued that such isolation was necessary either for protection of state interests or that a functional analysis of individual posts was impracticable. None directly addressed the Commission's argument that Art 48(4) could be used to circumvent the remainder of Art 48. Moreover, each government advanced arguments to the effect that the true intention behind Art 48(4) was that member states should be autonomous in relation to access to employment by non-nationals in their public services.

According to the Belgian government, if the concept of public service employment required interpretation, recourse should be had to the intention of the member states when the Treaty was being drafted. In support of a strong sovereignty approach, the Belgian government argued that as the Treaty did not fetter the power of the member states to determine the boundaries of the public sector, and as there was no Community concept of the objectives, scope and detailed rules of application of the acts of public authorities, it was 'logical to assume that when the Treaty was drafted the governments wished conditions of entry to public office to remain their preserve.'[18]

The United Kingdom's intervention is interesting as it sought to argue that it was 'evident' that Art 48(4) was intended to apply to the public service as a whole and not to individual activities or responsibilities. Any other approach, for example, a functional analysis of each post, would be impractical.

[17] At p 3886.
[18] At p 3887.

Germany also supported a 'state's rights' approach, arguing that no provision in the Treaty gave the Community the power to determine the sphere of operation of the public service; consequently, that power was 'reserved to the States themselves'.[19] Moreover, the German government argued that the free movement provisions were not intended as some incipient form of Community citizenship, but were intended to have strictly limited effects.

The German government concluded that:

> 'Accordingly it follows that the provision is simply intended to signify that freedom of movement is not meant to alter the legal situation existing before the Communities were established as regards the organisation of the state and in particular access for foreigners to the public service.'[20]

The French government in turn took a similar approach to the British as to the practicability of a functional approach to public service posts, and argued that demarcation of national public services remained 'a prerogative of the member states.'[21]

The Court's response, and that of the Advocate-General is equally interesting. In neither the judgment nor the Advocate-General's opinion is there discussion of the claim that Art 48(4) should be interpreted on the basis of an original intent of the authors of the Treaty. Nor do the Court or the Advocate-General address whether Art 48(4) is designed to isolate the public service as a whole from other aspects of Art 48 based on the perceived security needs of the individual member states. Rather, the discussion focuses on the danger identified by the Commission of allowing member states unfettered discretion to interpret and apply the concept. However, even in this regard the Court is not prepared to adopt the halfway approach suggested by the United Kingdom, ie supervising the application of Art 48(4) by deciding whether a particular institution is part of a state's public service. Rather, the Court adopts what the member states in the case rejected as 'impractical', ie a functional test to be applied to each post where nationality is seen as an issue of contention. Under this approach, the responsibilities and duties attaching to each post would have to be examined and only those posts which involved the exercise of state power and the safeguarding of the general interests of the state could be legitimately withheld from non-nationals. By adopting this functional approach, the Court has succeeded in narrowing the application of the public service exception to those positions which:

> 'involve direct or indirect participation in the exercise of powers conferred by public law and duties designed to safeguard the general interests of the state or of other public authorities.'[22]

The reasons provided by the Court in this case are particularly interesting

[19] At pp 3894–95.
[20] Ibid, at p 3895.
[21] At pp 3896–97.
[22] Case 149/79, [1980] ECR 3881, para 10.

in the context of the development of European citizenship, as the court stated that:

'such posts in fact presume on the part of those occupying them the existence of a special relationship of allegiance to the State and reciprocity of rights and duties which form the foundation of the bond of nationality.'

As the court was to reiterate in *Lawrie-Blum v Land Baden-Wurtemberg* Art 48(4), along with its counterparts in Art 48(3), is to be 'construed in such a way as to limit its scope to what is strictly necessary for safeguarding the interests which that provision allows the member states to protect.'

By adopting a functional approach to determining what positions come within the public service requirement, the court has largely restricted the ability of the member states to withhold employment in this sector for their own nationals, except insofar as the duties to be exercised in the post concern protection of State interests. Where there is a doubt, it is open to the individuals to challenge the member state's use of the public service exception clause.

Whether a functional analysis of each post is an adequate response to the issue has been questioned.[23] Perhaps it is too much to expect a comprehensive definition which would allow those who fall within the public service exception to be readily identified. However, the rationale the court provided in *Commission v Belgium* for a narrow concept of public service, ie the presumption of a special relationship of allegiance to the state and a reciprocity of rights and duties, raise issues of interest in the context of the Treaty on European Union's provisions on European citizenship, which will be discussed below. At this point, however, while accepting that a better response may have been possible, the point to be highlighted here is the extent to which the Court of Justice has once again limited the ability of the member states to rely on nationality as a ground for justifying discrimination.

CONCLUSION

It is suggested that the cases on Art 48 clearly show that the Court of Justice gives priority to establishing the viability of the free movement provisions over virtually all other considerations. While the EEC Treaty nominally gives rights to the member states to limit the free movement of labour, the development of the law on the use of the above exceptions demonstrates a clear desire by the European Court of Justice to limit the autonomy of the member states in favour of the achievement of the goal of ever-increasing

---

[23] See David O'Keeffe, 'Practical Difficulties in the Application of Art 48 of the EEC Treaty' (1982) 19 CML Rev 35; John Handoll, 'Article 48(4) EEC and Non-National Access to Public Employment' (1988) 13 ELR 223; O'Keeffe, 'Judicial Interpretation of the Public Service Exception to the Free Movement of Workers' in D Curtin and D O'Keeffe (eds) *Constitutional Adjudication in European Community and National Law* (Dublin, Butterworths, 1992) p 89.

integration. Indeed, it might even be claimed that the Court of Justice has exceeded the original intention of the member states by developing the law in this area in such a pro-integration and anti-state autonomy fashion. Whether one accepts Rasmussen's argument that the court has from time to time 'run wild',[24] Steiner's comment that '[in] seeking to promote freedom of movement, and to remove all obstacles to freedom of movement of persons within the Community, the Court has been prepared to sacrifice the letter of the law to what it sees as the spirit of the Treaty',[25] seems apt. To the extent that it recognises a margin of discretion for the members states, the exercise of this discretion is always subject to review by the Court. In essence, it appears that the Court of Justice views the free movement provisions as more than economic rights attaching to workers. Rather, as others have described these provisions, it seems to view Art 48 as the basis of an incipient[26] or embryonic[27] form of Community citizenship. In this context, the obligation which the Court of Justice appears to have set itself is to reduce the relevance of the member state's concerns over public security, public policy and public service employment in favour of the promotion of a sense of European citizenship. Yet it is not possible for the Court to eradicate the obstacles which the existence of internal borders and diverse member states have on the achievement of freedom of movement. Consequently, it remains possible to justify a certain amount of discrimination against non-nationals. However, as we have seen, this is predominantly public service employment.

The solution, of course, which would prevent discrimination based on nationality would be the achievement of a viable concept of European citizenship under which member state nationality would take second place. Thus, once an individual enjoyed the status of European citizenship, he would automatically have access to employment in a member state on exactly the same basis as those nationals of the member state concerned. It is interesting then to examine the provisions of the Treaty on European Union in as far as they address the issue of European citizenship. Article 8(1) of the Treaty on European Union announces that 'citizenship of the Union is hereby established. Every person holding the nationality of a member state shall be a citizen of the Union'. Article 8(2) states that 'Citizens of the Union shall enjoy the rights conferred by this Treaty and shall be subject to the duties imposed thereby'. Moreover, Art 8a(i) establishes that 'every citizen of the Union shall have the right to move and reside freely within the territory of the member states, subject to the limitations and conditions laid down in this Treaty and by the measures adopted to give it effect.'

---

[24] HJ Rasmussen, *On Law and Policy in the European Court of Justice: A Comparative Study in Judicial Policymaking* (Dordrecht, Nijhoff, 1986).

[25] J Steiner, *EEC Law* (London, Blackstone Press, 1992) (3rd edition) at p 178.

[26] See Richard Plender, 'An Incipient Form of European Citizenship' in FG Jacobs, (ed) *European Law and the Individual* (Oxford, North-Holland, 1976), p 39.

[27] Handoll, *op cit*, at p 240. For further discussion of this notion, see AC Evans 'European Citizenship' (1982) 45 MLR 497; Evans, 'European Citizenship: A Novel Concept in EEC Law' (1984) 32 AJCL 679.

On the one hand, Art 8a(i), as d'Oliveira has commented, has promoted 'the economically irrelevant people . . . to the status of persons'.[28] However, as he also highlights, the concept of European citizenship seems to be different in quality from that of national citizenship. Referring to the declaration which the Danes attached to their Act of Ratification of the Treaty, it becomes clear that European citizenship is not seen as equivalent to national citizenship.[29] Thus nationality *per se* is still a relevant consideration for the free movement provisions. This is particularly the case for public service employment, at least as long as such limitations as already exist in the Treaty, supporting legislation, and case law remain unchanged. It will take more than a declaration of the establishment of European citizenship before nationality is finally eradicated as a ground for justifying discrimination within the European Union.

---

[28] Hans Ulrich Jessurun d'Oliveira, 'European Citizenship: Its Meaning, Its Potential' in Renaud Dehousse, (ed) Europe After Maastricht – An Ever Close Union? (Munich, Beck, 1994) 126 at p 132.

[29] According to the Danish declaration:

> 1 Citizenship of the Union is a political and legal concept which is entirely different from the concept of citizenship within the meaning of the Constitution of the Kingdom of Denmark and of the Danish legal system . . .
> 2 Citizenship of the Union in no way in itself gives a national of another member state the right to obtain Danish citizenship or any of the rights, duties, privileges or advantages that are inherent in Danish citizenship.'

II

THE RIGHTS OF NON-EC IMMIGRANT WORKERS AND THEIR FAMILIES IN EC COUNTRIES OF EMPLOYMENT: A CASE FOR INTEGRATION

Ryszard Cholewinski

INTRODUCTION

Although immigrant workers and their families in European Community (EC) countries of employment who are not nationals of other member states may enjoy few rights under EC law, it is indisputable that they possess rights, which are guaranteed not only by domestic legal systems, but also in a number of international instruments specialising in the protection of migrants.[1] A closer examination of such instruments, however, reveals that the scope of this protection cannot be sufficient in the context of a Europe moving towards greater integration and a notion of 'European citizenship'. When compared with the legal status of EC and European Economic Area (EEA) nationals, the situation of non-EC immigrant workers and their families is strikingly and unjustifiably inferior.[2]

This chapter argues for the speedy integration of non-EC immigrant workers into the fabric of host societies. The choice of an appropriate concept of 'integration' is important. If the aim is (and it should be) to enable all persons and workers resident in EC countries to belong to and participate in a Europe in which they have an opportunity to fulfil their aspirations and to attain a decent standard of living, we should offer, on the basis of equality, a rightful place to all those who contribute, both economically and socially, to our Western European heritage, regardless

[1] The terms 'immigrant workers' and 'migrant workers' are used synonymously. The term 'migrants' refers both to migrant workers and to their families.

[2] Austria, Finland, Iceland, Norway and Sweden have been incorporated into the free movement of workers rubric since 1 January 1994 due to their ratification of the Agreement on the European Economic Area [1994] OJL 1/1. Austria, Finland and Sweden became full EC members as at 1 January 1995. The citizens of Norway voted against joining the EC in a referendum on 27 November 1994.

[3] It is important to emphasise at this juncture that integration is not the same as assimilation, a blending of all national, ethnic, and cultural differences into some new being called the 'European citizen', but rather it is viewed as a coherent interplay between the unique parts, like an orchestra whose individual and varied instruments come together to produce a harmonious melody. Cf T Hoogenboom, 'The Position of those who are not Nationals of a Community Member State' in A Cassese, A Clapham & J Weiler, (eds), *Human Rights and the European Community: Methods of Protection* (Baden-Baden, Verlagsgesellschaft, 1991) pp 351, 356.

of their nationality and notwithstanding that their origins may lie outside the continent.[3]

BACKGROUND

There were approximately ten million non-EC nationals legally resident in EC member states at the beginning of 1992,[4] nearly double the number of EC migrants.[5] According to the International Labour Organisation (ILO), there are also probably another 2.6 million illegally resident migrants in Western Europe and perhaps many more.[6] Indeed, non-EC migrant workers and their families have outnumbered their EC counterparts for many years.[7] Therefore, it is no exaggeration to speak of the EC's '13th nation'.[8] Unfortunately, the 'citizens' of this nation remain disenfranchised.

One-fifth of non-EC migrants come from the three countries of the Mahgreb region of North Africa.[9] The Southern European countries (once significant migrant-sending countries themselves) are receiving immigrant workers and their families from the Mahgreb and other developing regions of the world in increasing numbers, many of whom become employed without authorisation.[10]

[4] Commission of the European Communities, Communication from the Commission to the Council and the European Parliament, 'Immigration and Asylum Policies', COM(94) 23 final of 23 February 1994, 32, para 118 and Annex I, 22 (Table 9).

[5] According to 1992 figures, there were approximately 4.8 million EC nationals resident in other EC member states in comparison with about 9.5 million non-EC nationals. *Eurostat, Labour Force Survey 1992* (Luxembourg, Office for Official Publications of the European Communities, 1994) pp 36–7, Table 0.12.

[6] W R Böhning, 'Integration and Immigration Pressures in Western Europe' (1991) 130 *International Labour Rev* p 445, 449. This figure is a 1991 estimate and comprises migrant workers and their families, including seasonal workers and asylum-seekers who have not achieved refugee status and whose presence is not tolerated officially. For obvious reasons, the number of illegal migrants can never be the subject of precise calculations.

[7] Plender observes that free movement of labour within the EC has not resulted in an increase in migration for employment across the borders of member states. On the contrary. In 1959, when freedom of movement for workers was in its infancy, 75 per cent of migrant workers in EC member states originated from other member states. In 1973, however, when the free movement principle was beginning to be fully implemented, 75 per cent of migrant workers within the EC came from outside of the ECR – Plender, *International Migration Law* (Dordrecht, Martinus Nijhoff, 1988) p 215..

[8] See N Mole, 'Freedom of Movement in a Wider Europe: A Comparison of International Instruments' (1991) 1 AEHRYB 199, 206 and Hoogenboom, above n 3, p 352.

[9] There were over two million nationals from Algeria, Morocco and Tunisia legally resident in EC countries at the beginning of 1992. The majority (approximately 1.4 million) were living in France. Communication from the Commission to the Council and the European Parliament on Immigration and Asylum Policies, above n 4, Annex I, 19 (Table 8B).

[10] See M Biagi, 'Non-EEC Nationals and the Italian Labour Market: The Institutional Framework' (1992) 8 IJCLLIR 154; CBF. De Valderrama, 'The New Hosts: The Case of Spain' (1993) 27 International Migration Rev 169; M Eaton, 'Foreign Residents and Illegal Immigrants: *os Negros em Portugal*' (1993) 16 Ethnic & Racial Studies 536; N Sitaropoulus, 'The New Legal Framework of Alien Immigration in Greece: A Draconian Contribution to Europe's Unification' (1992) 6 INLP 89.

THE CASE FOR INTEGRATION

Integration of non-EC nationals lawfully resident in EC member states is advocated for three reasons:

(a) the realisation of social justice;

(b) the goal of economic efficiency encompassed in the successful completion of the internal market; and

(c) as a vital precursor in the struggle to eradicate ethnic and racial discrimination.[11]

First, the overriding justification must be the realisation of social justice. It is inequitable to discriminate between two groups of residents living side by side in many aspects of their working and living conditions, and to attempt to justify this discrimination on the basis that the members of one group have not acquired the citizenship of the country of employment, particularly if they have lived and worked there for a considerable length of time or were born in that country. Secondly, the concept of the temporary worker or 'guest worker', contrived in the 1950s and early 1960s to ensure that migrant workers would be able to make an economic contribution to the host society at minimum expense to that society, is outdated and no longer workable.[12] Today, the successful completion of the EC internal free market of goods, persons and services cannot take place when ten million persons are systematically excluded from its operation. Thirdly, we frequently read in our newspapers about horrific racist attacks perpetrated against asylum-seekers as well as against long-term immigrant residents.[13] The growth of extreme right-wing politics in Western Europe also remains a current topic of debate. The recent electoral gains of the far right in Austria and the open public support for these gains from Le Pen's National Front in France is a timely reminder of the dark vein of nationalism present throughout Europe.[14] Well-meaning and noble declarations to counter racism and

---

[11] *Cf* K R Simmonds, 'The Concertation of Community Migration Policy' (1988) 25 CMLRev 177, 200; R. Fernhout, '"The United States of Europe have Commenced", but for whom?' (1993) 11 NQHR 249, 260–262.

[12] This was the object of the 'rotation principle' which held an extremely limited conception of the migrant worker: 'The rotation principle implies a uni-dimensional view of the migrant; his economic contribution is welcomed, but at the same time his needs other than that to work and earn a living remain unsatisfied, and his freedoms are abridged: the migrant's role as a family member is ignored; he may be housed in a dormitory where the concept of privacy hardly exists; opportunities for occupational or geographical mobility are restricted; his cultural needs are neglected; and as a political actor he is in limbo.' R Rogers, 'Post-World War II European Labour Migration: An Introduction to the Issues' in R Rogers, (ed), *Guests Come to Stay: The Effects of European Labour Migration on Sending and Receiving Countries* (Boulder, Colorado, Westview Press, 1985) pp 5, 21. However, the rotation principle could not be fully implemented because of increasing family reunification. See also R Cholewinski, 'The Protection of the Right of Economic Migrants to Family Reunion in Europe (1994) 43 ICLQ 568, 571.

[13] Eg see articles on racism in Europe, (1993) *The Independent*, 18 June p 10; (1994) *The Independent*, 13 January, p 16.

[14] See A Bridge, 'Austria's Chancellor Determined to Hang on,' and Le Pen Hails Gains' (1994) *The Independent*, 11 October, p 10.

xenophobia issued by EC institutions[15] are seriously flawed if one of the groups they aim to protect remains *officially* marginalised.

The integration of immigrant workers and their families, especially those who have been resident in the country of employment for a long period of time, can only be successful if they are permitted to feel that they fully belong to the society in which they live and work. Short of citizenship entitlements, this process requires the protection of important rights, comparable with those held by EC nationals residing and working in other EC states, namely a whole range of economic, social, cultural, political and residence rights.

THE POSITION OF NON-EC NATIONALS IN THE DEVELOPMENT OF EC LAW AND EUROPEAN INTEGRATION

At its inception, it seems that the intention of those who drafted the EEC Treaty was to leave the possibility open to accommodate all workers lawfully resident in member states regardless of their nationality. This is clear from the working of EEC, Arts 7 (EC 6) and 48. The former provision enshrines the principle of non-discrimination on grounds of nationality and the latter espouses the freedom of movement principle. As observed by a number of commentators, neither principle is expressly limited to nationals of EC member states.[16] As EC law developed, however, the extensive rights it conferred were limited to EC nationals and the position of non-EC immigrant workers and their families remained inferior to that of EC nationals in EC countries of employment. Realistically, only a fundamental political commitment to the rights of the former will ensure that this group can take its rightful and deserved place in a Western European society.

EC secondary legislation

EC secondary legislation supports an impressive array of rights, particularly in the economic and social spheres. Without these rights, free movement of labour would quite simply be inoperable. The development and completion of the economic internal market would not be possible without concomitant

---

[15] Eg European Parliament, EC Council and Commission, Joint Declaration against Racism and Xenophobia of 25 June 1986 [1986] OJ C 158.

[16] S O'Leary, 'Nationality Law and Community Citizenship: A Tale of Two Uneasy Bedfellows' (1992) 12 YEL 353, 357; T Hoogenboom, 'Integration into Society and Free Movement of Non-EC Nationals' (1992) 3 EJIL 36, 41. See also R Plender, 'Competence, European Community Law and Nationals of Non-Member States' (1990) 39 ICLQ 599, 604 and Fernhout, above n 11, 255–256 with respect to EEC, Art 48. However, in Case 238/83, *Caisse d'Allocations Familiales v Meade* [1984] ECR 263, the Court of Justice implicitly held that EEC, Art 48 does not apply to non-EC nationals unless they are members of the worker's family (for family reunion see below).

progress in the social field.[17] The principal piece of legislation implementing EEC, Art 7 [EC, 6] and 48 is Regulation 1612/68EEC[18] which is clearly limited to nationals of EC member states.[19] The Regulation guarantees equal treatment for all EC workers in respect of access to a broad range of social rights. The Court of Justice has given a broad interpretation to this general principle of equality. A good example of such an interpretation can be found in the case of *Reed* concerning an English woman who wished to stay in the Netherlands with her English male partner, an EC migrant worker with a residence permit. Although the Court of Justice ruled that unmarried partners of EC workers, who have lived with them in a stable relationship, are *not* covered by the word 'spouse' in Art 10(1) of Regulation 1612/68/EEC which only applies to marriage partners,[20] she was permitted to stay with her partner on the basis that 'co-habitation' constituted a 'social advantage' enjoyed by Dutch nationals under Dutch law. Another example of this generous interpretation is the formulation of the concept of 'reverse discrimination' whereby nationals of EC member states who have exercised their free movement rights have been able to enjoy certain benefits on return to their country of origin which are unavailable to citizens who have not exercised these rights.[21]

Initiatives of EC institutions: Commission and European Parliament

The EC Commission and the European Parliament have attempted to improve the legal and social status of non-EC immigrant workers. The Commission's work in this regard has consisted of a number of policy documents which advocate equality in living and working conditions between third country nationals and EC nationals.[22] These efforts, however, have not

---

[17] International Confederation of Free Trade Unions (ICFTU), European Trade Union Confederation (ETUC), Union of Arab Mahgreb Workers – Union Syndicale des Travailleurs du Mahgreb Arabe. *Report to the Conference on Migrant Workers from the Mahgreb in the European Community* (Tunis, April 18–20, 1991) 13, para 2.12.

[18] Council Regulation 1612/68EEC of 15 October 1968 on freedom of movement for workers within the Community, as amended, OJ Sp Ed 1968–69, 475.

[19] Not all EC secondary legislation, however, bears this characteristic. For example, EC social security legislation is applicable to refugees and stateless persons from non-EC member States, and to members of their families and their survivors. See Art 2 of Council Regulation 1408/71/EEC of 14 June 1971 on the application of social security schemes to employed persons, to self-employed persons and to members of their families moving within the Community, as amended OJ Sp Ed 1971, 416, JO 1971 L 149/2.

[20] Case 59/85, *Netherlands v Reed* [1987] 2 CMLR 448.

[21] Eg Case C-370/90, *R v Immigration Appeal Tribunal and Surinder Singh ex parte Secretary of State for the Home Department* [1992] 3 CMLR 358 with respect to the right of family reunion in EC law. See also the discussion on family reunion below.

[22] Eg Commission of the European Communities, *Action Programme in Favour of Migrant Workers and Their Families,* COM (74) 2250 Bulletin of the European Communities, Supplement 3/76, 14; *Guidelines for a Community Policy on Migration,* COM(85) final of 7 March 1985, Bulletin of the European Communities, Supplement 9/85, 5; Communication from the Commission to the Council and the European Parliament on *Immigration and Asylum Policies,* above n 4, p 35, para 130.

thus far resulted in any fundamental changes to the *status quo*. An interesting development was a Commission decision issued in 1985 under EEC, Art 118 attempting to set up a prior communication and consultation procedure on migration policies in relation to non-member states.[23] Although this decision was overturned by the Court of Justice,[24] it was accepted that the policies of member states with regard to non-EC nationals can be raised under EEC, Art 118 because these policies will inevitably affect the employment and working conditions of EC nationals.[25] In 1988, the Commission revised its decision in compliance with the Court of Justice's ruling, but this amended decision has borne little fruit.[26]

The European Parliament has frequently advocated the social integration of non-EC immigrant workers on a par with national workers. For example, para A of its Resolution of 14 June 1990 on migrant workers from third countries[27] reiterates the premise that the completion of the single market implies a parallel social policy and notes that arrangements in this respect cannot possibly exclude the eight million (now ten million) non-EC migrants.

The Single European Act

The purpose of the Single European Act,[28] adopted on 29 June 1987, was to realise an internal market without internal frontiers by the end of 1992.[29]

---

[23] Commission Decision 85/381/EEC of 8 July 1985 setting up a prior communication and consultation procedure on migration policies in respect of non-member countries [1985] OJ L 217/25. The decision required each Member State to inform the Commission and other Member States in advance of draft measures and agreements pertaining to their country migrants with particular reference to such matters as entry, residence, equal pay and working conditions, and the integration of migrants and their families into the labour force, society, and cultural life of the host state. The decision also provided for a consultation procedure, the objective of which was to, *inter alia*, adopt a common EC position on migration from non-EC countries and to ensure that the individual State draft measures and agreements were in conformity with EC policy in this field.

[24] Cases 281/85, 283–285/85 and 287/85, *Germany and Others v EC Commission* [1987] ECR 3203, [1988] 1 CMLR 11. The Court of Justice considered the part of the decision dealing with the cultural integration of migrant workers as exceeding the scope of EC social policy. The Court also declared the decision void on the basis that the powers afforded the Commission under EEC, Art 118 were purely procedural in that the Commission may only initiate the consultation procedure and not pre-determine its outcome. In his opinion on the case, Advocate-General Mancini, *ibid* 3223 and 19 respectively, described the attitude of member states towards any measure relating to non-EC immigration as one of 'dissension, but above all coldness, distrust and vigorous defence of national sovereignty.'

[25] For commentaries on this case see K R Simmonds, above n 11 and C Greenwood, 'Nationality and the Limits of the Free Movement of Persons in Community Law' (1987) 7 YEL 185, 269.

[26] Commission Decision 88/384/EEC of 8 June 1988 setting up a prior communication and consultation procedure on migration policies in relation to non-member countries [1988] OJ L 183/35. See also Hoogenboom, above n 3, 402–403.

[27] [1990] OJ L 175/180.

[28] [1987] OJ L 169/1.

[29] See now EEC, Art 8a/EC, Art 7A which provides that 'the Community shall adopt measures with the aim of progressively establishing the internal market over a period expiring on 31 December 1992.' The second paragraph of Art 8a defines the internal market as 'an area without internal frontiers in which the free movement of goods, persons, services and capital is ensured in accordance with the provisions of this Treaty.'

The Act, however, contrary to some earlier expectations, did little to enhance the conditions of entry, residence, and access to the labour market for non-EC nationals. The EC Commission has clearly outlined that free movement of persons in this context should not be confused with the rights which flow directly from EEC, Arts 48 to 66.[30] At the time of adoption, two conflicting declarations were also issued reserving the sovereignty of member states in respect of, *inter alia*, the control of immigration from third countries, but also confirming the powers of the Commission 'as regards the entry, movement and residence of nationals of their countries.'[31] Any potential development towards a greater role for Community organs seems now to have firmly given way to state action on the intergovernmental level as a result of the Treaty on European Union.[32]

The Charter of the Fundamental Social Rights of Workers

The Charter of the Fundamental Social Rights of Workers,[33] adopted in December 1989, is a controversial EC initiative, particularly from the point of view of the United Kingdom government which chose not to support it. As a declaration, it has no binding legal effect, and is simply a recognition that the completion of the internal market cannot ignore the social ramifications.[34] Despite a reference in its Preamble to a guarantee of comparable treatment in respect of living and working conditions between member state nationals and nationals from third countries[35] and all-inclusive language in the main text, there is some doubt whether the Charter applies to non-EC

---

[30] Commission of the European Communities, Communication to the Council and to the Parliament, *Abolition of Border Controls*, SEC (92) 887 final of 8 May 1992, Annex I, 10.

[31] The first was a general declaration on Arts 13–19 of the Act (the provisions concerned with the internal market): 'Nothing in these provisions shall affect the right of the member states to take such measures as they consider necessary for the purpose of controlling immigration from third countries, and to combat terrorism, crime, the traffic in drugs and and illicit trading in works of art and antiques.' Secondly, a political declaration was attached to the Act as a whole and reads as follows: 'In order to promote free movement of persons, the member states shall co-operate without prejudice to the powers of the Commission, in particular as regards the entry, movement and residence of nationals of third countries. They shall also co-operate in the combating of terrorism, crime, the traffic of drugs and illicit trading in works of art and antiques.' See also Hoogenboom, above n 16, 49–50.

[32] Fernhout, above n 11, 257–258; 'Third Pillar' of the Treaty on European Union (see below).

[33] Reprinted in Commission of the European Communities, Directorate-General for Employment, Industrial Relations and Social Affairs, *Social Europe 1/90* (Luxembourg: Office for Official Publications of the European Communities, 1990) 46–50.

[34] Paragraph 2 of the Preamble to the Charter asserts that 'in the context of the single European market, the same importance must be attached to the social aspects as to the economic aspects and . . . therefore, they must be developed in a balanced manner.'

[35] Paragraph 8 declares that it is for 'member states to guarantee that workers from non-member countries and members of their families who are legally resident in a member state of the European Community are able to enjoy, as regards their living and working conditions, treatment comparable to that enjoyed by workers who are nationals of the member states concerned.'

workers.[36] Subsequent reports of the Commission, however, appear to have dispelled this uncertainty.[37] In the 1992 Protocol on Social Policy annexed to the Treaty on European Union, the same 11 member states expressed the wish 'to continue along the path laid down in the 1989 Social Charter.' Under Art 3(3) of the Agreement on Social Policy, which is itself annexed to the Protocol, the Council is obliged to act unanimously on a proposal from the Commission, after consulting the European Parliament and the Economic and Social Committee, in the area of, *inter alia*, 'conditions of employment for third-country nationals legally residing in Community territory.' It is too early to say whether the provision will lead to the augmentation of the rights of non-EC nationals. The area of action is limited to 'conditions of employment' and, consequently, any measures flowing from Art 3(3) are unlikely to assist significantly with the *full* integration of non-EC immigrant workers and their families into EC countries of employment.

Treaty on European Union

The Treaty on European Union,[38] which amends the Treaty establishing the European Economic Community, is the final affirmation of the non-applicability of fundamental EC principles to non-EC nationals. In essence, it assigns their fate to the results of intergovernmental co-operation among EC member States. The concept of European citizenship is restricted to nationals from those countries.[39] An integral part of this concept is the right

---

[36] For a comprehensive analysis of the contents of the Charter see B Bercusson, 'The European Community's Charter of Fundamental Social Rights of Workers' 53 MLR 624, Bercusson notes, *ibid* at 626–627, that the final draft of the Charter replaced the word 'citizens' with 'workers'. The all-embracing nature of the term 'workers', may therefore apply to workers from third countries. In a later article, however, Watson reluctantly concedes that because of, *inter alia*, the lack of reference to third country nationals in the main text, 'they are . . . plainly excluded from the Charter.' P Watson, 'The Community Social Charter' (1991) 28 CMLRev 37, 65.

[37] Eg, *Second Report from the Commission to the Council on the Application of the Community Charter of the Fundamental Social Rights*, COM(92) 562 final of 23 December 1992, 12–13, para 21. In this report, the Commission refers to EC action in respect of third country nationals under the section of the Charter entitled 'Improvement of Living and Working Conditions'.

[38] [1992] OJ C 191.

[39] EC, Art 8. See also EC, Art 8a(1) which reads: 'Every citizen of the Union shall have the right to move and reside freely within the territory of the member states, subject to the limitations and conditions laid down in this Treaty and by the measures adopted to give it effect.' This provision clearly applies to those EC citizens who are not economically active. As a result, it would cover all those seeking to reside in member states, including students and retired persons, who were the subjects of the three Council Directives of 28 June 1990: Directive 90/364/EEC on the right of residence [1990] OJ L 180/26; Directive 90/365/EEC on the right of residence for employees and self-employed persons who have ceased their occupational activity [1990] OJ L 180/28; and Directive 90/366/EEC on the right of residence for students [1990] OJ L 180/30, are-issued as Directive 93/96/EC [1993] OJ L 317/594, following the annulment of the original Directive by the Court of Justice in Case C-295/90, *Are Students' Rights: European Parliament v EC Council* [1992] 3 CMLR 281. The right of residence is extended by these Directives to non-economically active EC nationals provided they do not become a burden on the social assistance system of the host member state.

to vote and to stand as a candidate in municipal elections and in elections to the European Parliament.[40] Non-EC or third country nationals are mentioned in the Treaty, but only in the so-called 'Third Pillar' which contains provisions on co-operation in the fields of justice and home affairs.[41] Therefore, non-EC nationals are to be the subjects of action at the intergovernmental level. A right of initiative, however, is given to the Commission which may result in the Council adopting joint positions and joint actions (by a qualified majority), or in the drawing up of conventions and their recommendation to member states for adoption.[42]

If the intergovernmental process, occurring both within and outside the ambit of the EC, harmonising national laws relating to asylum and advocating the elimination of internal border controls,[43] is to be taken as a model for future developments, equal treatment between non-EC nationals and EC nationals in their working environment is unlikely to be realised for some time to come. Although the reference to the former in the Third Pillar of the Treaty on European Union clearly pertains to matters which are of importance to them such as their conditions of entry, movement and residence (including family reunion and access to employment),[44] it is also made in the context of such 'related' concerns as combating unauthorised immigration[45] and 'police co-operation for the purpose of preventing and combating terrorism, unlawful drug trafficking and other serious forms of international crime.'[46] The *rights* of non-EC immigrant workers and their families are unlikely to be rapidly advanced in such a context.[47]

---

[40] EC, Art 8b On the implementation of these rights, see respectively, Council Directive 94/80/EC of 19 December 1994, laying down detailed arrangements for the exercise of the right to vote and to stand as a candidate in municipal elections by citizens of the Union residing in a Member State of which they are not nationals [1994] OJ L 368/38. Council Directive 93/109/EC of 30 December 1993 on the detailed arrangements for the exercise of the right to vote and stand as candidate in European Parliament elections for Union citizens residing in a member of state of which they are not a national [1993] OJ L 329/34.

[41] TEU, Title VI.

[42] TEU, Art K3(2).

[43] See respectively: Convention determining the state responsible for examining applications for asylum lodged in one of the member states of the European Communities, signed at Dublin 15 June 1990 (1991) 30 ILM 425; Convention applying the Schengen Agreement of 14 June 1985 between the governments of the states of the Benelux Economic Union, the Federal Republic of Germany and the French Republic on the Gradual Abolition of Checks at their Common Borders, signed at Schengen 19 June 1990 (1991) 30 ILM 68 (this Convention has since been acceded to by Greece, Italy, Portugal and Spain); Commission of the European Communities, Communication from the Commission to the Council and the European Parliament, *(1) Proposal for a Decision based on Art K3 of the Treaty on European Union establishing the Convention on the Crossing of the External Frontiers of the Member States; (2) Proposal for a Regulation based on Art 100c of the Treaty Establishing the European Community Determining the Third Countries whose Nationals must be in Possession of a Visa when crossing the External Borders of the Member States,* COM(93) 684 final of 10 December 1993.

[44] TEU, Art K1(3)(a)–(b). It is noteworthy that the term 'right' is not used in relation to this list.

[45] TEU, Art K1(3)(c).

[46] TEU, Art K1(9).

[47] Cf the political declaration appended to the Single European Act, above n 42.

THE LIMITED FREE MOVEMENT RIGHTS OF NON-EC NATIONALS UNDER EC LAW

Derived rights

EC law does cater for non-EC nationals in some respects. The right to family reunion permits the EC migrant worker to be joined by his or her spouse and dependants regardless of their nationality.[48] Once in the country of employment, non-EC family members have free access to the labour market.[49] The freedom of movement principle would be redundant without corresponding rights for family members of the migrant worker.[50] The broad interpretation given to the right of family reunion by the Court of Justice also means that non-EC nationals who fall into this category find themselves in a relatively secure legal position. However, these are not independent rights but derived from the status of the primary rights-holder. The concept of 'reverse discrimination', referred to earlier, may assist significantly in overcoming national immigration restrictions, but if EC nationals have not exercised their freedom of movement rights, reunion with non-EC family members is subject to the (usually) stricter conditions of domestic law.[51]

Non-EC nationals may also acquire limited free movement rights under EEC, arts 59 *et seq*, the provisions concerned with the freedom to provide services. The Court of Justice has ruled that a company originating in one EC member state and providing services in another member state is not required to obtain work permits from the national immigration authority for non-EC nationals in its lawful employment.[52]

Association and co-operation agreements

The EC has also entered into a number of association and co-operation agreements with non-member states, such as Turkey, the Mahgreb countries

---

[48] Reg 1612/68/EEC, Art 10. The *right* to family reunion is limited to spouses, children under 21, or to children over 21 if they are still dependent on the worker, and to dependent parents and grandparents (Art 10(1)). Member states only have an obligation *to facilitate* the reunion of other dependent relatives with the migrant worker (Art 10(2)).

[49] Reg 1612/68/EEC, Art 11.

[50] T Stein & S Thomsen, 'The Status of the Member States' Nationals under the Law of the European Communities', in Max Planck Institute of Comparative Law, (ed), *The Legal Position of Aliens in National and International Law*, vol 2 (Berlin, Springer Verlag, 1987) pp 1775, 1801.

[51] Case 35–36/82, *Morson and Jhanjan v Netherlands* [1982] ECR 3723, [1983] 2 CMLR 221. Similarly, non-EC nationals cannot rely on EC law to claim a right to remain on the death of the spouse if the latter did not exercise free movement rights. Cases C-297/88 and C-197/89, *Dzodzi v Belgian State* [1990] ECR I-3763.

[52] Case C-113/89, *Rush Portuguesa Lda v Office National d'Immigration* [1990] ECR I-1417, [1991] 2 CMLR 818; Case C-43/93, *Vonder Elst v Office des Migrations Internationales (OMI)* [1994] ECR I-3803. For a fuller discussion of some of the case law referred to above see W. Alexander, 'Free Movement of Non-EC Nationals. A Review of the Case-Law of the Court of Justice' (1992) 3 EJIL 53, 55–59.

and Central and Eastern European countries, which confer a range of rights on their nationals in respect of equal work and employment conditions, access to the labour market, and social security. Generally-speaking, implementation of these agreements is entrusted to Councils of Association or Co-operation Councils composed of representatives from EC institutions, EC member states and the non-member state concerned. The Court of Justice has observed that these agreements and the decisions adopted thereunder by the relevant implementing body are an integral part of the EC legal order[53] and, if sufficiently clear and precise, are also capable of having direct effect in member states.[54]

It is arguable that these agreements, however, can only constitute stop-gap measures and that their patchwork approach is insufficient in assisting the full integration of non-EC immigrant workers and their families into the society of the country of employment. Although those agreements that confer limited free movement rights on some non-EC workers and their families have undoubtedly resulted in the creation of a higher 'intermediate' status for this group,[55] this process will inevitably lead to further social stratification unless it is plainly seen as a step on the road to the full integration of all non-EC immigrant workers and their families.

THE UNIVERSAL AND REGIONAL HUMAN RIGHTS CONTEXT

Thus far, this paper has exposed the inferior position of non-EC migrants in comparison with their EC counterparts. It should be emphasised that the vulnerable position of the former is similar to that experienced by migrant workers and their families elsewhere in the world. Generally speaking, the specialist international instruments adopted for the protection of migrants fall far short of the comprehensive provisions found in EC law. An in-depth examination of these specialist instruments is beyond the scope of this chapter. Nonetheless, a few salient examples of some of the more enlightened provisions together with the principal shortcomings are discussed.

---

[53] Case C-192/89, *SZ Sevince v Staatsecretaris van Justitie* [1990] ECR 3461, [1992] 2 CMLR 57, para 9.

[54] In Case 58/93, *Yousfi v Belgium* [1994] ECR I-1353 and Case C-18/90, *Kziber v Office National De L'Emploi* [1991] ECR I-199, Art 41(1) of the EEC-Morocco Co-operation Agreement ([1973] OJ L 264/1), concerned with equal treatment in the field of social security, was held to be directly effective. In Case C-355/93, *Eroglu v Land Baden-Württemberg*, [1994] ECR I-5113, Case C-237/91, *Kus v Landeshaupstadt Wiesbaden* [1993] 2 CMLR 887 and *Sevince, ibid*, various access to employment provisions in decisions issued by the Association Council under the EEC-Turkey Association Agreement and Protocol ([1973] OJ C 113/1) were also found by the Court of Justice to confer direct effect.

[55] N Burrows, 'The Rights of Turkish Workers in the Member States' (1994) 19 ELRev 305, 307.

The most recent instrument, the United Nations International Convention on the Protection of All Migrant Workers and Members of Their Families,[56] is an ambitious and lengthy document aiming to protect both legally resident and illegally resident migrant workers. With regard to undocumented migrants, the Convention's provisions are more liberal than EC efforts which are confined to policy statements primarily focusing on preventing illegal immigration, with only passing references to the protection of their rights and mainly to those rights arising out of past employment.[57] More recently, however, the Commission has advocated ratification of the Convention by EC member states.[58] A closer examination of the Convention's provisions reveals that important rights which would greatly facilitate integration, such as the right to family reunion and free access to employment,[59] are seriously circumscribed in deference to state sovereignty. Moreover, since its adoption in December 1990, the Convention has only been ratified by two labour-sending countries, Egypt and Morocco, as 30 June 1994.[60]

The other universal system concerned with the protection of migrant workers exists under the auspices of the ILO. Generally-speaking, international labour standards are applicable to all workers regardless of their nationality. The pertinent instruments concerned with migrant workers are Convention No 97 of 1949 concerning Migration for Employment (Revised) and Convention No 143 of 1975 concerning Migrations in Abusive Conditions and the Promotion of Equality of Opportunity and Treatment of Migrant Workers, and the accompanying recommendations.[61] In contrast with the UN Convention, the two ILO Conventions are in force, although they have not been widely ratified.[62] In many respects, the

[56] UN GA Resolution 45/158 of 18 December 1990.

[57] Eg *Guidelines for a Community Policy on Migration*, above n 22, 10. The views of the Commission with respect to illegal migrants in the Guidelines are taken from the objectives in a 1976 proposal for a Directive on the harmonisation of laws in the member states to combat illegal migration and illegal employment, which was presented to the Council of Ministers in 1976, but which never came to fruition. As indicated in the section on the Treaty on European Union above, efforts to adopt a common approach with regard to the prevention of illegal migration are to be developed on the intergovernmental level and outside of the ambit of the EC. For another example, see the Schengen Agreement, above n 53.

[58] Communication from the Commission to the Council and the European Parliament on *Immigration and Asylum Policies*, above n 4, pp 29–30, para 110.

[59] Arts 44 and 52, 53.

[60] United Nations, 'International Instruments Chart of Ratifications as at 30 June 1994', UN Doc ST/HR 4/Rev 10. The Convention requires 20 ratifications to enter into force (Art 87). This is also the threshold before the supervisory body, the Committee for the Protection of the Rights of All Migrant Workers and Their Families, can come into operation (Art 72).

[61] Recommendation No 86 of 1949 concerning Migration for Employment (Revised) and Recommendation No 151 of 1975 concerning Migrant Workers. The texts of these ILO Conventions and Recommendations are reproduced in International Labour Organisation, *International Labour Conventions and Recommendations 1919–1981* (Geneva, International Labour Office, 1982), pp 785–810, 821–833.

[62] As at 1 January 1995, Convention No 97 had been ratified by 40 countries including eight EC member states (Belgium, France, Germany, Italy, Netherlands, Portugal, Spain, United Kingdom). Convention No 143 had been ratified by 17 countries and by only three EC member states (Italy, Portugal, Sweden).

provisions in these treaties, and in particular the later Convention (No 143), are more forward-looking than those of the UN Convention, largely because international labour standards are drafted by non-governmental groups, employers' and workers' representatives in addition to government delegates. Examples of such enlightened provisions include the state obligation to remove all restrictions on access to employment after the migrant worker has worked for two years or completed the first employment contract if this is of a shorter duration,[63] and the duty to *promote* (and not merely guarantee) equality in a number of areas.[64] The 1975 Convention is also concerned (in Part I) with illegal migrant workers, and although its main thrust in this regard is to prevent migrations in abusive conditions, it emphasises that the basic rights of *all* migrant workers are to be safeguarded (Art 1).

Regionally, the Council of Europe is also concerned with the protection of migrant workers. Two human rights instruments are of particular relevance: the European Social Charter (Arts 18 and 19) and the European Convention on the Legal Status of Migrant Workers. As at 1 January 1995, the former had been ratified by all EC member states whereas only France, Italy, the Netherlands, Portugal, Spain and Sweden had deposited ratifications in respect of the latter in addition to two non-EC countries (Norway and Turkey). The principal problem with these instruments, however, is that they apply on the basis of reciprocity, that is to say migrant workers may only expect to receive protection if both the country in which they live and work and their country of origin have ratified the treaty in question. Of course, if the nationals concerned come from countries beyond Europe, such as the Mahgreb region of North Africa, they will always fall outside the protective scope of these instruments. The provisions in these instruments are of mixed quality. Article 19 of the Charter lists a number of rights pertaining to migrant workers, including a short clause guaranteeing equality between migrant workers and state party nationals in respect of 'remuneration and other employment and working conditions, membership of trade unions and enjoyment of the benefits of collective bargaining, and accommodation.'[65]

These rights have been given an extensive and liberal interpretation by the Committee of Independent Experts, the body entrusted with the

---

[63] Convention No 143, Art 14(a).

[64] Convention No 143, Art 10 which reads: 'Each Member for which the Convention is in force undertakes to declare and pursue a national policy to promote and guarantee, by methods appropriate to national conditions and practice, equality of opportunity and treatment in respect of employment and occupation, of social security, of trade union and cultural rights and of individual and collective freedoms for persons who as migrant workers or as members of their families are lawfully within its territory.' This clause should be contrasted with Art 6 of Convention No 97 which only proscribes inequality of treatment arising out of laws, measures or administrative action taken by public authorities and does not contain any express obligation to promote equality and to eliminate discrimination in practice.

[65] Art 19(4). This provision is modelled on Art 6 of ILO Convention No 97, *ibid* Art 19(4) has not been accepted by two EC member states who are parties to the Charter (Austria and Denmark).

implementation of the Charter.[66] The Convention on the Legal Status of Migrant Workers purports, as reflected by its title, to comprehensively cover this subject. However, a closer examination reveals many deficiencies:

- it only applies to migrant workers '*authorised* by another Contracting party to reside in its territory in order to take up paid employment' (and is, therefore, inapplicable to undocumented workers);[67]
- there is no right of access to employment;
- the family reunion provision is heavily circumscribed;[68] and
- there is no scheme in place for facilitating the acquisition of permanent residence.

A further Council of Europe instrument briefly worth considering (though in a rather more negative context) is the Convention on the Reduction of Cases of Multiple Nationality and Military Obligations in Cases of Multiple Nationality, ratified by 12 EC member states as at September 1993. The aim of this instrument is, *inter alia*, to discourage dual nationality. However, this approach, has been diluted by a recent Protocol, which essentially leaves it to the discretion of states' parties to permit dual nationality in respect of, amongst other things, second-generation migrants.[69] Facilitating dual nationality for second-generation migrants would not only improve their legal status and thus enable them to benefit from the freedom of movement rights under EC law, but, more importantly, would also be a truer expression of their dual identity.

Another human rights instrument of relevance in Europe (although by no means a 'specialised' instrument), which applies to all persons who find themselves within the jurisdiction of those states which have accepted it, is the European Convention on Human Rights (ECHR), ratified by all EC member states. The ECHR, however, is almost exclusively concerned with civil and political rights. Economic, social, cultural, and residence rights, of most concern to non-EC immigrant workers who wish to be fully integrated into their host society, are, with few exceptions, absent. Indeed, some of the ECHR provisions clearly hinder the acquisition of rights by non-nationals,

---

[66] For example, the Committee has suggested that Art 19(4)(c), concerned with equal treatment in respect of accommodation, might involve an obligation by member states to undertake a special programme of assistance to encourage the construction of housing specifically for the benefit of migrant workers and their families. Council of Europe, Committee of Independent Experts of the European Social Charter, *Conclusions II*, 67, quoted in Council of Europe, Social Affairs, *Case Law on the European Social Charter* (Council of Europe, Strasbourg, 1982) p 160.

[67] Art 1(1). Emphasis added.

[68] Art 12.

[69] Second Protocol Amending the Reduction of Cases of Multiple Nationality and Military Obligations in Cases of Multiple Nationality, Art 1. As at 1 September 1995, this Protocol had received no ratifications. It has been ratified by two states (France and Italy). See also R Cholewinski, 'Strasbourg's "Hidden Agenda"? The Protection of Second-Generation Migrants from Expulsion under Article 8 of the European Convention of Human Rights' (1994) 12 NQHR 287, 304.

particularly political rights.[70] The ECHR, however, has played an important role in safeguarding long-term resident aliens, and particularly second-generation migrants, from expulsion or the threat of expulsion.[71] Its more effective enforcement machinery, in comparison with other Council of Europe human rights instruments, also means that, although limited in scope, the ECHR can be a useful tool in promoting the rights of non-EC immigrant workers and their families.

This fleeting survey of universal and regional human rights standards concerned with the protection of migrant workers and their families effectively confirms that the unique regime operating in the EC in respect of migrants who come from other EC member states can be described as the quintessential system of protection, not only in terms of containing the most enlightened standards, but also in terms of possessing the most effective system of supervision and enforcement of their rights.

CONCLUSION: THE NEED FOR AN EC SOLUTION

To rely solely on the specialist international instruments concerned with the protection of migrants in order to safeguard the rights of non-EC immigrant workers and their families is surely the wrong way forward. In order to preserve its *raison d'être*, the EC *itself* must find an equitable solution. This solution must make way for the integration of this neglected group into the EC free movement of workers system. One principled way forward would be to return to the original understanding of EEC, Arts 7 (EC, 6) and 48 which were never intended to be restricted to non-EC nationals.[72] Given the potential opposition to such a radical move, extension to the freedom of movement principle and the rights which follow would probably have to be implemented gradually and come into full operation after, say, a period of four years' legal employment. Such a proposal would mean of course that equality between *established* non-EC migrants and EC migrants would have to be realised immediately.[73]

---

[70] See especially Art 16 which expressly allows states parties to impose restrictions on 'the political activity of aliens' in respect of the rights to freedom of expression (Art 10), freedom of peaceful assembly and freedom of association with others (Art 11), and the right to enjoy the rights and freedoms set out in the ECHR without discrimination (Art 14).

[71] See the case law under Art 8 of the ECHR concerned with the right to respect for family and private life: *Berrehab v Netherlands* Eur Ct HR, 1988, Ser A, No 234–A; *Moustaquim v Belgium* Eur Ct HR 1991, Ser A, No 193; *Beldjoudi v France* Eur Ct HR 1992; Ser A, No 234–A. For an exposition of this case law see Cholewinski, above n 69.

[72] Fernhout, above n 11, 264.

[73] Fernhout, *ibid* 263. Fernhout disagrees with the argument that this prospect would greatly increase migration to the EC by emphasising that four years *legal* employment would be required. Of course, this could effectively mean 'a licence to exploit' for a period of four years. The two-year period (or less if the first employment contract is shorter than two years) laid down in Art 14(a) of ILO Convention No 143 of 1975 is more ideal and preferable from a human rights standpoint, but given the attitude of the majority of EC member states to this instrument and the restrictive policies in place in respect of immigration to Western Europe generally, the four-year period is probably a politically more viable goal.

Whatever the method chosen, politicians from EC member states must act to urgently address the plight of non-EC immigrant workers and their families and their blatant and unjustifiable inequality with EC nationals. The Treaty on European Union essentially defers to state sovereignty in this respect, and contrary to popular belief, must be seen as a menacing step backwards in the overall process of European integration.

12

THE PROTECTION OF MINORITIES
UNDER THE EUROPEAN CONVENTION
ON HUMAN RIGHTS

Geoff Gilbert

The European Convention on Human Rights[1] does not contain any provision guaranteeing minority rights. 'The Convention does not provide for any rights of a . . . minority as such, and the protection of individual members of such minority is limited to the right not to be discriminated in the enjoyment of the Convention rights on the grounds of their belonging to the minority (Art 14 of the Convention).[2]

On the other hand, minority groups may be recognised as having *locus standi* to bring cases questioning breaches of the ECHR:

> In order to be recognised two conditions must be satisfied: the claimant must fall within any of the categories of petitioners mentioned in Art 25 and he must *prima facie* be able to claim to be a victim of a breach of the Convention. As regards the first applicant, it is clear that the first condition is satisfied. The Liberal Party is an association of persons with a common interest for the purposes of the municipal law of the United Kingdom. As such, it falls clearly within one of the categories of petitioners set out in Art 25 of the Convention as a non-governmental organisation or a group of individuals.[3]

Thus, while an individual member and the minority group itself can bring applications before the Commission, they can only do so under the existing provisions; there is no direct protection for the minority group as a group. The effect of this restriction needs to be addressed. While many group

[1] 213 UNTS 221; ETS No 5; 45 AM J INT'L L Supp 24 (1951): hereinafter, ECHR.

[2] *App No 8142/78 X v Austria*, 18 D+R 88 at 92–93 (1979). **NB**: Nor does the American Convention on Human Rights, 9 INT LEG MAT 673 (1970), refer to minority rights. A Protocol to the ECHR was proposed in 1959 that would have provided protection to 'national minorities' as such, but it was never proceeded with—see Capotorti, '1977 Study on the Rights of Persons Belonging to Ethnic, Religious and Linguistic Minorities', (1991) at para 51: (hereinafter, Capotorti 1977). And see Thornberry, *International Law and the Rights of Minorities*, 1991 at pp 305–306.

    The difficulties that the lack of an express minorities provision creates are evident from the *Belgian Linguistics*, see below n 7 at p 7, case, where what is in effect a claim to mother-tongue education had to be couched in six complaints alleging discrimination in the provision of and access to state education and funding. Since there was an educational system provided, although teaching was in Dutch, there was no effective discrimination: nonetheless, the cultural identity of the group was threatened.

[3] *App No 8765/79, The Liberal Party et al v United Kingdom*, (1982) 4 EHRR 106 at 120–121.

rights will entail measures guaranteeing non-discrimination and other fundamental freedoms relevant to individual claims, the protection and promotion
of the minority as such, will be a coincidental happenstance. The case of *K
v France*[4] reveals how a person might not suffer discrimination, but would
be denied the right to assert his cultural identity. The applicant spoke
French, but as part of a concerted campaign to promote his Breton identity,
he claimed the right to an interpreter before a French court. The
Commission held his claim under Arts 6 and 14 was inadmissible:

> The applicant also invokes Art 14 in this regard, alleging that he was discriminat-
> ed against as a member of a national minority. The applicant, however, has not
> shown that he was treated differently from any other accused who, being capable
> of understanding the proceedings, sought to defend himself in another language.

If minority rights were recognised as such though, it is possible that
Breton would be accepted as one of the national languages.[5] The applicant
had not been treated any differently from any other French speaker in
France. His cultural and linguistic identity was, however, denied him in
public life.

Nevertheless, as matters stand, applicants seeking to preserve the rights of
their minority group have to rely on Art 14 of the ECHR. Article 14 is
purely a non-discrimination provision:

> The enjoyment of the rights and freedoms set forth in this Convention shall be
> secured without discrimination on any ground such as sex, race, colour, language,
> religion, political or other opinion, national or social origin, association with a
> national minority, property, birth or other status.

Article 14 does not establish an autonomous right not to suffer discrimination. It is dependent upon the other provisions of the ECHR:

> According to the constant case law of the Convention organs Art 14 has no
> independent existence, but plays an important role by completing the other nor-
> mative provisions of the Convention and the Protocols. Article 14 safeguards indi-
> viduals, placed in similar situations, from any discrimination in the enjoyment of
> the rights and freedoms set forth in those other provisions. A measure which as
> such could be in conformity with one of the normative provisions may therefore
> nevertheless violate that provision taken in conjunction with Art 14, if it is applied
> in a discriminatory manner. It is as if Art 14 formed an integral part of each of
> the provisions laying down specific rights and freedoms.[6]

A wide interpretation of discrimination in Art 14 could provide minority

---

[4] *App No 10210/82*, 35 D+R 203 at 207 (1983).
[5] He may still not have been granted an interpreter, but he may have been able to address the
court using the Breton language. See also, *App No 2333/64, Isop v Austria*, 8 Yb ECHR 338
(1965), and *Cadoret & Le Bihan v France*, Comm Nos 221/1987 & 323/1988, Adoption of
Views 11 April 1991, cited in (1991) 6.2 *Interrights Bulletin* at p 36—in that case, the
Human Rights Committee surprisingly held that the right to use Breton in court and the
failure to provide interpreters did not even raise an issue under Art 27 ICCPR.
[6] *App No 10316/83, M v United Kingdom*, 37 D+R 129 at 134 (1984); see also, *App No
788/60, Austria v Italy*, 4 Yb ECHR 166 and 6Yb ECHR 796.

groups with effective protection of their collective rights. If it is read to encompass indirect discrimination and affirmative action to eradicate institutionalised discrimination, then many group rights can be enforced through individualised Art 14 applications. The standard definition of discrimination is found in the *Belgian Linguistics Case*:[7]

> In spite of the very general wording of the French version (*sans distinction aucune*), Art 14 does not forbid every difference in treatment in the exercise of the rights and freedoms recognised. This version must be read in the light of the more restrictive text of the English version (without discrimination).
>
> . . .
>
> It is important, then, to look for the criteria which enable a determination to be made as to whether a difference in treatment, concerning the exercise of one of the rights and freedoms set forth, contravenes Art 14. On this question the Court, following the principles which may be extracted from the legal practice of a large number of democratic states,[8] holds that the principle of equality of treatment is violated if the distinction has no objective and reasonable justification. The existence of such a justification must be assessed in relation to the aim and effects of the measure under consideration with regard being had to the principles which normally prevail in democratic societies. A difference of treatment in the exercise of a right laid down in the Convention must not only pursue a legitimate aim: Art 14 is likewise violated when it is clearly established that there is no reasonable relationship of proportionality between the means employed and the aim sought to be realised.[9]

While the Court's view seems to evince a concept of direct discrimination alone, it is possible to read into the judgment an acceptance of group promotion through a justified difference of treatment. If so, then actions by states that favour minorities at the expense of majorities may be justified under Art 14, whereas claims by an individual or group that such actions be undertaken by a state would fail since there is no express provision for the promotion of minority rights under the ECHR.[10] According to *McFeeley v United Kingdom*,[11] the test for whether Art 14 has been violated is as follows:

> The Commission, in determining whether a difference in treatment contravenes Art 14 must first consider whether the distinction has an objective and reasonable justification taking into consideration the aim and effect of the measure in question, having regard to the principles which normally prevail in democratic societies, and second, whether there is a reasonable relationship of proportionality between the means employed and the aims sought to be realised.

---

[7] *Case Relating to Certain Aspects of the Laws on the Use of Languages in Education in Belgium (Merits)*, Judgment of 23 July 1968, Series A, Vol 6.

[8] Since the case was decided in 1968, the United Kingdom has passed legislation applying indirect discrimination and some limited action measures – see Race Relations Act 1976, ss 1 and 35.

[9] Above n 7, at 34.

[10] See *X v Austria*, above n 2.

[11] *App No 8317/78*, (1981) 3 EHRR 161 at 214–215. The test crystallised in *McFeeley* comes from the court's decision in the *Belgian Linguistics Case*, above n 7, at 34–35.

The discretion granted to the Court and Commission by the concepts of, *inter alia*, reasonableness and proportionality, should permit to those institutions the latitude to reach decisions which would avoid the constraint of there being no express minorities provision in the ECHR.

However, before considering judicial practice, some matters relating to the grounds for discrimination need to be examined, if only briefly. Article 14 prohibits discrimination on grounds of race. However, in *East African Asians v United Kingdom*,[12] the Commission was prepared to hold that in appropriate circumstances race discrimination may amount to a violation of Art 3, as constituting inhuman and degrading treatment. Whether it is right to single out one form of discrimination for special treatment is open to question, but it does enhance the protected status under the ECHR of racial minority groups.

Furthermore, while Art 14 protects the right not to suffer discrimination in the enjoyment of Convention rights and freedoms on the basis of the applicant's political opinion, the singular decision of the Commission in *X v Italy*[13] seems[14] to have held that it is legitimate to discriminate against fascists to protect democratic institutions.[15] The potential for state abuse is evident in that it permits governments to deem opposition parties to be a threat to the new democracies. While sympathising with the Commissions instincts in this case, it is necessary for the facts of the case to be clarified so that its limits can be established.

STANCE OF THE EUROPEAN COMMISSION AND COURT OF HUMAN RIGHTS

Having established that Art 14 itself and the leading interpretations of it leave it open to the Commission and Court to protect minority rights through a broad reading of the idea of discrimination, it is necessary to examine how the deliberative organs of the ECHR have dealt with group rights cases brought before them in terms of individual discrimination. As might be expected, there is no categorical denial of group rights, but the balance is in favour of a repudiation of protection. Nevertheless, before looking at the repeated failure to protect minority rights under the ECHR, it

[12] (1970) 13Yb ECHR 928 at 994, (1981) 3 EHRR 76. See also Thornberry, above n 2, at p 303.
[13] *App No 6741/74*, 5 D+R 83 at 85 (1976).
[14] The lack of certainty on this matter flows from the fact that the report is extremely sketchy, the French and English versions, combined, taking up less than three full sides of the volume.
[15] The case also raises problems in that it failed to refer to Art 17, 'Nothing in this Convention may be interpreted as implying for any State, group or person any right to engage in any activity or perform any act aimed at the destruction of any of the rights and freedoms set forth herein or at their limitation to a greater extent than is provided for in the Convention.' Nor did it refer to the leading authority on the rights of fascists, *De Becker*, 2 Yb ECHR 214 (1958–59).

is worth noting those occasions when the Commission or Court has suggested that it is prepared to go beyond individual direct discrimination. It is all very well for the Commission and Court to assert that there is no minority rights protection in the ECHR, but it has to be examined as to whether their use of Art 14 and certain other provisions has effectively improved the collective position of minorities in member states, either by granting recognition[16] or even protection.

In *Belgian Linguistics*,[17] the Court was prepared to hold that it would intervene where there was direct discrimination in the enjoyment of Convention rights between two groups without justification. While this decision reflects no more than that a group has *locus standi* in the same way as an individual, it may be useful in enhancing group rights; for example, where the state supports two sets of schools in an area, each using a different language, and allows children from anywhere in the state to attend one, but only local children to attend the other, then the court will intervene, incidentally promoting education in the second group's mother-tongue.[18]

Further, if Art 14 is intended to lead to equal treatment of all individuals and groups, then, as the decision in *Christians Against Racism and Fascism v United Kingdom*[19] makes clear, treating essentially different groups in an identical fashion may, in fact, violate Art 14. In appropriate cases, therefore, treating the minority in the same manner as the majority may be discriminatory. Where the minority suffers prejudicial treatment at the hands of the majority, distinctions would have to be made to protect that minority. In the 1988 case of *Plattform 'Ärtze für des Leben' v Austria*[20] the Court went so far as to impose an obligation on states to take positive measures in order to permit one group to exercise its right to peaceful assembly under Art 11.[21] Such an interpretation of Arts 14 and 11 should ensure that minority groups can demonstrate to promote their needs and cause.

More pro-actively, the Commission held, *obiter*, in *Liberal Party et al v United Kingdom*[22] that there may be occasions when Art 3 of Protocol 1, together with Art 14, could be violated if voting behaviour indicated that religious or ethnic groups could never be represented in the legislature 'because there was a clear voting pattern along these lines in the majority.' The result, if followed, would be that a minority group would suffer 'discrimination', even though its members had the same voting rights as the majority population. This view endorses the Commission's earlier judgment

---

[16] There is, for instance, a case proceeding through the Strasbourg system challenging a conviction by Greek courts for distributing leaflets referring to the Muslim minority of western Thrace as 'Turks'. If Greece is found to have violated the ECHR, then implicit recognition is given to the minority and its 'identity' is promoted.

[17] Above no 7, at 70.

[18] See *Belgian Linguistics*, above n 7, at 61–71.

[19] App No 8440/78, 21 D+R 138 at 152 (1980); hereinafter, the *CARAF* case.

[20] Series A, Vol 139, (1988) 13 EHRR 204 at 210.

[21] Cf *CARAF*, above n 19, and App No 8191/78, *Rassemblement Jurassien & Unité Jurassienne v Switzerland*, 17 D+R 93 (1979).

[22] Above n 3, at 123.

in *Lindsay*,[23] ie that it is proper to discriminate if it improves the effectiveness of a Convention right for the benefit of a minority:

'A system of proportionate representation will lead to the minority being represented in situations where people vote generally on ethnic or religious lines and one group is in a clear minority throughout all electoral districts. Where such a situation exists only in a specific region of a country – as it does in Northern Ireland – the Commission cannot find that the application of a system more favourable to the minority in this part of the country is not in line with the condition that the people should be able to express its opinion freely. Rather on the contrary, a system taking into account the specific situation as to majority and minority existing in Northern Ireland must be seen as making it easier for the people to express its opinion freely.

The applicants have also complained that the application of the proportional representation system would amount to discrimination contrary to Art 14 of the Convention in conjunction with Art 3 of Protocol 1 because the majority in Northern Ireland will gain less seats than a comparable majority in the rest of the United Kingdom. As the Commission has stated above, the United Kingdom has specific reasons for applying a different electoral system in one part of the country, namely the protection of the rights of a minority. The electoral system complained of is, therefore, based on reasonable and objective criteria which justify the differentiation applied. Moreover, it does not appear that there is no reasonable relationship of proportionality between the means employed and the aim sought to be realised. Therefore, there is no discrimination under Art 14 . . .'

Taken together, the *Liberal Party* and *Lindsay* cases give a discretion to states to discriminate in favour of minorities to ensure their electoral representation. Since one of the reasons behind the ECHR was to entrench the democratic principles of its member states, then promoting the electoral participation of minority groups seems to represent the realisation that equality can only truly be achieved through representation.

More radically still, in *G and E v Norway*,[24] the Commission, *obiter*, was prepared to accept that under Art 8.1:

'a minority group is, in principle, entitled to claim the right to respect for the particular life style it may lead as being "private life", "family life" or "home".'

The *dictum* seems directed towards ethnic minorities rather than linguistic ones, for instance, but it takes the Court and Commission beyond mere non-discrimination, as established under Art 14, and provides authority for the protection of minority rights. Nevertheless, not only is Art 8.1 different in nature, since it prohibits interference in family life, Art 8 is also circumscribed in para 2, such that the rights set out in para 1 may themselves be interfered with in accordance with the law, so long as it is necessary in a

---

[23] *App No 8364/78, Lindsay et al v United Kingdom*, [1979] 3 CMLR 166 at 170–171.
[24] *App Nos 9278 & 9415/81*, 35 D+R 35–36 (1983).

democratic society for one of the enumerated purposes. In the instant case, the reindeer-shepherding, hunting and fishing lifestyle of the Lapps would be interfered with to some extent by the new hydro-electric dam, but it was justified in part because the dam would assist 'the economic well-being of the country'[25] However, in *Buckley v United Kingdom*,[26] a case concerning the rights of gypsies, the Commission were prepared to find that English planning laws interfered with the applicant's way of life and violated Art 8 (the case is now going to the Court).

Therefore, the Commission and Court have, on occasions, moved beyond the simple direct discrimination and have adopted certain positions, which to varying degrees, protect and promote the minority as such. However, such decisions are rare and most applications which try to advance group rights are rejected as manifestly ill-founded. Even in *G and E v Norway*,[27] the Commission also observed that there was no express guarantee of minority rights in the Convention, only a prohibition against discrimination. Moreover, as Norwegian citizens the Lapp applicants had all the same rights as other citizens including the right to vote; despite there being no Lapp representation in the Norwegian Parliament. The mere fact Lapps could vote and stand for election denied their having suffered discrimination.[28]

In *Belgian Linguistics*, the Court refused to recognise minority rights, even as an incidental part of non-discrimination. The Court seemed to be of the opinion that members of a group are faced with a voluntary choice when deciding whether to accept state policy or to try and preserve their identity:

> '[In] so far as the legislation leads certain [French-speaking] parents to separate themselves from their children, such a separation is not imposed by this legislation: it results from the choice of the parents who place their children in schools situated outside the Dutch unilingual region with the sole purpose of avoiding their being taught in Dutch, . . . one of Belgium's national languages.'[29]

Moreover, even where a harsh provision would cause hardship to the group, the court will not interfere unless there is an unprincipled and arbitrary distinction.[30]

Of more concern with regard to the rights of minority groups in general, was the court's refusal to examine demographic change in an area. At the hearing in 1968, the most up-to-date official data showed that in 1947, 47 per cent of the population of one of the administrative areas under consideration was French-speaking.[31] Yet, the court still spoke of the district as one

---

[25] *Cf* The Art 27 International Covenant on Civil and Political Rights case, *Kitok v Sweden*, CCPR/C/33/D/197/1985, 10 August 1988: cited in Thornberry, above n 2, at pp 211–213.
[26] *App No 20348/92*, Commission, 2 March 1995.
[27] Above n 24, at 35.
[28] Above n 24. The application was declared inadmissible. *Buckley*, therefore, represents a potentially major development.
[29] Above n 7, at 43.
[30] Above n 7, at 50.
[31] Above n 7, at 51. Unofficial statistics suggested that by 1968 that figure had risen to 65 per cent.

which by tradition was Dutch-speaking.[32] Given that minority groups must reach a certain minimum threshold before the state has to take account of their needs, the way that the court failed to explore the true nature of the situation even calls into question how correct its decision would be on whether mere discrimination was reasonable and proportionate in the circumstances.[33] Therefore, applications concerning the rights of minorities have to overcome several general limitations which promote assimilation and strict equality of treatment over preservation of identity, as well as a failure to carry out even the most basic assessments in order to see if there had been simple discrimination against the group.

The Commission and Court have also refused to protect minority groups when interpreting substantive provisions of the ECHR. The rights, usually sought by minority groups, relate to the preservation of cultural traditions or the use of language, either in education or in public life.

Among the various alleged breaches of the Convention complained about in the *Kalderas Gipsies* case,[34] the applicants alleged that German marriage laws violated their rights under Art 8. German domestic law did not formally recognise gipsy marriages, such that the husband's name did not appear as that of the father on the birth certificate. The complaint failed because Art 6(5) of the German Basic Law treats illegitimate children the same as legitimate ones,[35] but that ignores the point that the cultural traditions of the gipsies have been deemed inadequate in the eyes of the law. If a minority rights provision existed under the ECHR, then the issue of the illegitimacy of the children would not have arisen since the marriage formalities themselves, in all likelihood, would have been the focus of the judgment.

With regard to mother-tongue education, the Commission and court have been equally as unyielding. According to the court in *Belgian Linguistics*,[36] adopting a minimalist stance, the scope of the right to education in Art 2 of Protocol 1 is merely to guarantee access to already established means of instruction in the general and official educational system:

'The Convention lays down no specific obligations concerning the extent of these means and the manner of their organisation or subsidisation. In particular, the first sentence of Art 2 does not specify the language in which education must be conducted in order that the right to education should be respected.[37]

...[The] Court notes that Art 14, even when read in conjunction with Art 2 of the Protocol, does not have the effect of guaranteeing to a child or to his parent the right to obtain instruction in a language of his choice.'[38]

[32] Above n 7, at 56. The dissenting judges issued a separate opinion which was even stricter in relation to demographic changes—*ibid* at 89 *et seq.*
[33] See *McFeeley*, above n 11.
[34] *App No 7823 & 7824/77, Kalderas Gipsies v FRG and the Netherlands*, 11 D+R 221 (1977).
[35] Above n 34, at 232–233.
[36] Above n 7.
[37] Although the Court did state the obvious proviso that it ought to be one of the national languages.
[38] Above n 7, at 31 and 35.

Furthermore, the court also dealt with the separate question of whether it was discriminatory for a state to provide subsidised education to one language group while it failed to support schools using a different language. The principles are not necessarily as universally relevant because of the sharp regional division in Belgium between French and Flemish speakers – if language groups were dispersed randomly throughout the state, then the court's reasoning may not be applicable. Nevertheless, the almost absolute disregard for basic minority rights reveals the need for an express provision rather than having to rely on a broad interpretation of non-discrimination:[39]

> 'Article 14 does not prohibit distinctions in treatment which are founded on an objective assessment of essentially different factual circumstances and which, being based on the public interest strike a fair balance between the protection of the interests of the community and respect for the rights and freedoms safeguarded by the Convention.
>
> This legislation – tends to prevent in the Dutch-unilingual region, the establishment or maintenance of schools which teach only in French. Such a measure cannot be considered arbitrary. To begin with, it is based on the objective element which the region constitutes. Furthermore, it is based on a public interest, namely to ensure that all schools dependent on the state and existing in a unilingual region conduct their teaching in a language that is essentially that of the region.'[40]

The evident thrust of the Belgian legislation was one of progressive assimilation of linguistic minorities in each of the regions through the educational system. Such a policy conflicts with the principle of preserving the identity of the group that lies behind minority rights provisions, yet, on the face of it does not amount to discrimination.

The right to use one's mother-tongue generally in public life has not fared well before the Commission or court, either.[41] In *Clerfayt and Legros v Belgium*,[42] the issue was whether elected representatives could use their mother-tongue in legislative debates and when voting. The Commission pointed out that no Convention article 'explicitly guarantees "linguistic freedom"'[43] and went on to state that the ECHR:

> does not guarantee an elected representative's right to use the language of his choice . . .'.[44]

Since there was no substantive right in either the Convention or Protocol 1, then, following the *jurisprudence constante* of the Court and Commission,[45]

---

[39] See above, pp 153–6.
[40] Above n 8, at 44. On the other hand, the Court's assumption was based on demographic data from over 20 years earlier.
[41] See also the *Isop* case, above n 5.
[42] *App No 10650/83*, 42 D+R 212 (1985). The case finally turned on whether the Commission had jurisdiction over the procedural affairs of the various assemblies – at 222.
[43] Above n 42, at 221.
[44] Above n 42, at 222.
[45] Above n 6.

there could be no violation of Art 14. However, to force one linguistic group to use the language of the other group amounts to a policy of public linguistic assimilation.[46] Such a policy may be justified where there is a great disparity in the relative size of each group, but in the municipalities in question there were a large number of French-speaking residents.

The politics of language in Belgium subsequently gave rise to another case.[47] The facts were complex, but the language in which the elected representative took the oath when being sworn into Parliament determined on which regional council he would sit and which language-bloc he would vote with in Parliament. Once again, the problem arose that the substantial French-speaking minority in a nominally Dutch-speaking region could elect representatives who would either join the French language-bloc, but would not then sit on the Dutch regional council which dealt with their constituencies, or who would sit on that council, but would then not be part of the French language-bloc for important constitutional votes in Parliament. The Court saw this limitation on voters' choice as justified in that it was part of an attempt to:

'achieve an equilibrium between the Kingdom's various regions and cultural communities by means of a complex pattern of checks and balances. The aim is to defuse the language disputes in the country by establishing more stable and decentralised organisational structures. This intention, which is legitimate in itself, clearly emerges from the debates in the democratic national Parliament and is borne out by the massive majorities achieved in favour [of the relevant legislation] ... In any consideration of the electoral system in issue, its general context must not be forgotten. The system does not appear unreasonable if regard is had to the intentions it reflects and to the respondent State's margin of appreciation within the Belgian parliamentary system – a margin that is all the greater as the system is incomplete and provisional.'[48]

The Court is probably technically correct in its interpretation of Art 3 of Protocol 1, but its reasoning betrays the lack of a minority rights provision in the ECHR and the concomitant result that the court is preoccupied with individual rights. Minority rights treaties recognise the need to protect the group in regions as well as in the state overall. While each linguistic group in Belgium has its own region, pockets of the French-speaking minority in the Dutch unilingual area lack full representation. The dissenting judgment in *Mathieu-Mohin* appreciated this in coming to the view that Art 3 of Protocol 1 in conjunction with Art 14 had been breached.

'In our opinion, such a situation, excluding, as it does in practice, representation

---

[46] It might be noted that until 1980 councillors could use both Dutch and French – above n 42, at 219.

[47] *App No 9267/81, Mathieu-Mohin and Clerfayt v Belgium*, Series A, Vol 113, (1988) 10 EHRR 1.

[48] Above n 47, at 18. How 'incomplete and provisional' can be seen from the fact that Belgium is increasingly decentralising its powers to regional councils to such an extent that the kingdom will soon be effectively divided in two – see (1991) *The Guardian* p 10, 22 November and p 7, 11 February 1992.

of the French-speaking electorate of Halle-Vilvoorde at regional level, does not ensure "the free expression of the opinion of the people in the choice of the legislature" as stipulated in Art 3 of Protocol No 1, and it creates a language-based distinction contrary to Art 14 of the Convention. None of the reasons put forward to justify this incompatibility appears to us to be convincing. In the first place, it is true that the French-speakers elected in Halle-Vilvoorde could belong to the (Flemish) regional Council if they agreed to take the oath in Dutch. In that eventually, however, the representatives concerned would lose their status as French-speakers in Parliament, and this – in addition to the psychological and moral aspect of the issue – would have important political consequences, given the role played by the parliamentary language groups.'[49]

The dissenting judges have interpreted Art 14 to include principles of indirect discrimination to reach this opinion, but an express minority rights provision would obviate the need for semantic argument and allow discussion of the facts in their appropriate context.

Finally in relation to decisions on substantive provisions that tell against minority groups, the Commission and Court have given judgments that restrict a minority's right to demonstrate under Art 11 because of the possible reaction amongst the majority. The decisions in *Christians Against Racism and Fascism*[50] and *Rassemblement Jurassien*[51] provide that a minority group must take counter-demonstrators as it found them and that a state could take account of the behaviour of others in determining the limits it might impose on rights asserted under the ECHR:

'It is not in dispute that the applicant association does not advocate violence. Its difference in this respect from the other organisations is, however, not in issue. What is in issue is the likelihood of demonstrations to result in public disorder, and in this respect it was not unreasonable for the authorities to apply an objective criterion rather than a subjective test relating to the violent or peaceful intentions of the organisers of such demonstrations.'[52]

While the decision in *Plattform 'Ärtze für des Leben' v Austria*,[53] above, forces states to take such measures as are necessary to permit a group to exercise its Art 11 rights, the Commission and Court will apply the usual margin of appreciation, such that if in the state's opinion it is not possible to guarantee public order even if the authorities use all reasonable powers at their disposal, then the principles in *CARAF* and *Rassemblement Jurassien* would still be applicable to restrict the rights of the minority group.

Thus, while there has been some movement in favour of protecting minority groups by means of a wide interpretation of discrimination in Art 14, the general trend has been to deny to minorities as such the rights and freedoms of the ECHR, even where the result is harsh. Given the develop-

[49] Above n 47, at 20.
[50] Above n 19.
[51] Above n 21.
[52] The *CARAF* case, above n 19, at 152.
[53] Above n 20.

ments taking place in Eastern Europe and the resurgence of interest in minority rights as a topic, it is time that the deliberative organs of the ECHR were provided with a mechanism whereby they could directly address the needs of minority groups.[54] Such an opportunity may become available through the proposed Minorities Protocol, but that is still some years off.

[54] See the Framework Convention on National Minorities adopted by the Council of Europe in December 1994 and the work of the OSCE in this field.

13

HUMAN IMMUNODEFICIENCY VIRUS IN THE WORKPLACE: PREJUDICE AND OBJECTIVITY

Bob Watt

INTRODUCTION

This chapter will demonstrate that discrimination against people infected with the human immunodeficiency virus[1] is widespread and severe. It will be argued that such discrimination is founded upon two components:

(a) a rational fear of contracting an incurable, unpleasant and fatal disease: a reaction which is often swamped by
(b) the stigma attached to AIDS (and PWAs) based on its strong association with disfavoured characteristics or lifestyles.

It will continue by analysing the legal treatment afforded to PWAs in the United States of America where they area treated as 'handicapped' or 'disabled' under a variety of statutes. They are placed in a 'protected group', members of which may benefit from anti-discrimination law.

However, the focus of anti-discrimination law in the US AIDS cases has been to consider whether the detriment imposed upon particular PWAs is 'justified'. In a number of circumstances the detriment imposed upon the PWA has been held to have been properly imposed.

The central question to be addressed is whether the classification of PWAs as belonging to a 'protected group' is useful, or whether it merely adds to their stigmatisation. The author proposes an alternative policy and legal mechanism for ensuring public confidence in workplaces in general and healthcare provisions in particular, which should serve to limit the stigmatisation of PWAs. This alternative approach has the advantage that it is usable in jurisdictions where there is no statutory protection for disabled people. Furthermore, the author raises the question as to whether a special anti-discrimination statute or the application of a more general statute to PWAs is the most appropriate legal solution to the problems of stigmatisation faced by PWAs.

---

[1] Usually abbreviated as HIV. I shall use the designation PWAs (People with Aids) to refer to those people infected with the virus irrespective of whether they have only undergone sero-conversion or whether they display the appropriate number (two) of symptoms and laboratory signs (two) to be classified as suffering from AIDS. This follows the convention adopted in my earlier work for distinguishing between those suffering from AIDS and those diagnosed as HIV seroconverts. See 'HIV, Discrimination, Unfair Dismissal and Pressure to Dismiss' (1992) 21 Industrial Law Journal 280–292, 280, n 1.

STIGMA AND HATRED

Sociological literature defines the concept of stigma in a variety of ways.[2] However, the most useful starting point for our purposes is the analysis proposed by English:[3]

> 'In the final analysis, stigma might best be characterised to be the negative perceptions of so-called normal people to all individuals who are different from themselves.'

However, this seems to understate the problem, for as will be seen below the level of hatred which seems to be directed towards PWAs is grotesque. For example in *Support Ministries for Persons with AIDS Inc et al v Village of Waterford NY et al*,[4] in which a zoning ordinance passed to prevent the establishment of a hospice for PWAs was challenged by way of judicial review, the court noted that:

> 'To conclude that PWAs are stigmatised is an understatement; they are widely stereotyped as miasmic, untouchable physically and morally polluted . . . They are shunned socially and often excluded from public life.'[5]

When the court gives permission for the hostel it thought it necessary to read into the record a strong warning placing the inhabitants of the village, including the Mayor as one of the central protestors, on notice of the penalties which could be imposed for harassing the staff or users of the hospice.[6]

This level of venom requires some explanation. A partial explanation may be achieved by pointing out that the stigmatisation of PWAs may rest upon all of the three bases of stigma identified by Goffman.[7] These he identifies as:

(a) 'abominations of the body', taken to be diseases and deformities;
(b) 'blemishes of individual character' (which he identifies as including homosexuality and addiction, two of the identified high risk factors for transmission of the virus); and
(c) 'tribal stigma' which may be interpreted as stigma based upon membership of an identified and despised group in society.

It seems logical to conclude that where a person bears all three stigmatising factors he will be more highly stigmatised than a person who is shunned on one ground alone. However, even this combination of factors would not be sufficient to explain the treatment meted out to those identified as infected with the human immunodeficiency virus. PWAs have been treated in the following ways:

---

[2] See Robert M Page *Stigma* (London, Routledge & Kegan Paul 1984) especially Chapter 1.
[3] See RW English in *Correlates of stigma towards physically disabled persons*, Marinelli and Dell Orto (eds) (New York, Springer, 1977) p 162 quoted in Page *op cit* p 1.
[4] 808 F Supp 120 (NDNY 1992).
[5] 808 F Supp 120, 132, citing *Cain v Hyatt* 734 F Supp at 679.
[6] 808 F Supp 120, 139.
[7] E Goffman, *Stigma* (Harmondsworth, Penguin, 1968) p 14 *et seq*.

'(The) removal of a teacher with AIDS from teaching duties; refusal to rent an apartment to male homosexuals for fear of AIDS; firebombing of the home of hemophiliac children who tested positive for AIDS; refusal by doctors and health-care workers to treat people with or suspected of having AIDS; refusal of co-workers of an AIDS victim to use a truck used by the victim; filing of a charge of attempted murder against an AIDS victim who spat at police; requiring an AIDS victim to wear a mask in a courtroom; denial of access to schools to children with AIDS; threatening to evict a physician who treated homosexuals; boycotting of a public school after a child with AIDS was allowed to attend; firing of homo-sexuals who displayed cold symptoms or rashes; refusal of paramedics to treat a heart attack victim for fear he had AIDS; refusal by police to drive an AIDS victim to hospital; police demands for rubber masks and gloves when dealing with gays; refusal to hire Haitians; and urging of funeral directors not to embalm the bodies of AIDS victims.'[8]

It seems unlikely that an irrational stigma alone can account for this beha-viour, thus some other explanation is needed. The British Public Health Laboratory Service[9] reports that 9,290 cases of AIDS were reported in England and Wales in the period 1982 to May 1994 of which 6,283 patients were known to have died. Since some 1,500 of these cases of AIDS where only confirmed within the previous year it is quite clear that the prognosis for PWAs is very poor. The courts, at least in the United States, have taken a similarly bleak view. In the words of the court in *Doe v Washington University*:[10]

'Nor is the third factor, the severity of the risk to third parties, at issue since HIV is the precursor to AIDS which is, for all practical purposes, 100 per cent fatal.'

It seems likely that it is the objective fear of contracting the virus which lies at the heart of the hatred faced by PWAs and a recognition and isolation of this factor may lead to the possibility of reducing stigma and hatred. Clearly the courts and legislature may influence public opinion so as to out-law stigmatising acts and by so doing may influence public opinion so as to lessen stigma, but no judicial or legislative act can lead to the lessening of the objective risks of transmission.

Legislature and the courts in the United States have focused upon the objective risks of a person infected with the human immunodeficiency virus transmitting it to others, and it is to be hoped that this action will lead to a lessening of the stigma.

[8] *Estate of William Behringer v Medical Center* 592 A 2d 1251 (SCNJ Law Div 1991), 1272 n 12.
[9] PHLS HIV Bulletin 6(6) June 1994, p 13.
[10] 780 F Supp 628 (USDC ED, Missouri, ED 1991), 632.

THE LEGAL CATEGORISATION OF PWAS IN THE UNITED STATES AND THE DEFINITION OF 'OTHERWISE QUALIFIED'

In *School Board of Nassau County Florida v Arline*[11] the Supreme Court held that a person suffering from a contagious disease could be regarded as *handicapped* within the meaning of that term in the Rehabilitation Act 1973. This is so, provided that the severity of the disease is such that it results in a substantial limitation of one or more major life activity. Arline who suffered from (non-AIDS-related) tuberculosis was protected by virtue of s 504 of the Act against dismissal provided that she was *otherwise qualified* for her post as elementary school teacher.

The Rehabilitation Act 1973, s 504 provides that:

> 'No otherwise qualified individual with handicap . . . shall, solely by reason of his handicap, be excluded from the participation in . . . or be subjected to discrimination under any program or activity receiving Federal financial assistance.'

The term 'otherwise qualified' was enacted to ensure that any employee could perform the normal functions of the job. In the light of the passage of the Americans with Disabilities Act 1990[12] it is now plain that a private employer is similarly bound and the term 'otherwise qualified' must be read as including a person who with, or without, 'reasonable accommodation' can perform the essential functions of the employment position.

In *Arline* the Supreme court decided furthermore that a person 'who poses a significant risk of communicating an infectious disease to others in the workplace' would not be 'otherwise qualified' for the job. This determination of whether a person was 'otherwise qualified' would, in the view of the Supreme Court, normally require an individualised inquiry. This inquiry should include; findings of facts, based on reasonable medical judgments given the state of medical knowledge, about:

(a) the nature of the risk – how the disease is transmitted;
(b) the duration of the risk – how long is the carrier infectious;
(c) the severity of the risk – what is the potential harm to third parties; and
(d) the probabilities that the disease will be transmitted and will cause varying degrees of harm.

After the Court of Appeal in *Chalk v USDC Central California & Orange County Supt Schools*[13] confirmed that the Rehabilitation Act 1973 applied to PWAs, the stage was set for the use of the *Arline* test to determine whether such a person could use it to defend themselves against disadvantage or discrimination at work.

---

[11] 480 US 273, 107 S Ct 307, 94 L Ed 2d 307 (1987).
[12] Congressional debates surrounding the Americans with Disabilities Act make it plain that PWAs are covered by the ADA – see Watt n 1 above, (1992) 21 ILJ 280 at p 287 esp n 27 referring to the work of Robert Burgdorf (1991) *Harvard Civil Rights – Civil Liberties Law Review* 433–552 at p 447.
[13] 840 F 2d 701 (9th Cir 1988).

A succinct statement of the use of the four-part *Arline* test in a human immunodeficiency virus case is to be found in *Doe v Washington University*.[14] While Doe, a dental student, lost his case the analysis there provides a paradigm for it shows that only one of the *Arline* factors is of practical utility in AIDS cases. The court said:

'The first of these factors, the nature of the risk, is not at issue in the case at bar. All parties acknowledge that HIV could be transmitted to a patient if the plaintiff's blood were to enter the patient's mouth accidentally. The second factor, the duration of the risk, is equally not refuted since presently there is not known cure for the HIV infected individual and plaintiff consequently will remain infectious for the rest of his life. Nor is the third factor, the severity of the risk to third parties, at issue since HIV is the precursor of AIDS which is, for all practical purposes, 100 per cent fatal.

The court believes that it is the fourth factor, the probability that the disease will be transmitted, that is really at issue. This area is at the heart of this country's debate surrounding HIV infected individuals, as there has been only limited study of the risk of HIV transmission from infected health-care workers to patients.'

It is instructive to see how this modified *Arline* test has been used in a variety of circumstances.

THE RISK OF TRANSMISSION OF THE HUMAN IMMUNODEFICIENCY VIRUS

In *Doe v District of Columbia*[15] a successful applicant for employment in the fire service discovered that he was HIV seropositive before taking up employment. He advised the Fire Department of this fact and his appointment was deferred and he was subsequently dismissed. He challenged this decision on the grounds that he was protected as a 'handicapped person' under the Rehabilitation Act but, since he was in good health, he was 'otherwise qualified'. Doe applied for a mandatory injunction obliging the Fire Department to engage him. The court decided that his seropositivity gave him membership of a protected group under the Rehabilitation Act 1973, s 504 but that he could be excluded if his medical condition meant that there was a 'direct threat' or 'significant risk' of transmission of the virus to others. Thus the court followed the modified *Arline* analysis and concluded – on the evidence placed before it by doctors and firefighters – that there was no chance of the virus being transmitted. This evidence considered by the court included a detailed description of the duties of a firefighter and the protective clothing issued by the Fire Department. The court

---

[14] 780 F Supp 628 (USDC ED Missouri, ED 1991), p 632.
[15] 796 F Supp 559 (DDC 1992).

focused its attention upon the likelihood of the transfer of blood from Doe to a member of the public or to a colleague and concluded that the risk was 'so remote as to be unmeasurable'.[16] The court then concluded that since Doe did not present a 'direct threat' to other firefighters or to members of the public that he was 'otherwise qualified' under the *Arline* test.

The court furthermore considered the evidence that Doe had been excluded because he was stigmatised and said:

'The district relied upon the alleged public perception of persons with HIV in declining to give Doe employment. Chief Alfred testified that he "would be crazy not to consider the public's perception in formulating a policy regarding the employment of HIV+ persons . . .

The Constitution cannot control such prejudices, but neither can it tolerate them. Private biases may be outwith the reach of the law, but the law cannot directly or indirectly give them effect. "Public officials sworn to uphold the Constitution may not avoid a constitutional duty by bowing to the hypothetical effects of private . . . prejudice that they assume to be both widely and deeply held."'[17]

While the *Ray*[18] case does not concern employment, it deals with the circumstances faced by some young PWAs in school which is clearly an analogous situation. Mr and Mrs Ray were HIV seronegative, they had four children, three haemophiliac boys who were HIV seropositive and a sero-negative daughter. The boys had contracted the virus by being treated with contaminated Factor VIII administered to promote blood clotting. This seropositivity became known to the children's school and all four children were excluded. Candy Ray, the daughter was re-admitted before the action was brought by the Rays. An action for a preliminary injunction was brought against the school district requiring them to re-admit the children to integrated schooling. This was granted on the basis that the parents showed that they had a strong chance of success if the case came to full trial. The court considered that the plaintiffs were likely to succeed on the basis of *Arline*, and reasoned:

'Unless and until it can be established that these boys pose a real and valid threat to the school population of De Soto County they should be readmitted. The court recognises the concern and fear which is flowing from this small community particularly from the parents of school age children in De Soto County. However the court may not be swayed by such community fear, parental pressure or the possibility of lawsuits. These obstacles, real as they may be, cannot be allowed to vitiate the rights of the children . . .'[19]

[16] 796 F Supp 559 (DDC 1992), 569. See the useful list of decisions considered in reaching this conclusion of fact: *Chalk*, see below, 840 F 2d 701 (9th Cir 1988), *Martinez v School Board of Hillsborough County* 711 F Supp 1066 (MD Fla 1989), *Doe v Dolton Elem School Dist* 694 F Supp 440 (ND Ill 1988), *Ray*, see below, 666 F Supp 1524 (1987), *Dist 27 Comm School Board v Board of Educ* 130 Misc 2d 398, (NYSupp Ct 1986), *Jasperson v Jessica's Nail Clinic* 216 Ca App 3d 1099 (Cal Ct App 1989).

[17] 796 F Supp 559 (DDC 1992), 570. Quotation derived from the dissenting judgment of White J in *Palmer v Thompson* 91 S Ct 1940, 1962–1963 (1971).

[18] *Ray v School District of De Soto County* 666 F Supp 1524 (MD Fla 1987).

[19] *Ray v School District of De Soto County* 666 F Supp 1524 (MD Fla 1987), 1535.

The court thus decided that the three Ray boys be re-admitted to normal schooling. However, they imposed a number of conditions upon the children, their parents and the school. The court insisted that Centre for Disease Control and American Paediatric Association Redbook Guidelines be scrupulously observed by the children and their parents, and that a monitoring committee be established. The children were furthermore banned from all contact sports, all practices which might lead to the transfer of bodily fluids, were to be given special sex education.

The court took a strong line to protect the rights of the children and of the community, and expressly disregarded the irrational stigma.

This rational analysis of the risks of transmission clearly opens the possibility that cases will arise in which the courts will conclude that the detriment imposed upon the PWA was justified. A number of such cases have arisen in the United States courts.

In *Doe v Washington University*[20] a dental student who has HIV+ was excluded from degree scheme on 'academic grounds'. The faculty believed that because of his seropositivity that he would never be able to qualify as a dentist because they could not allow him to work in the dental clinic and thus accumulate 1,452 hours of clinical practice needed to qualify. The court refused to interfere. While it accepted that Doe was – in principle – covered by the Rehabilitation Act 1973, the court adopted the well-known position that elemosynary bodies (and *a fortiori* academic institutions) are entitled to summary judgment unless it can be shown 'that there is no rational basis for a decision or it was motivated by bad faith or ill will unrelated to academic performance'.

The court considered the steps the faculty had taken to establish the risk of transmission of the virus, and examined the steps they had taken to find alternative means for the student to complete his course and enter practice. Since the faculty had shown that a board of 40 professionals, 33 of whom were medically qualified, had concluded that Doe could not complete the course without posing a serious risk of transmission to third parties, thus failing the *Arline* test, the court was satisfied that the faculty had behaved rationally. The board had also considered the possibility of the student working in a clinic for PWAs, but concluded that he could not gain sufficient breadth of experience there.[21] This the court accepted.

The second example of a court deciding that a PWA was not 'otherwise

---

[20] See above n 11, 780 F Supp 628 (USDC ED, Missouri, ED 1991).

[21] This conclusion seems, on the face of it, suspect because if PWAs do not generally require the full breadth of dental treatment – as evidenced by the limited experience which could be gained in such a clinic – there might well be something to be said for having an albeit less experienced dentist with special knowledge. While Doe might fall short in some area he would, at least, have a deeper knowledge of the special problems of oral infection, with eg *Candida albicans*, faced by PWAs.

qualified' under the *Arline* formula, because he posed a 'serious risk' of transmission of the virus to others is to be found in *Bradley v U Texas MD Anderson Cancer Center*.[22] Brian Bradley revealed to the newspapers that he was HIV+ and had worked as a surgical technician assisting in operations. On this revelation he was reassigned to the hospital purchasing department, without other loss of status or privileges. He claimed that the hospital had discriminated against him, contrary to the provisions of the Rehabilitation Act 1973. After losing in the district court he appealed, but the 5th circuit of the Court of Appeal applied the *Arline* test and affirmed the decision below. The court held that the hospital had showed that there was a 'significant risk' of transmission of the virus when Bradley performed his job in the way that he had been accustomed to, and that even having a substitute for certain parts of Bradley's job did not constitute 'reasonable accommodation' on safety and efficiency grounds.

The most striking example of a rational analysis of the risks of transmission of the virus, and that risk being held to be so great that withdrawal of surgical facilities was the only option, is to be found in *Estate of William Behringer MD v Medical Center at Princeton et al*.[23] The *Behringer* case contains a number of issues concerning breaches of confidence and discrimination by imposition of conditions and withdrawal of privileges. This chapter will focus upon the reasonableness of the restrictions imposed upon Behringer, an HIV+ facio-maxillary surgeon.

The court considered these in a very highly rational way and eventually secured agreement between expert witnesses that the risk of actual transmission of the HIV was calculated as being between 1 in 130,000 to 1 in 145,000 for a single patient. However, this chance rises with the number of operations conducted so that if the surgeon performed 500 operations the chance of any one of those patients contracting the HIV is 1 in 126. This, the court held, was a rational basis for restricting the type of work which the surgeon could perform to non-invasive procedures.

Finally it is necessary to consider the situation which arises when the employer, and the court, find themselves unable to conduct a rational examination of the risk of transmission. These circumstances arose in the *Leckelt* case.[24] Kevin Leckelt, a licensed practical nurse, was known to be homosexual and his partner ws hospitalised with AIDS symptoms. When this latter fact came to light the hospital management instituted an investigation into Leckelt's health. They discovered that he was suffering from symptoms which were generally indicative of immunodeficiency. In his first interview with hospital management he agreed to provide the employer with the results of an HIV antibody test, but after further consideration resiled from

---

[22] F 3d 922 (5th Cir 1993).
[23] 592 A 2d 1251 (SCNJ Law Div 1991).
[24] *Leckelt v Board of Commissioners of Hospital District No 1* 901 F 2d 820 (5th Cir 1990).

this, saying that 'he did not believe that any law required him to divulge the test results and that he was concerned about losing his job if he was sero-positive.' The hospital dismissed Leckelt because of his continued refusal to supply his test results, a dismissal upheld as justified on that ground at first instance and at appeal.

Clearly Leckelt was dismissed by reason of his conduct, but the Court of Appeal went on to hold that the District Court was correct in finding that, although he could be taken to be handicapped under the Rehabilitation Act 1973, s 504 and, therefore, specially protected by that Act, he was not quali-fied for the post of practical nurse because the hospital was unable to deter-mine the extent of his capabilities without determining whether he had seroconverted.

PROTECTED CLASS AND 'GENUINE OCCUPATIONAL DISQUALIFICATION'

The basis of the legal treatment of PWAs in the United States has been to establish that they fall within a class of persons whose rights are specially protected by law. The most sophisticated system of classification is that pro-vided by the Americans with Disabilities Act 1990 which provides a three-fold definition of the protected class:

(1) Those who do in fact suffer from the disability.
(2) Those who have a history of disablement even though the disabling condition may have been cured.
(3) Those who are wrongly perceived as having a disability.[25]

Clearly most of the people discussed above fell into the first limb of the definition. If Candy Ray, the HIV seronegative sister of the three Ray broth-ers had not been voluntarily readmitted to school she could have founded an action on the third limb.

Members of the protected class who are so classified because they are infected with, for example, the human immunodeficiency virus are *prima facie* protected against discrimination unless, under the *Arline* doctrine, they pose a serious risk of transmitting the disease. One might say that the effect of *Arline* has been to provide protection unless the plaintiff has a 'genuine occupational disqualification'. This disqualification varies from occupation to occupation dependent upon the actual risks of transmission.

One might then expect PWAs to be anxious to secure recognised mem-

---

[25] See 42 USC §12102, and discussion by Brian Doyle in 'Employment rights, equal opportun-ities and disabled persons: the ingredients of reform' (1993) 22 Industrial Law Journal pp 89–103, section 2 'The protected class'.
[26] See above n 18 and associated text, and the instances of discrimination beyond the reaches of the law detailed in Burgdorf cited above n 13.

bership of the protected class. The difficulty with this is however, as the courts have recognised, that there is stigma beyond the reaches of the law.[26] Furthermore the difficulty with granting special protection to identified groups, no matter how deserving the group might be, is that there is likely to be a backlash against them.[27]

If PWAs avoid being dashed upon the shores of stigma they risk becoming entangled in a Sargasso of 'me too' claims. There are reports of employers in the United States refusing to hire Haitians because of the high incidence of the human immunodeficiency virus amongst that group and discrimination against homosexuals has been exacerbated on both sides of the Atlantic because of a misplaced fear of AIDS.[28] Members of these groups would be protected in the United State because they could claim protection under the third limb of the Americans with Disabilities Act definition.

The problem with the 'protection for mislabelled persons' limb is that so many people can fit themselves into such a class without seriously distorting it. The British Public Health Laboratory Service classifies people who have lived in, or have visited, Africa, along with bisexuals, injecting drug users and haemophiliacs as being at high risk of contracting the human immunodeficiency virus. Moderate risk groups include people with many heterosexual partners, people who have lived in, or visited, the Americas, and people who were transfusion or transplant recipients. If effective legal protection is provided for *bona fide* PWAs and 'genuine' mislabelled persons while all others have to endure daily disadvantages because of an over-supplied labour market or limited resources, it would come as no surprise to find that less scrupulous citizens would try to fit themselves into the protected class by means of the third limb of the Americans with Disabilities Act definition.

ALTERNATIVE TO THE 'PROTECTED CLASS'

Vigilance, and the vigorous protection of their rights, seems to be the only possible legal response to stigmatisation of PWAs. However, responding to the problem of 'me to' seems more difficult within the 'protected class' framework. Furthermore in jurisdictions such as the United Kingdom where PWAs do not benefit from any legal protection such a mechanism is unavailable and PWAs remain unprotected.

The United States courts have found a mechanism to avoid this pitfall in circumstances where membership of a protected class is difficult to establish

[27] For a valuable discussion of the dangers of a 'backlash' inherent in 'positive action' programmes see the discussion by Christopher McCrudden in 'Rethinking Positive Action' (1986) 15 Industrial Law Journal, p 219.
[28] See text associated with nn 9, 17–19 above and *Buck v The Letchworth Palace Ltd* IT 36488/86 (unreported).
[29] US 432, 105 S Ct 3249, 87 L Ed 2d 313 (1985).

because its boundaries are unclear. Thus the majority of the Supreme Court in the 14th Amendment – equal protection of the law – case *City of Cleburne Texas v Cleburne Living Center*[29] adopted an alternative route.

Here there was a proposal to build a home for the 'mentally retarded'[30] in the City of Cleburne. Local residents responded by lobbying for, and eventually obtaining the passage of a zoning ordinance which precluded any such development. The Supreme Court struck down the ordinance as violating the equal protection clause.

The Court seems to have had a great deal of difficulty in deciding whether the 'mentally retarded' could be fitted into any discrete class at all. 'Mentally retarded' could be used to describe, thought the Court, any group of people from the slightly dim-witted to those with severe learning difficulties caused by organic dysfunction. The Court was much happier with a more pragmatic analysis, focusing upon an inquiry as to the reasons for the disadvantageous treatment meted out to the aspirant residents. The Court concluded, on the evidence, that the reasons for the disadvantage were based upon the concerns of local householders and business people for their property value and profits. The Court would have upheld the ordinance were it based upon a rational concern, such as for the residents' safety. The respondent City attempted to claim that the neighbourhood was unsafe for mentally retarded people because it constituted a 500-year flood plain.[31] This was dismissed by the Court.

This approach suggests that the classification of persons as belonging to some or other protected class is, at least, otiose and may be damaging where the plaintiff fails to prove that they fit into the protected class. The Court in *Cleburne* managed to arrive at a result which protected the rights of the plaintiff group without identifying them as a group, while leaving the possibility of another court finding otherwise upon different facts.

Arguably, therefore, in human immunodeficiency virus cases it would be better to focus more sharply upon the type of activity which was proposed in the employment, and to consider the probability of harm resulting in the course of that activity if the actor were to be HIV seropositive.

In some employments, for example, obstetric and facio-maxillary surgery,[32] it may be that the risks of transmission of the virus are great even when the highest practicable level of precautions are employed because of the physical demands upon the surgeon. Therefore, it may be that persons employed in these capacities should be obliged to undergo routine human immunodeficiency virus antibody testing at regular intervals and should be subject to redeployment should they prove seropositive.

---

[30] These were the words used by all parties to the action.

[31] Meaning that it would flood once in 500 years!

[32] See *Estate of William Behringer MD v Medical Center at Princeton et al* 592 A sd 1251 (SCNJ Law Div 1991).

[33] 'HIV, Discrimination, Unfair Dismissal and Pressure to Dismiss' (1992) 21 Industrial Law Journal, pp 280–292.

I have argued elsewhere that the British law of unfair dismissal is adequate to protect PWAs[33] and it could be that the development of discrimination law into this area in the United States is a result of the lack of generally available protection against unfair dismissal there. It is possible, therefore, that this development is as misguided as the development of anti-gender discrimination law to control sexual harassment.[34]

[34] Janet Dine & Bob Watt 'Sexual harassment: moving away from discrimination' (1995) 58 Modern Law Review pp 343–63.

Part III

DISCRIMINATION IN PARTICULAR SECTORS

14

THE COST OF REMOVING DISCRIMINATION FROM SOCIAL SECURITY SCHEMES

Christopher McCrudden

This chapter addresses the following issues. First, what costs arise from the *status quo* and what remedial costs arise from moving to a position of equality, who might bear these costs, and what would the consequences be of allocating them to different parties. Secondly, to what extent are cost considerations taken into account in terms of the determination by the Council of the scope of the definition of equality between women and men in social security. Thirdly, how does the European Court of Justice deal with the issue of costs in relation to the determination of direct effect, the definition of the right and the provision of the remedy. Before turning to these points, however, some preliminary points would be pertinent.

GENERAL CONTEXT OF SOCIAL SECURITY DEVELOPMENTS IN THE COMMUNITY

Social and economic changes are imposing new or reinforcing existing demands on the social security system. Two of the most important factors are unemployment and an ageing population, experienced in all member states. When most member state pension schemes were established, there were fewer pensioners than workers; this is now changing.[1] As women have a longer life expectancy, approximately two-thirds of pensioners will be women.[2] Recent years have also seen an increase in the number of people claiming unemployment related benefit an a rise in the level of long-term

---

[1] In Germany, France, the UK and Italy, dependency ratios of the population aged over 65 to the population age 15–64 were between 24.1 per cent and 22.9 per cent in 1992 (Harrison, *Pension Provision in the EC: Opportunities for the Private Sector in the Single Market* (Financial Times Management Report, 1992) p 12). By 2035 the same ratio will be between 32–42 per cent, and in Germany nearly 50 per cent (*ibid*). For further figures see Department of Social Security, *Containing the Cost of Social Security, The International Context* (HMSO, London, 1993). The dependency ratios of the population over 60 to that between 15–59 are clearly higher, see Eurostat, 1993.

[2] ILO, *Social Security and Social Protection: Equality of Opportunity between Men and Women* (ILO, TMSSE/1993), p 3.

unemployment. In this context, member states are seeking to contain the cost of social security systems, which in 1990 represented on average 26 per cent of GDP.[3] This aim is being pursued through a number of policies, including linking uprating to prices rather than earnings,[4] raising contributions, reducing unemployment benefit and/or its duration, increasing work incentives, reducing or restricting disability benefits, reforming pensions, freezing family benefits and reducing social assistance. Some member states, including the poorest, are also seeking to shift the responsibility for provision to the private sector and encouraging more private provision.[5] In all member states there is currently a debate over what policies should be pursued, what level of benefits can be afforded in each country, and at a more fundamental level what role the welfare state should be playing.[6] Governments are concerned with the future financing of social security, particularly pension programmes, the role of social security in unemployment, and increased 'targeting' of benefits to those most in need.

There is thus an increasing pressure in members states not to introduce measures which will impose greater demands on welfare systems. The implications for the issue of equality in social security are that where equality will lead to greater costs for the welfare system, its implementation is likely to be resisted.

NATURE AND INCIDENCE OF COSTS

What costs may be encountered? Costs will be defined widely to include direct and indirect financial implications as well as disadvantages which extend beyond the purely economic. Paul Gewirtz[7] has developed a useful distinction between, on the one hand, what he calls costs of the right and, on the other, transitional costs of remedies for violations of the right. The former are 'the distributive costs entailed by the end-state vision embodied in the right itself'. The latter are 'the costs imposed in order to move from the current situation to that end state'. An example would be, in the context of equalisation of state pension age, the cost of overriding the ideological

---

[3] DSS *Containing the Cost of Social Security – the International Context* (HMSO, London, 1993) (the figure includes spending on health).

[4] In the UK pensions have been uprated in relation to prices since 1981. Recently, France announced that pensions would continue to be uprated in line with prices for at least a further five years following a temporary move to price indexation in the 1980s. In 1992 Italy also enacted a provision to uprate all benefits by RPI-1 per cent. (Latter figures supplied by the UK Department of Social Security).

[5] Greece, Ireland, Portugal, Spain, UK, Italy. Details from DSS 1993, *Containing the Cost of Social Security – the International Context* (HMSO, London, 1993).

[6] See in the UK, Hills *The Future of Welfare: A Guide to the Debate* (Joseph Rowntree Foundation, 1993), which disputes the premise that in the UK policy is completely 'boxed in' by fiscal and demographic constraints and offers a range of policy options.

[7] Gewirtz 'Remedies and Resistance' 92 Yale Law Journal, 92(4), March 1983, 587, at p 607.

assumption and preference which underpinned the original decision to have differential ages (the cost of the right) and, once a decision has been taken that these ideological assumptions and preferences are no longer valid, the costs of moving to an equalisation of pensions ages (transitional costs). We seek to include both types of costs in this chapter.

COSTS OF THE *STATUS QUO*

The sources of gender inequality in social security systems are well documented. They arise from systems based on a traditional concept of the family where the husband is the head and the sole breadwinner, and the wife is seen as the economic dependant whose social security entitlements are derived through the husband. Inequality also arises from the non-recognition of caring for adults of children as economically valuable work, and from social, economic and working conditions restricting women's access to the labour market and advancement in it.

An important point needs to be kept in mind, however. Women are not a homogeneous group with the same interests. There are substantial differences of class and income group, age and disability, and between those who are single or married, mothers or childless. Some women may be incorporated into the social security system through rights derived from their husbands' contributions and receipt of benefits for dependents; others may be claiming directly as heads of households. Not all women will need to depend on social security; others may have sufficient income to provide for themselves independently either of a husband or the state. The latter tends to be a very small minority group, however. While only a minority rely wholly on the income of their partner, the economic independence achieved by most women from their present or ex-partners and/or the state, is limited.[8]

REMEDIAL COSTS

We turn now to consider our second category of costs, those involved in moving from the *status quo* to a position of equality.

Costs to the victim/victim group

It may seem paradoxical that moving from the *status quo* which, as we have noted above, disadvantages women in a number of respects should also incur costs on women. Again, it should be remembered that women are not an homogeneous group; while some may suffer more from the *status quo*

---

[8] For a detailed discussion of these issues see McCrudden and Black in *Equality of Treatment between Women and Men in Social Security* Chapter 7, p 169.

than others, some may incur greater costs, or at least not derive benefits, from a change in that *status quo*. For example, it is sometimes argued that removing the disadvantages to (some) women from means-tested benefits through individualisation of benefits could reduce the incentives for married women to seek employment, so undermining their access to an independent income through paid employment.[9] Some reports have, therefore, suggested that individualisation of benefits should be pursued through non means-tested benefits.[10] Further, it is sometimes argued that changes which involve an improvement in the benefits women receive from employers will in fact pose costs on women generally, as they will become more expensive to employ, making employers more reluctant to employ them.[11]

It is not our intention to examine all of the different types of reforms which have been proposed for social security systems to see what their impact on women would be.[12] Instead we will focus on two issues: the cost of equalising state pension ages, and the costs of unisex rating in pensions and insurance.

Equalisation of pension ages

Most member states either already have equal pension ages or have adopted decisions to achieve this on a transitional basis, with the exception of Italy.[13] Most have, or are planning to implement a minimum pension age of 65. France has a minimum age of 60, and Belgium a flexible pension age of 60–65.[14] The nature of implementation varies: Portugal will equalise pension ages at 65 over a three-year period beginning in 1994; the UK has recently stated that the state pension age will be raised to 65, but that equalisation will be phased in between 2010 and 2020; Greece has equalised the state pension age at 65, but only for all new members to the national insurance scheme.

In countries where women's retirement age is increased, women will thus incur first, the cost of having their entitlement postponed, and secondly, depending on the nature and length of the transitional period, an upset of their legitimate expectation to retire at 60. The longer the transitional period, the less this expectation is frustrated. Equalisation at 65 is opposed by those who see the postponement leading to greater poverty for women. However, it is also argued that those women earning above the lower earnings level may benefit from an extra five years in the labour market in which

---

[9] P Esam and R Berthoud *Independent Benefits for Men and Women* (Policy Studies Institute, 1991), and Lister 'Women's Economic Dependency and Social Security' (EOC, 1992), p 3.

[10] Lister 'Women's Economic Dependency and Social Security' (EOC, 1992, p 65.

[11] This argument has been used by the UK government, and accepted by the Court of Appeal, but not by the House of Lords to justify indirect discrimination. See *R v Secretary of State for Employment, ex parte EOC* [1994] 2 WLR 409 (HL).

[12] For a summary of some of the different types of systems see A Dilnot and S Webb, 'A Practical Framework for the Analysis of Social Security Reform', (1991) 12 *Fiscal Studies* 33, and Hills *The Future of Welfare: A Guide to the Debate* (Joseph Rowntree Foundation, 1993).

[13] Italy passed legislation in 1992 to raise state pension age to 60 and 65 from 55 and 60 for men and women respectively, phased in between 1993 and 2002.

[14] DSS, *Options for Equality in State Pension Age* Cmnd. 1723 (London, 1991), p 34.

to make contributions towards a pension.[15] The impact will also depend on whether any policies are adopted to improve the position of those on low incomes between 60 and 65, mainly women, for example, policy options to target the savings made from equalising at 65 to provide support for those women in low income groups and without an occupational or personal pension, carers, and women returners to the labour market.[16]

If the state pension age had been equalised at 60, then more immediate costs of having to wait until 65 would not be incurred. However, the argument has also been made that as equalisation at 60 would have incurred greater expenditure, those women working would have to finance the expenditure through higher taxes.[17] Further, 'levelling up' to 60 may pressure governments to introduce an earnings or contributions requirement in order to minimise the full costs, a strategy which might have a disadvantageous effect on women for the reasons discussed above.

The issue of frustrated expectations also arises in the equalisation of pension ages for occupational pension schemes. If equalised to 65 this would frustrate the legitimate expectation of those women covered to retire earlier. However, as the transitional periods envisaged for equalisation of state pension ages would not be available under *Barber*, the frustration would be far greater as the change would be immediate. Such immediate equalisation at 65 has in fact been criticised as 'turning *Barber* on its head'.[18]

Unisex rating

Equalising contributions and benefits is seen as having the principal effect of raising premiums and introducing cross subsidies between men and women. In relating to premiums it is argued that in pooling low and high risk groups, insurance companies will assume a more unfavourable mix than they expect, so that the average premium would be higher than if the groups were assessed separately. The low risk group will be aware that the premium is levelled towards the high risk group, and so will under-insure. The high risk group will recognise that the price is lower than it would otherwise be for their risk level and so will over-insure. Then insurance will become increasingly concentrated in the high risk group, causing premiums to rise further. To contain the risks, insurance companies will direct their marketing towards the low risk group and possibly restrict the range of insurance options they offer.[19]

---

[15] See for example, ILO, *Social Security and Social Protection*, see n 2 above at p 10; Social Security Advisory Committee, *Options for Equality in State Pension Age: A Case for Equalising at 65*, (HMSO, 1992), para 3.9.

[16] See Social Security Advisory Committee, *ibid*, Chapter 4.

[17] Social Security Committee, Public Expenditure on Social Security, Minutes of Evidence, 1992/93 HCP 615-i, para 70 (Mr Peter Lilley, Secretary of State for Social Security).

[18] Labour Research Department, *Pensions and Equal Treatment* (LRD, September 1991). For a discussion of different companies' approaches see H Desmond, 'A Tangled Web: *Barber* and Beyond – a research report' (1993) 23 ILJ 235.

[19] Institute of Actuaries and Faculty of Actuaries *Report of the Working Party on Discrimination in Insurance and Pensions* (London, 1988), pp 91–2.

Further, classifying different risk groups as one results in cross subsidies. This is a common feature of insurance classifications: non-smokers subsidise smokers, joggers the unfit. In grouping men and women into one classification, unisex rating would mean women would cross-subsidise men in life contracts (where men have the higher risk), and in disability and annuity contracts, men will subsidise women.[20] Women will thus pay more for their life assurance, while gaining higher annuity and disability payments.

Respondent and respondent group costs

Three types of costs may be identified which affect in particular the respondent or the respondent group. There is, first, the specific cost of any remedy imposed, though the extent of such costs will depend on the nature of the remedy. If, for example, 'levelling up' is required then the costs will necessarily be greater to the respondent than if levelling down is permitted. Secondly, we can identify costs which derive from loss of efficiency, though the extent of these costs will depend on whether the discrimination in question was efficient or not (this will be pertinent, for example, in the context of life assurance). Thirdly, we can identify the 'cost' of regulation itself and the interference with autonomy of action which this brings. It will be useful, first to distinguish between state and occupational social security provision.

State, social security and the equalisation of pension ages

It is in the context of funding pensions that the demographic factors of an ageing population are principally of significance. In the UK, equalisation has been identified as having a direct effect on expenditure on the state pension, and other direct effects, principally on revenue from income tax, national insurance contributions or social security taxes, and indirect taxes; and on spending on contributory benefits and income related benefits.[21] The costs of equalisation vary depending on a wide range of factors, the most obvious of which are the age which is chosen, the ratio of working population to retired persons, and the measurement of pension entitlements (whether prices or earnings uprated).[22] The assumptions made in the calculations are disputed, leading to disputes over the figures themselves. The UK Department of Social Security, for example, has estimated that the net cost to the exchequer of equalising the pension at age at 60 in the UK would be £3.4bn in 2035,[23] recently revised to £4bn at 1993/94

---

[20] *Unisex Pricing in Long Term Insurance, an independent report by actuarial consultants Tillinghast for the Equal Opportunity Commission* (EOC, April 1992), p 2.

[21] DSS, *Options for Equality in State Pension Age* Cmnd. 1723 (London, 1991), Appendix, para 16.

[22] For a discussion of these assumptions, see *ibid.*

[23] *Ibid,* Appendix 1. The cost in 2025 was estimated at £4.5bn, *ibid,* p 39. All figures based on prices up-rating.

prices.[24] The net savings of equalising at 65 are estimated at £3bn in 2035.[25] Equalising at 63 would have cost approximately £0.5bn.[26] However, alternative figures indicate that equalisation at 60 would not involve such high costs, and that equalisation at 65 could in fact impose costs.[27]

The dispute over equalisation of pension ages reflects the fact that the costs question is an area of considerable disagreement, first over the figure themselves and secondly as to the political assumptions on which these cost analyses are based. The discussion above related solely to the British situation. Other examples from which lessons may be drawn may include France when it has been said that the effective equalisation of state pension ages at 60 has not had any drastic effects on the economy.

Employers

In the employment context, one of the principal issues is that of unisex rating for occupational pension schemes. The figures are again disputed, here on the basis of differing estimates as to existing and future levels and lengths of scheme membership, working patterns, final salary levels and investment returns, etc. The figures also vary with the four different interpretations which have been made as regards the retrospective effect of *Barber*.[28] For example, it has been estimated that had *Barber* been made fully retrospective, this could have cost employers in the UK approximately £50 billion, £15 billion in the Netherlands and £500 million in Ireland.[29] Cost estimates for limited retrospective effect (service post-*Barber*) are around £2 billion. A survey for the UK National Association of Pension Funds (NAPF) found that by the end of 1991 75 per cent of schemes had equalised pension ages, most at 65.[30] As noted above, the figures are disputed and a NAPF survey in the UK indicates that many major schemes state that even the most costly interpretation would not be unaffordable.[31] However, smaller schemes may not be as able to meet the costs quite as easily as the bigger, well-established schemes.

---

[24] DSS, *Equality in State Pension Age*, Cmnd. 2420 (HMSO, London, 1993), p 33. The figure for 2025 is £5bn. The effect on expenditure is estimated to be £6bn in 2025 and £5bn in 2035, *ibid*, p 34.

[25] *Ibid*, p 33. The figure for 2025 is £3.5bn; expenditure effects are estimated at £5bn in 2025 and £4bn in 2035, *ibid*, p 34.

[26] The figure for 2025 is still £1bn; expenditure effects are estimated to be saving of £0.5bn in 2025, and negligible savings in 2035, *ibid*, p 34.

[27] B Davies, *A Question of Fairness: Can we Afford Equality at 60?* (Trades Union Congress, November 1993).

[28] For an exposition of these, see Advocate-General van Gerven's Opinion to the *Ten Oever, Neath, Moroni* and *Coloroll* cases, April 1993.

[29] Argument of UK government in *Coloroll* etc, other figures from (1989) 49 EOR 2.

[30] NAPF, 22.2.92, quoted in Desmond, 'A Tangled Web: *Barber* and Beyond – a research report', (1993) 23 ILJ 235.

[31] Survey of the National Pension Fund Association, figures quoted in *Pensions and Equal Treatment* (LRD Booklet, September 1991) pp 18–19. This also quotes an estimate of the cost of equalising at 60 to be £10 billion.

Identifiable third parties costs

Turning now to costs to identifiable third parties, several costs may again be identified. To those who ordered their affairs in a manner which is adjudged in separate proceedings to be unlawful, there are the costs derived from the disruption of settled expectations. There are also the costs of uncertainty in some situations where the scope of an expanding right is unclear.

Men

As regards the comparison group, the incidence and nature of the costs which may arise will actually depend on the remedy given. If the equalisation is achieved through 'levelling down' the comparator group will incur a clear cost, the difference between the old and the new positions. So if, for example, the result of requiring equality in benefits was to reduce the level of benefits received by all, the comparator group would suffer a reduction in income. If the equalisation is achieved through a 'levelling up' which bin fact results in the comparator group being treated more favourably, clearly no costs are incurred. So, for example, the equalisation of the pension age at 60 would make most men financially better off between the ages of 60 and 65.[32]

As regards insurance policies, it has been argued that unisex rating will drive premiums up, which will be to the disadvantage of men where they form the low risk group (morbidity, for example). However, the effect on premiums may be affected by competition driving premiums down, and by the actual mix of the classification group, in this case the male/female ratio. Currently, in most forms of private insurance, men are heavily over-represented. Their current rates are likely to dominate unisex premium calculations.[33]

Insurance companies: unisex rating

The essence of the insurance business is that individuals are classified as members of a group on the basis of known risk factors which enable as accurate an assessment as possible of the cost to the insurer. Preventing insurance companies from classifying on the basis of sex, it is argued, would prevent them from taking a certain group of risks into consideration, which would in turn threaten their solvency and seriously damage the commercial viability of the industry.[34]

Others draw a distinction between practices which take the distribution of

---

[32] DSS, *Options for Equality in State Pension Age* Cmnd. 1723 (London, 1991), para 6.24.

[33] J Keithley, *Sex Discrimination and Private Insurance: A Social Policy Perspective*, Joint Seminar: Institute and Faculty of Actuaries and Equal Opportunities Commission, 26.5.89, p 24, Tillinghast Report for EOC.

[34] Institute and Faculty of Actuaries, *Discrimination in insurance and pensions*, pp 5–6.

risks into consideration when estimating overall costs, but then spread premium costs and benefits on a basis which disregards the characteristics of the insured individual.[35] On this basis, some estimate that unisex rating would have little significant impact on the business volumes, profitability and solvency of the long-term insurance market.[36]

Public interest costs

Lastly, we can turn to the costs to the society more generally, what might be seen as costs to the 'public interest', though that term is necessarily rather hazy. Several different types of cost may be identified. In relation to a situation where state expenditure is increased to provide the level of equality, then the taxpaying public will have to finance this expenditure. In relation to employers, if equality measures result in inefficiency, then there will be reduced profitability, and a less healthy economy may result. However, as we have seen, costs are also borne by those who suffer under the *status quo*. The public interest could, and some argue should, be given a broader definition not only to take into account efficiency of the economy, but substantial equality of individuals. The argument, inevitably, becomes one of equity versus efficiency; is society better off as it recognises equal treatment of individuals?

Impact on the economy

The impact on the economy of measures which would increase demands on the welfare system would be that these measures would have to be financed, either through cuts in other areas of expenditure, or through increased state income from taxes, or both. Particular measures would have particular effects. The UK government argues, for example, that equalisation of state pension ages at 60 would mean that men would retire earlier, reducing the size of the workforce, pushing up real value of wage rates and there would be adverse effects on employment, competitiveness and output.[37] The UK government also argues that equalising at 65 would mean real wages would fall, there would be favourable effects on employment, output and international competitiveness. The rate of unemployment would be broadly unchanged under both, but personal savings might fall to a small extent under the latter. These arguments are disputed by those who argue that equalising at 60 would reflect the earlier age at which people are taking voluntary retirement, and that the effects on employment, for example, would not be as the government anticipated.[38]

---

[35] This is the approach recommended by Advocate-General van Gerven in his opinion to the *Ten Oever, Neath, Moroni* and *Coloroll* cases, April 1993.

[36] Tillinghast Report for EOC, p 2.

[37] Based on DSS, Options for Equality (see n 14 above), paras 6.15–6.24.

[38] On the latter, see Davies, *Question of Fairness* (see n 27 above).

Insurance

In providing people with a private, ie non-state funded, means of protection from risks of sickness and old age, and for providing for dependents on death, insurance plays a valuable social role. In the context of the effect of unisex rating it is argued that if this would result in under-insurance or an unhealthy insurance industry there would be a demise in private provision against risks, and consequently greater burdens on the state.[39] However, as noted above, the implications of unisex rating for the insurance industry are disputed.

Employer provided benefits

There is an argument, advanced frequently in the UK, that greater burdens on employers will lead to decreased profitability, a decline in the share price and ultimately increased unemployment. The UK government argued in *Coloroll* etc that making *Barber* fully retrospective would lead to an increase of 100,000 in unemployment. It is also argued that making women more expensive to employ will mean employers are less willing to employ them.[40]

COSTS AND THE DIRECTIVES

We have examined some aspects of the costs which are borne by the victim or victim group of remaining with the *status quo*, and the costs which are borne by that group,. the respondent group, identifiable third parties, and the public interest as a consequence of some obvious remedial measures. The incidence and nature of costs and who bears them will depend on the nature of the benefit lost or withheld, on the nature of the market in which the actors are operating, on the nature of the respondent, on the nature of the remedy and on the nature of the compliance strategy adopted by the respondent.

We turn in this section to consider the extent to which these costs are taken into account in the formulations of the current EC legal standards in this area. The most obvious way in which costs may be taken into account is in the scope and definition of the right itself. This requires consideration both of the legislative provisions themselves – in some cases the Directives have taken costs into account explicitly – and of the approach taken by the Court of Justice – in some cases the court has defined a right in such a way as to take into account certain costs.

---

[39] Institute and Faculty of Actuaries, *Discrimination in insurance and pensions*, p 5 emphasises this social role.

[40] This has been argued in the UK to be a justification for indirect discrimination, see *R v Secretary of State of Employment, ex parte Equal Opportunities Commission* [1994] 2 WLR 409.

More problematic (and more interesting, perhaps) is the situation where costs are taken into account in the application of remedies for violations of these EC legal standards. Costs apparently insufficient to override Community interests at the rights-defining stage 'are afforded a second veto at the remedy stage to prevent practical vindication of those rights.'[41] This too requires consideration both of the legislative provisions themselves – again, in some cases the Directives have taken costs into account explicitly – and of the approach taken by the Court of Justice – in some cases the court has limited remedies because of their cost implications.

Regarding the approach taken by the Directives, we should consider both the existing Directives and the draft Directive. We can see that certain costs have been taken into account both in the focus of Dir 79/7 on employment status (eg not addressing issues such as child care provisions) and by the simple expedient of creating exceptions to the general principle where inclusion was thought to create too great a cost: for example, the inclusion of exceptions in Art 7(1) of the 1979 Directive, and the exclusion of widowers' pensions from the equality requirement in Art 3(2). A second legislative technique is phased implementation of the Directive as a whole. Discussions before the adoption of both the Equal Pay Directive and the Equal Treatment Directive left social security issues to be dealt with in future directives. Both Dirs 79/7 and 86/378 permit long periods for member states to implement the Directives, and the costs of implementation were an important element behind these delays. The third legislative technique has been the adoption of transitional arrangements of implementation for specific issues, such as the inclusion of transitional arrangements regarding pension ages in the draft Directive and the transitional period provided for the application of unisex actuarial factors in employee contributions in Dir 86/378.

In most cases, however, the Directives are silent on the issues of costs, and the main forum in which the debate has taken place has been the courts of the member states and the European Court of Justice. In the next section we turn to consider the approach taken by the court.

COSTS AND THE EUROPEAN COURT OF JUSTICE

Costs and the definition of the right

Altering the scope of the rule through the definition of the rights to be protected has immediate cost implications. If the rights are narrowly defined, then the requirement will have less impact simply because it applies in fewer situations, making fewer demands on the *status quo*. In discussing the definition of the right, we will be focusing on those situations where discrimination, either direct or indirect, exists, but is not held to fall within the legal

---

[41] Gewirtz, *Remedies and Resistance* (n 7 above), p 602.

provisions on equal treatment. This may be either because the exceptions in Directives are held to permit the discrimination, or because the scope of the right is inherently restricted. In these instances, narrow definition of the right will mean continuance of the *status quo*. Therefore, the incidence of costs of the discriminatory practice will not change. the costs will be incurred by the victim group. We will consider three aspects of the definition of the right: the issue of direct effect; the interpretation of the scope of the Directives and the exceptions which they contain; and the definition of indirect discrimination and objective justification.

In considering the incidence and nature of costs, above, a distinction was drawn between cases where the respondent was the employer and where it was the state in its capacity as welfare provider. The cases defining the scope and definition of rights indicate that the court adopts a slightly different approach in these two cases. The definition of 'pay' in Art 119 has been subject to a wide interpretation (see, for example, *Defrenne*,[42] *Bilka*,[43] *Barber*[44] etc), but the court has in the consideration of social security systems displayed a sensitivity for member state autonomy in the determination of social policy, and the judgments have been affected accordingly.

Direct effect and the scope of Art 119

Arguments have been put forward by respondents that the court should not recognise a provision, be it Art 119 of the Treaty or a Directive provision, as having direct effect because of the administrative and financial complexities of its implementation. Such an argument was explicitly rejected in *Defrenne* in relation to Art 119, and in *FNV*,[45] *McDermott and Cotter*[46] and *Borrie Clarke*[47] in relation to Art 4(1) of Dir 79/7. These followed the decision in *Becker*[48] where the court held that financial and administrative complexities which arose from the member states' failure to implement on time should be borne by the government, not passed onto individuals.[49] The court has thus been unwilling to hold that financial considerations should affect the issue of whether or not a provision has direct effect.

Respondents have also argued that the scope of Art 119 should be restricted on financial grounds. In *Burton*[50] the UK government argued that to apply Art 119 to voluntary redundancy schemes would discourage their provision by employers. Such schemes served a useful social and economic purpose in industries which would otherwise have to resort to compulsory

---

[42] Case 80/70 *Defrenne v Belgium* [1970] ECR 445.
[43] Case 170/84 *Bilka-Kaufhaus GmbH v Weber von Hartz* [1986] ECR 1607.
[44] Case 262/88 *Barber v Guardian Royal Exchange* [1990] ECR 1889.
[45] Case 71/85 *Netherlands v FNV* [1986] ECR 3855.
[46] Case 286/85 *McDermott and Cotter v Minister for Social Welfare* [1986] ECR 723.
[47] Case 384/85 *Borrie Clarke v Chief Adjudication Officer* [1987] ECR 2865.
[48] Case 8/81 *Becker v Bundesanstalt für Arbeit* [1982] ECR 53.
[49] *Ibid*, para 47.
[50] Case 19/81 *Burton v British Rail Engineering Board* [1982] ECR 555.

redundancies.[51] In *Newstead*[52] the UK government argued that financial difficulties regarding pension provision, for example, those arising from women's
longer life expectancy, meant that the issue must fall under Arts 118 and 117;
financial rules adopted in this area could not, it argued, be put in question by
a simple application of Art 119. While in both cases the court did in fact
hold that Art 119 did not apply, it made no reference to these arguments.
However, it is clear from the interpretation given to Art 119 in other cases,
and particularly from the *Barber*[53] judgment, that the court is not prepared
to hold that financial ramifications should inhibit its interpretation.

Interpretation of exceptions

We have noted above that the Directives take account of cost in an immediate and direct manner simply through creating exceptions to the general
principle. How has the court interpreted them, and to what extent has the
consideration of costs influenced that interpretation?

In determining rights, the court is engaged in balancing competing interests.
The proportionality principle requires the court to weigh the interest pursued
by the rule in question against the interest that rule infringes the principle of
equal treatment. The court has repeatedly emphasised that the principle of
equal treatment is a fundamental right, and so exceptions to it should be narrowly construed (see, for example, *Roberts*,[54] *Marshall*,[55] *Beets*,[56] *Jackson and
Cresswell*,[57] C-173/91 *Commission v Belgium*[58]). However, while a broad
interpretation has been given to the word 'pay' in Art 119 and the employment context (above) in the field of social security the court has not adopted
such an expansive approach in the interpretation of the scope of Dir 79/7.

The interpretations given to Dir 79/7 indicate that there must be a clear
economic/direct and effective link between the benefit and the protection
provided against one of the risks specified in Art 3(4) for it to fall within the
scope of the Directive (*Drake*,[59] *Smithson*[60]). The court will look to the substance rather than the form of the payment in order to prevent the Directive
falling foul of formalistic compliance by member states (*Drake, Smithson*),
emphasising the need to achieve harmonious implementation of the
Directive 'amid the tangle of national systems and rules'.[61]

---

51 The case was not decided on these grounds and the argument was not referred to. However,
    a similar 'social policy' justification has been argued in the UK to justify indirect discrimina-
    tion in the employment context: *R v Secretary of State for Employment, ex parte Equal
    Opportunities Commission* [1994] 2 WLR 409.
52 Case 192/85 *Newstead v Department of Transport* [1987] ECR 4753.
53 Case 262/88 *Barber v Guardian Royal Exchange* [1990] ECR 1889.
54 Case 151/84 *Roberts v Tate and Lyle* [1986] ECR 703.
55 Case 152/84 *Marshall v Southampton and SW Hants Area Health Authority* [1986] ECR 723.
56 Case 262/88 *Beets Proper v F van Lanschot Bankiers NV* [1986] ECT 706.
57 Cases 63/91 and 64/91 *Jackson and Cresswell v Chief Adjudication Officer* [1992] ECR I-4737.
58 Case 173/91 *Commission v Belgium* [1993] ECR I-563.
59 Case 150/85 *Drake v Chief Adjudication Officer* [1986] ECR 1995.
60 Case 243/90 *R v Secretary of State for Social Services, ex parte Smithson* [1992] ECR I-467.
61 Opinion of Advocate-General van Gerven in *Jackson and Cresswell*, para 14.

However, although this substantive approach means that the mode of payment is not the decisive test for whether there is a direct and effective link (*Smithson*), for example, that benefits paid to a third party arising out of one of the risks in Art 3(1) are covered by the Directive (*Drake*), in its interpretation of the scope of the Directive the court has not adopted a fully purposive approach to the interpretation of the provision. It has emphasised that benefits which are designed to provide income for those with insufficient means to meet their needs do not fall within the scope of the Directive. In adopting this interpretation the court has rejected the purposive approach to Art 3(1) suggested by Advocate-General van Gerven in his Opinion in *Jackson and Cresswell*.[62] The court held that minimum subsistence benefits do not fall within Dir 79/7 whether a person is suffering from an Art 3(1) risk or not,. as the level of benefit was determined by an assessment of needs which took no account of the existence of those risks.[63] The fact that the method of calculation of those benefits may affect sole mothers' ability to take up access to employment or training was not sufficient to bring it within the scope of the Directive.

The court thus did not adopt the test of practical effect suggested by Advocate-General van Gerven, but that of legislative intent, proposed by the UK government. The intention of the benefit was to provide income for those with sufficient means to meet their needs; this was the significant factor, not the impact of the methods of calculating those benefits. This approach confirmed that taken in *Smithson* where the court adopted a similar restrictive approach, stating that the fact that the existence of a risk covered in Art 3(1) is taken into account in determining the amount of a benefit whose purpose is to protect against poverty is not a sufficiently direct link to bring that benefit within Dir 79/7.

The issue of costs was not argued in either *Jackson and Cresswell* or *Smithson*, although there would clearly have been financial implications of a judgment that such benefits did fall within the Directives. However, recent cases which involve what are seen as more serious financial implications for the state have indicated the significant role which can be played by considerations of cost in the definitions of the exceptions. Several recent cases have involved the interpretation of the scope of Art 7(1)(*a*) of Dir 79/7. Here the purpose of the exceptions has been interpreted as prevailing over the overall aim of the Directive, which is progressively to implement equality.

In *R v Secretary of State for Social Services, ex parte Equal Opportunities Commission*,[64] a social security system in which men paid contributions for longer than women but received the same pension was held to fall within the exception on the grounds that to hold otherwise 'would disrupt the complex

---

[62] Cases 63/91 and 64/91 *Jackson and Cresswell v Chief Adjudication Officer* [1992] ECR I-4737. The Advocate-General suggested that although subsistence benefits were not expressly covered by the article, its aim was ultimately to protect against loss of income or poverty and so these benefits should fall within it: Opinion, para 16.

[63] *Jackson and Cresswell*, para 20.

[64] Case 9/91, [1992] ECR I-4297.

financial equilibrium of those systems, the importance of which could not be ignored'.[65] The court held that the exception was provided to enable member states progressively to adapt their pensions system to avoid the severe financial and regulatory consequences which would otherwise result, subject to the requirements in Arts 7(2) and 8(2) of the Directive. Interpreting Art 7(2) to require a measure which would upset the financial equilibrium of pension schemes would render the provision of the exception nugatory.[66] In his Opinion Advocate-General van Gerven suggested that the proportionality principle played a smaller role than usual because the procedures laid down by these provisions for the balancing of interests meant that it was not for the court to undertake that process itself. The court can only do so exceptionally, for example, where the procedure laid down was not taken seriously by the member state, or where discrimination may be eliminated without excessive legislative or financial difficulties. However, the court stressed that discrimination should be allowed only if it was necessary in order to achieve the objectives which the Directive is intended to pursue by allowing member states to retain a different pension age for men and women.

The court has emphasised in a series of subsequent cases that Art 7(1) of Dir 79/7 only allows such forms of discrimination as are *necessarily and objectively linked* to differences in age for the purposes of granting old age and retirement pensions. In *Thomas*,[67] discrimination was held to be justified by the provision only if it was 'objectively necessary in order to avoid disrupting the complex financial equilibrium of the social security system or to ensure consistency between retirement pension schemes and other benefit schemes'.[68] The court distinguished between contributory benefits (at issue in *ex parte EOC*) and non-contributory benefits (the subject of *Thomas*). It held that the granting of non-contributory benefits at certain ages had no direct influence on the financial equilibrium of contributory pension schemes, and discrimination between men and women on non-contributory schemes was not necessary to preserve the financial equilibrium of the entire social security system. It should be noted that in contrast to *ex parte EOC* the issue of costs was not raised by either side, merely that of administrative convenience.

A similar stress on a necessary and causal link between the difference in retirement ages and the provision of calculation of benefits was emphasised in *Remi van Cant*.[69] Belgium had equalised its pension age, but retained differences in the calculation of the benefit for men and women. The judgment

---

[65] Para 15.
[66] Paras 16–18.
[67] Case 328/91 *Secretary of State for Social Security v Thomas* [1993] ECR I-1247.
[68] *Ibid*, para 12.
[69] Case 154/92 *Remi van Cant v Rijksdeinst voor pensioenen*, [1993] ECR I-3811. See also the Opinion of Advocate-General Jacobs, C-173/91, 2 December 1992 (the court held that the benefit in question fell under Art 119, so arguments as to Dir 79/7 were not ultimately relevant to the decision).

simply stated that Art 7(1) could not be used to justify such a difference. In his Opinion Advocate-General Darmon argued that the necessary link between the difference in retirement age and difference in benefit had disappeared. Moreover, the arguments that the discriminatory system was necessary for the financial equilibrium of the social security system were relevant only to the fundamental requirements which justified the existence of different retirement ages. Once the ages had been equalised, these ceased to be relevant.[70]

Thus Art 7(1) of Dir 79/7 has been held to justify benefits which discriminate on the basis of retirement age if they are necessary to maintain the financial equilibrium of a member state's social security system, but the courts have been wary of construing this link in a general manner. The decision in *van Cant*, particularly, will clearly have implications for transitional provisions that member states introduce for the implementation of equal pension ages. In relation to the scope of the Directive, the court has stated in effect that it is the intention of the member state legislature rather than the impact of the benefit which is important. Although the cases of *Jackson and Cresswell* and *Smithson* had financial implications for both parties, it is notable that neither side put forward arguments based on cost.

INDIRECT DISCRIMINATION AND 'OBJECTIVE JUSTIFICATION'

General principles

Indirect discrimination arises where a policy or practice, not on its face discriminatory, in practice adversely affects more women then men (or *vice versa*), unless the policy or practice is objectively justifiable.[71] Although the determination of indirect discrimination and the scope of the objective justification is for the national courts, interpretation of their meaning has arisen in a number of cases. Indirect discrimination has been held to include different benefits paid to part-time workers,[72] and the court has recently also held that where two posts are of equal value, and where there is a substantial pay differential between them and one is staffed primarily by women and the other by men, there is *prima facie* discrimination.[73] As developed in *Bilka*[74] objective justification has two elements:

---

[70] Opinion of Advocate-General Darmon, C-154/92, *Remi van Cant* [1993] ECR I-38114.
[71] Case 96/80 *Jenkins v Kingsgate (Clothing Productions) Ltd* [1981] ECR 911; Case 170/84 *Bilka-Kaufhaus GmbH v Weber von Hartz* [1986] ECR 1607.
[72] See *Jenkins* (hourly wages); *Bilka* (occupational pension schemes); Case 171/88 *Rinner-Kühn* [1989] ECR 2743 (statutory sick pay benefits); Case 33/89 *Kowalska* [1990] ECR I-2591 (collectively agreed severance pay); Case 184/89 *Nimz* [1991] ECR I-297 (access to pay increments).
[73] Case 127/92 *Enderby v Frenchay Health Authority* [1994] ICR 112.
[74] Case 170/84 *Bilka-Kaufhaus GmbH v Weber von Hartz* [1986] ECR 1607.

(a) the objective to be achieved by the practice must be legitimate, corresponding to a genuine need on the part of the respondent, and sufficiently important to take precedence over the principle of equal treatment; and

(b) the means must be suitable and necessary for attaining that purpose.

It is through the determination of what may be a legitimate objective and the assessment of 'necessary and appropriate means' that the court has limited the application of the right, and considerations of cost have come into play. The court has stated that financial considerations can influence the interpretation of 'objective justification'. An employer's economic objectives can be legitimate, as *Bilka* indicated, and may include different criteria such as the worker's flexibility or adaptability to hours and places of work, training or length of service (*Danfoss*[75]) as long as there can be attributed to the particular needs and objectives of the undertaking. The court held further in *Enderby*[76] that awarding different rates of pay for different but comparable jobs could be justified if the state of the employment market was such that this was necessary in order to attract candidates, although the national courts had to determine precisely what proportion of the increase is attributable to market forces.[77]

Indirect discrimination in social security

The court has held that social security systems can be indirectly discriminatory.[78] It has not adopted the suggestion proffered by Advocate-General Darmon in both *Rinner-Kühn*[79] and *Ruzius-Wilbrink*[80] that a distinction should be drawn between legislative provisions and private employment contracts. Whereas a presumption of indirect discrimination should be raised in the latter, the Advocate-General argued, it should not in the former. The legislature, 'as trustee of the public interest must take account of a large number of social, economic and political factors, of which the ratio of men and women is just one aspect'. It should not be presumed to be guilty of discriminatory conduct. The ECJ has not adopted such a restrictive approach, and as noted above, has indicated that social security legislation may be *prima facie* indirectly discriminatory.

In the field of social security it has become clear, however, that social policy objectives of member states can provide objective justification for a discriminatory practice. The issue of 'objective justification' illustrates the somewhat different situation of the court *vis-à-vis* employers (whether state or private sector) and member states acting as welfare providers. In the case of employers, the court has required a 'genuine need', and action which is necessary and suitable to meet that need. In the case of social security, the

---

[75] Case 109/88 *Danfoss* [1989] ECR 3199.
[76] Case 127/92 *Enderby v Frenchay Health Authority* [1994] ICR 112.
[77] Paras 26 and 27.
[78] See Chapter 5 McCrudden *Equality of Treatment between Women and Men in Social Security*.
[79] Case 171/88 *Rinner Kühn v FWW Spezial Gebaudereinigung GmbH* [1989] ECR 2743.
[80] Case C-102/88 *Ruzius-Wilbrink* [1989] ECR 4311.

court has shown a sensitivity to member states' autonomy to determine its social policy. Although generalisations will not suffice as justifications (*Rinner-Kühn*) and a stated objective has been rejected on the grounds that it is not consistently pursued (*Ruzius-Wilbrink*), measures which are indirectly discriminatory are justified where they are necessary to achieve 'one of the essential aims of its social policy' (*Rinner-Kühn*, C-229/89 *Commission v Belgium*,[81] *Molenbroek*[82]).

In *Teuling*[83] it was held that the social objective of providing minimum subsistence carried greater weight than that of equal treatment in the case of social security benefits. Rules determining the amount of benefits on the grounds of marital and family status were held to be *prima facie* indirectly discriminatory, but were justified on the basis that they were necessary to ensure adequate minimum subsistence by compensating those with dependants for the greater burdens which they bore in comparison with single persons. In its judgment the court displayed a sensitivity to the autonomy of member states to determine their own social policy within the confines of their resources. The court emphasised that such a guarantee of minimum subsistence income was an integral part of the social policy of member states. Community law did not prevent a member state controlling its social expenditure by having regard to available resources. In this context, taking account of the differing burdens of those with dependants was justifiable.

Costs have figured prominently in arguments of member state governments to justify the indirectly discriminatory effects of social security provisions. In C-229/89 *Commission v Belgium* preferential treatment in social security benefit was given to those with dependants. The Belgian government argued that this was designed to provide to each individual an income for a limited period, within the limits necessarily set by budgetary resources. Those limits meant that benefits had to take into account the income of the spouse or partner of the unemployed. Any change would be to the detriment of those with dependants and single persons and would thus be a retrograde measure in the social field. The court held, taking these arguments into account, that the principles and objectives of the benefit formed an integral part of social policy which it was a matter for the member state to determine. Member states could take into account the greater needs of those with dependants.[84] The court held that the system corresponded to 'a legitimate objective of social policy [of member states] involving increases suitable and requisite for attaining that aim and therefore justified by reasons unrelated to discrimination on the grounds of sex'.[85]

In *Molenbroek*, the court was asked whether a pension benefit which was calculated by taking into account the income earned by a spouse of non-

[81] Case 229/91 *Commission v Belgium* [1991] ECR 2205.
[82] Case 226/91 *Molenbroek v Bestuur van de Sociale Verzekeringsbank* [1992] ECR I-5943.
[83] Case 30/85 *Teuling v Bedrijfsvereniging voor Chemische Industrie* [1987] ECR 2497.
[84] Paras 20–25.
[85] Para 26.

pension age was indirectly discriminatory, or whether it could be justified given that its purpose was not to provide a minimum subsistence level. The court held that such a system was *prima facie* indirectly discriminatory, but that following C-229/89 *Commission v Belgium*, it was objectively justified if the means chosen corresponded to a legitimate aim of social policy and was that which was apt and necessary to achieve the aim sought. The court stressed the universal nature of the benefit, and the fact that it was designed to provide a minimum level of income, even if in some cases it was not necessary to achieve that minimum level in fact.

In the above cases, the arguments have centred on the impact on other aspects of social policy of holding the social security provision to be indirectly discriminatory. Costs have been raised as an integral part of this argument, particularly in the context of a potential 'levelling down' which might result through financial constraints. However, in a more recent case the financial implications of holding a provision to be indirectly discriminatory were specifically raised. In C-343/92 *Roks*, the Raad van Beroep, Netherlands, asked (*inter alia*) three related questions. First, whether indirectly discriminatory provisions of social security law can be objectively justified by budgetary considerations. Secondly, is this the case where the cost of setting aside the measures leads to socially unacceptable consequences for the national security budget and/or the financing of social security? Thirdly, is recurring expenditure of Fl 85m (£240m, ECU 183m) per annum combined with a one off cost of Fl 100m (£280m, ECU 215m)[86] to be regarded as an unacceptable consequence of this kind? The Court of Justice[87] accepted that budgetary considerations may influence a member state's choice of social policy, and affect the nature or scope of the measures of social protection it wishes to adopt. However, budgetary considerations 'cannot themselves constitute the aim pursued by that policy'[88] and cannot, therefore, justify indirect discrimination. To allow this 'would be to accept that the application and scope of as fundamental a rule of Community law as that of equal treatment between men and women might vary in time and place according to the state of the public finances of the member states'.[89]

On the whole, it seems fair to conclude that in relation to indirect discrimination in the social security context the court is sensitive to the fact that significant issues of member state policies as to social security are being called into question. Because of this, both issues of cost, but primarily questions of appropriateness of court interference, influence its determination of 'objective justification'.

---

[86] Approximate figures at exchange rates as at 27.11.93.
[87] *Sub nom* Case C-343/92, *MA De Weerd, née Roks, and others v Bestuur van de Bedrijfsvereniging voor de Gezondheid, Geestelijke en Maatschappelijke Belangen and others* [1994] ECR I-571.
[88] *Roks*, para 35.
[89] *Roks*, para 36.

COSTS AND THE PROVISION OF THE REMEDY

The second area in which the court may take costs into account, as discussed above, is in the definition of the remedy. Here also there are limits on the ECJ's competence: it cannot prescribe the remedy which employer or state should adopt, it can only stipulate that such a remedy be non-discriminatory. The issue is thus linked to that of implementation, both of which are fully discussed elsewhere.[90]

CONCLUSION

The problems of the judicial assessment of cost and benefits when it takes an interest balancing approach are, however, considerable, and inevitably rough justice can result. The blame must lie with the Council which left the issues open. The court is in a very difficult position in this context. The lack of information on costs in terms of either academic research (save in the limited area of state pension age or occupational pensions), published statistics of member state governments or Commission research, increases the difficulty of the court in taking costs into account. There is, for example, no *fiche d'impact* (impact statement) for any of the Directives, including the draft Directive. Further, court decisions are either all or nothing, and unless it is provided for in legislation either by national governments or the Council, it is very difficult for the court to provide for progressive implementation of its decisions, which can minimise the frustration to expectations and reduce the impact of costs by spreading them over time.[91] It is not surprising that the court has adopted an interest balancing approach in defining remedies. Indeed, in some ways it is more desirable from the point of view of those supporting the right that costs should be taken into account in the cost of remedies rather than in the definition of the right. At least then the full right is preserved 'as an aspiration that may be vindicated in other ways or places'.[92]

A difficulty, with adopting an interest balancing approach such as the ECJ has done has, however, been put in another context by Gewirtz:

> 'Politically, rejecting rights maximising may lead the courts to approve a general conception of interest balancing that undervalues the importance of vindicating rights, or may open the way for judges hostile to the right to dilute its force by excessively diluting the remedy in particular cases; psychologically, judges may systematically undervalue individual rights if allowed to balance them against broad social interests. Therefore, even if one believes that interest balancing is the

---

[90] See McCrudden ed (*op cit*) at p 169 *et seq*.

[91] See the comments made in relation to the equalisation of state and occupational pensions ages, above. For an example of where the court has heeded the Directive's exceptions on the ground of the need for progressive implementation, see C-9/91 *R v Secretary of State for Social Services, ex parte EOC* [1992] ECR I-4297.

[92] Gewirtz *Remedies and Resistance* (see n 7 above), p 606.

best approach in theory, concern about possible abuses in its application might lead to renunciation of the approach altogether. It may be better to insist upon rights maximising, even if it sometimes will lead to inappropriately sweeping remedies, since the greater danger is that legitimating any form of interest balancing will lead to inappropriately narrow remedies'.

MADAM BUTTERFLY AND MISS SAIGON: REFLECTIONS ON GENUINE OCCUPATIONAL QUALIFICATIONS

Gwyneth Pitt

OVERTURE

Discrimination law in the United Kingdom is based on a notion of formal equality that expresses itself in the general principle that all discrimination on grounds of sex and race is wrong. Discrimination against men is treated as equivalent to discrimination against women and discrimination against white people as bad as discrimination against members of ethnic minorities. Indeed, this is spelt out in s 2 of the Sex Discrimination Act (SDA) which states:

'the provisions . . . relating to sex discrimination against women are to be read as applying equally to the treatment of men'.

It is notable that two of the most important decisions on English and European sex discrimination law, *James v Eastleigh BC*[1] and *Barber v Guardian Royal Exchange*[2] were actually victories for men, the latter resulting in a situation where many women have ended up having to work for more years in order to qualify for occupational or state pensions.

The point has frequently been made that formal equality is inappropriate because it focuses on difference rather than the disadvantaged position associated with differences, and thus fails to address many of the problems resulting from difference.[3] While direct discrimination and victimisation are defined as less favourable treatment on grounds of sex or race, and indirect discrimination in terms of detriment, the thrust of the legislation is to suggest that any use of sex or race as a criterion is flawed: decisions should be colour-blind and gender-blind. It follows that exceptions are regarded as aberrations requiring special overriding reasons, permissible only in the most limited and strictly controlled circumstances. According to the philosophy behind the legislation, ideally exceptions should not be necessary at all.

---

[1] [1990] 2 AC 751 (HL).
[2] [1990] ICR 616 (ECJ).
[3] See, for example, Hepple, 'Has twenty-five years of the Race Relations Act in Britain been a failure?' and Lacey, 'From individual to group?' in eds Hepple and Szyszczak, *Discrimination: the Limits of Law*, (Mansell, London, 1992) Chapters 2 and 7.

This chapter contains some themes, as yet not fully orchestrated, reflecting on one of the exceptions permitted by British legislation in relation both to sex and race discrimination; namely, the 'genuine occupational qualification' in both Acts relating to *authenticity*, where the nature of the job calls for a woman or a man or a person of a particular race in dramatic performances 'for reasons of authenticity'.[4] This may seem a little esoteric, but it will be argued that reflecting on the issues in a theatrical context can actually be rewarding in considering the elimination of discrimination in general.

ACT I – MISS SAIGON

Cameron Mackintosh, producer of the musical, *Miss Saigon*, decided in July 1990 to transfer it to Broadway with the original London stars. This provoked the disapproval of American Equity. The actors' trade union was not on this occasion making its usual complaint that the actors in the British version were not sufficiently famous to justify using them rather than Americans; rather it objected to the fact that the star part of the Engineer, a Eurasian pimp, would be taken by a white Welshman, Jonathan Pryce.

American Equity banned Pryce from appearing. Mackintosh responded by cancelling the show (which had already taken $14m in advance ticket sales). It was argued that by its stance the union was denying 34 Asian-American actors who had been cast in other roles their chance of work and recognition. It was argued that by casting Asian-Americans in the minor roles (and advertising expressly for Orientals to replace other minor roles in the British version) the producer was guilty of applying double standards. It was argued that Mackintosh had tried and failed to find an Asian actor who had the requisite ability and charisma for the part of the Engineer, and that his general good faith was indicated by the fact that he had cast a black actor in the lead role (as a European aristocrat) in another musical, *The Phantom of the Opera*.

Within a few weeks, American Equity backed down and the show was rescheduled. In December 1990 it was reported that Cameron Mackintosh was financing the British Chinese Theatre, a company which aimed 'to reinterpret the classics of the English stage with oriental casts'. In April 1991 *Miss Saigon* opened on Broadway to critical acclaim and in June 1991 Jonathan Pryce and Lea Salonga (who played the eponymous heroine of *Miss Saigon*) won the Tony awards for Best Actor and Best Actress

---

[4] RRA 1976 s 5(2)(a): 'the job involves participation in a dramatic performance or other entertainment in a capacity for which a person of that racial group is required for reasons of authenticity'.

SOA 1975 s 7(2)(a): 'the essential nature of the job calls for a man for reasons of physiology (excluding strength or stamina) or, in a dramatic performance or other entertainment, for reasons of authenticity, so that the essential nature of the act would be materially different if carried out by a woman'.

in a musical. A happy ending for a story about a show with an unhappy ending.

Is it a case of double standards to insist on ethnic Asians in the minor roles and yet cast a white man as the star? Apparently it was possible to discover an Asian actress good enough to star as Miss Saigon: Lea Salonga, a Filipina, (who was unknown before this success). If the interests of authenticity required the casting of actors of the same racial group as the characters they were playing in the minor parts, why did it not extend to the starring role of the Engineer? (This character was originally meant to be Asian, but was changed to Eurasian to help accommodate Jonathan Pryce.) If racial authenticity was not required, how did the unknown Lea Salonga manage to displace the numerous white singing actresses who have starred in all the other hit musicals of the 1980s?

It is a curious fact that when there are discussions of the meaning of the authenticity exception, taking the part of Hamlet or Ophelia or Antony or Cleopatra – acting – is usually given as the explanatory example. Yet in reality, it is a very inconsistent one. No thought of racial authenticity has ever disturbed a producer of *Antony and Cleopatra* or *The Royal Hunt of the Sun*, and most of all, the role of Othello is still seen as one of the major peaks for white classical actors to scale. While it has been argued from time to time that a black actor should be cast, it has never become as serious an issue in the United Kingdom as it has in the United States.

There are probably two issues underlying the objections of Asian actors to Jonathan Pryce as the Engineer and of black actors to whites playing Othello. The main one is the lack of fair shares; that they are denied opportunities to appear because of conscious or unconscious discrimination. Where conscious, this discrimination is frequently claimed to be justified on grounds of authenticity. The other objection is the lack of taste shown in making up a white actor to appear as a member of another race, particularly when that is done by trying to reproduce or, arguably, caricaturing, characteristics which are associated with their denigration as a race by other groups (eg, taping the eyelids, emphasising the lips). It was for such reasons that as long ago as the 1960s British Equity set its face against entertainments like *The Black and White Minstrels*.

The problem with trying to reserve Othello or the Engineer for minority actors is that overall it would reduce opportunities for non-white actors – who by the same token could be excluded from King Lear, Ophelia and Rosalind. There could also be difficult and ultimately absurd arguments over how far authenticity should go: should only Jewish actors play Shylock, an actor with the appropriate physical disability play Richard III, heterosexual actors for Romeo and Juliet?

Societal casting

The 'fair shares' complaint could be answered to some extent by what the

Americans call 'societal casting',[5] ie where a role is such that it really does not matter what the race or sex of the actor is, black actors or women may be cast in the role without, in any sense, altering the meaning for the audience.

The trouble is that this policy has been followed only to a very limited extent in the United Kingdom – and usually only in situations where it would be normal to see a woman or a black or Asian person in real life (ie where it is 'authentic'). So you *do* get black or Asian actors in working class soaps or as nurses in hospital series, but not, for example, black judges, solicitors, airline pilots or architects.[6] In 1968, what was then called the Coloured Artists' Advisory Committee stated in its report to Equity:

> 'In practical terms, as things are at the moment, the chances of a coloured artist being considered for a part of, say, a bank manager or chartered accountant in a play with no racial connotations and simply on the basis of his ability to play the role, are even more remote than the chances of a suitably qualified coloured person gaining employment as either a bank manager or a chartered accountant.'[7]

The position has not changed in more than 25 years. Not only does this result in a reduction of opportunities for actors from ethnic minorities in particular (although women actors over 40 may have similar problems), it also has a tendency to reinforce negative stereotypes of blacks and Asians as people on the lowest rungs of society.

This can be contrasted with the United States, where societal casting is deployed more frequently. Devotees of *LA Law* may well have formed the opinion that there are lots of black judges, lots of women judges, even a fair number of black women judges in California. However, according to an article a few years ago in a Yale Law Journal symposium[8] on how law is portrayed on television, this is actually not the case and Californian courts are as dominated by white males as are the courts in most other places.

However, even if societal casting were used on a wide scale in the United Kingdom, the impact would still be very limited because almost by definition, the situations where the sex or race of an actor does not matter are seen as confined to minor roles. The main parts are for whites, unless a special point is being made. There is no particular reason why this should be so. Take, for example, the popular Inspector Morse. He could as well be played by a black actor as by a white. Admittedly, he is based on a literary character, but from a series of books which are not, it is suggested, of such classical literary status that tampering with the character should be seen as literary *lese-majesté*. It may be objected that there are barely any black inspectors in England, let alone in the Thames Valley police – to which it may be replied that the Thames Valley force does not actually have on its

---

5 See Benedict Nightingale, 'Casting couched in a colour code', *The Times Saturday Review*, (1991) 18 May.
6 The part of Usha, a British-Asian solicitor in *The Archers*, a radio serial taken by a British-Asian actress: authenticity or fair shares?
7 Equity Annual Report 1967–68, *What Equity is Doing*, Appendix B.
8 S Gillers 'Taking *LA Law* more seriously', (1989) 98 Yale LJ 1607.

strength many Wagner-loving, real beer bores who are super-sensitive about their first name and knock off *The Times* crossword in under half an hour.

Cross-cultural casting

Minority actors can get the starring roles if they put on a cross-cultural production where all the roles are cast from among the same minority: this is apparently what the British Chinese Theatre Company, referred to above, has been set up for. Similarly, in 1991 there was an all-black performance of *The Importance of Being Ernest*. This differs from all-black productions like *Carmen Jones* or *Five Guys Named Moe*,[9] because it takes a play which is normally cast with white actors and casts actors of a different race instead.

This would seem to be a legitimate way of expanding opportunities for minority actors, provided that it can be satisfactorily distinguished from, and therefore not legitimise, all-white productions. It can help to deal with the problem that black actors may have less experience than white counterparts and thus lack the opportunity to develop to a level where they can confidently handle leading parts on the rare occasions when they may actually be available (as with the Engineer). However, such productions are difficult to mount in the commercial theatre, because they are perceived as unlikely to appeal to white audiences and thus cannot attract backing. This can result in the marginalisation of the production and those involved with it.

Integrated or colour-blind casting

The Coloured Artists' Advisory Committee sought to persuade Equity to adopt the policy of integrated casting in 1967, when they defined it as, 'simply the casting of actors on the basis of their individual ability as actors and regardless of their racial origin, or the colour of their skins'. Equity adopted a policy of integrated casting in 1983. It supports:

- the casting of artists in productions (dance/drama etc) so that the cast/ensemble, in its entirety, is multiracial in composition;
- the casting of performers ... on the basis of their individual abilities as performers regardless of their racial origins;
- the range and type of work [should be] in no way restricted, or bounded by stereotypical traditions and conventions;
- the establishment and practice of an equal opportunity programme in every aspect of the entertainment industry;
- the casting of artists in productions that exceeds tokenism.[10]

The policy was accepted by the Royal Shakespeare Company as long ago as 1968, which means, for example, that in Shakespeare's history plays there

[9] Both of which have been described by one critic as 'minstrel shows' on the ground that it is still essentially provision of entertainment by blacks for white audiences: this is another problem, but a different one from the one under discussion here.
[10] Equity's Policy Statement on Integrated Casting.

may be a black Duke of Bedford or Earl of Salisbury; that a black actress may play Cordelia to a white Lear and so on. Audiences may sometimes object but, the argument goes, audiences have to suspend their disbelief all the time: acting is about pretending to be someone else and audiences have to enter into it.[11] We are all used to 'imagining' sets in minimalist productions – why should this suspension of belief not go one step further? On this basis Josette Simon, who is black, performed to great acclaim as the Marilyn Monroe figure in Arthur Miller's *After the Fall* in 1990 and Hugh Quarshie has played leading roles with the RSC, including Hotspur and Tybalt.

Integrated casting should be distinguished from 'conceptual casting', which is not random. Rather, a role is cast across race in order to make a point – to indicate separateness or difference or to show a new perspective (for example, Frances de la Tour as a female Hamlet; the National Theatre's 1960s all-male production of *As You Like It* and most recently, Fiona Shaw as Richard II at the National Theatre in summer 1995).

The argument for integrated casting appears sound; but as a policy it is subject to a major flaw: that it is entirely dependent on the goodwill of the producer or director, who in the end will make the decision as to whether a role should be cast across race. A *Times* leader at the time of the *Miss Saigon* furore contended that while a director would obviously prefer to cast someone who approximated physically in age and appearance to the character she will be asked to play, an actor of outstanding ability (and with good make-up!) could overcome her physical unsuitability and be completely convincing:[12] that is ethnic authenticity is to be preferred, but as a factor, not a requirement for the part. Jonathan Pryce was taken so to have overcome his physical unsuitability.

Put in this way, the problem is set in relief. It means, of course, that for the majority of roles, black actors will have to be outstandingly good and much better than their white counterparts to get a look in. And it is more likely in practice that white actors will be regarded as able to overcome their physical unsuitability for a part like the Engineer. The reason given at the time was that there was no sufficiently good Asian actor in the United Kingdom or the United States; but, as noted already, in the absence of opportunities to develop, this would not be surprising, if it was indeed the case (a theme to be taken up again in Act II).

It seems probable that integrated casting is most likely to be a reality only where there is a standing company of actors from whom all productions are cast, as is broadly the case with the RSC. Where there are open competitions for a number of places, in any field, women and minorities are far more likely to get a share. Once established within the company, they can hardly be given nothing to do, and as they have the chance to demonstrate

---

[11] '. . . can this cockpit hold the vasty fields of France? Or may we cram within this wooden O the very casques that did afright the air at Agincourt?' (from the Prologue, *King Henry the Fifth*).

[12] *The Times*, (1990) 4 September.

their abilities, the more likely they are to get parts commensurate with them.

ACT II – MADAM BUTTERFLY

This brings us to Act II: Madam Butterfly, which contains just two short scenes.

The first makes the point that when you turn from straight theatre to the world of opera and ballet, insistence on authenticity dissolves almost entirely. Of course, when it comes to opera or ballet, the skills needed are in much shorter supply than in the non-musical theatre. Thus, it is much more the case that talented individuals will be cast in starring roles regardless of authenticity.[13] There are black stars in opera, such as Willard White, Kathleen Battle, Grace Bumbry, Jessye Norman, who have no equivalent in straight theatre. What this suggests is that if opera and ballet audiences can suspend their disbelief, there should be no greater difficulty for theatre audiences. The authenticity argument is, therefore, unconvincing.

The second relates to the argument noted in Act I that there was no Asian actor good enough to be the Engineer. It is an argument which is used all the time in relation to women as well (who has not heard how an organisation would love to have more women, but that women simply do not apply for the posts, or that the problem is in the prior training at school or university because there are just not enough women at that stage?) These regrets are frequently coupled with the pious hope that things will soon change, as there are now more women training in the lower ranks. This line of conversation is sometimes heard in relation to law, although the author and her contemporaries will recollect that nearly a half of law graduates were women over 20 years ago.

The point is merely this – it is remarkable how such difficulties disappear when a job can only be done by a woman – for example, a leading soprano role. Consider the life of an opera singer: the unsociable hours, the travelling, the care for diet and surroundings, the long build to a career, the training and rehearsals. One could hardly think of anything less suitable for anyone who wished to have a permanent relationship and a family – yet there is no shortage of suitable women at all levels in opera. Could it be that obstacles are found not to be insurmountable once it is accepted that a job can only be done by a woman? And perhaps if it were ruled that the part of the Engineer could only be taken by an Asian actor, or Othello only by a black actor, such difficulties would also be seen to disappear. Recollect that it was possible to find a suitable Asian actress for the role of Miss Saigon; could this be because the work would have had no credibility if both major

---

[13] This is perhaps truer of opera than of ballet. While there are several black and Asian dancers in most ballet companies, including the Birmingham Royal Ballet, a notable exception has been the Royal Ballet.

roles had been taken by white actors, so one had to be cast authentically? And if it could be done for one, why not for two?

It comes back to the question of how far employers can be expected to put themselves out to give equal opportunities: if they are compelled to do things, difficulties often turn out to be not insuperable after all. An analogy could be drawn in relation to maternity rights, where Susan McRae's study for PSI found that although many employers anticipated that it would be very difficult for them if they had to accommodate women on maternity leave, those employers who actually had experience of women on maternity leave had not in fact found it a problem.[14] Consider too the way university departments who have had problems in recruiting students with 'A' levels in the right subjects (for example, German, Engineering, Classics) have not closed down for lack of suitably qualified candidates; rather, they have discovered that it is possible to take people without these erstwhile 'essentials' and bring them to the requisite level in the end.

FINALE

So what, by way of a finale, are we to conclude from this? First of all, a lawyer may be chastened to observe the almost total irrelevance of sex and race discrimination law in this area. The authenticity exceptions in the Sex Discrimination Act and Race Relations Act seem to have had no impact on the debate about the position of minority actors within British Actors' Equity, nor to have any potential to assist the position of black or Asian actors. The initiative within Equity was in 1967–68 and was prompted by a dispute over the employment of non-British black actors rather than the Race Relations Acts 1965–68. Subsequent developments bear little relation to legislative movement. In recent years, much of the focus in Equity literature has been on the position of actors with disabilities, again well ahead of any legislative protection. The irrelevance of the authenticity exceptions must raise questions as to their continuance.

Secondly, it seems that the experience of minority actors, and in a similar way, women, indicates the hollowness of some of the explanations for their invisibility. If societal casting were adopted as a strong policy, there would be greater expansion of opportunity and, more importantly, the high visibility of the acting profession would mean that it could play a powerful role in helping to *include* under-represented groups into mainstream society.

Indeed, 'societal casting' ought, in this writer's view, to be more generally permissible and adopted by employers in order to ensure a balanced workforce and to give credence to their claims to be equal opportunities employers. Where employing institutions purport to be serving the whole community, a clear indication of this can be given by employing people from the whole community. This, it seems to me, would have been a better

14 S McRae, *Maternity Rights in Britain*, (1991) Policy Studies Institute.

justification than the 'personal welfare' exception for wanting to designate the post of housing manager for someone of Asian or Afro-Caribbean origin in *Lambeth v CRE*.[15]

This does, of course, presuppose an asymmetrical model of discrimination – a distinction between 'good' and 'bad' discrimination, Such a distinction can be made, however, according to whether it is designed to be *inclusive* or *exclusive*. Contrary to existing law, this requires a consideration of motive;[16] but this, it is submitted, is not a fatal flaw; furthermore, such a policy would not violate the right of each individual to be treated with equal respect and concern.[17]

[15] [1989] ICR 641 (EAT).
[16] See, for further discussion, Bob Watt in Chapter 12 above.
[17] This argument is developed in more detail in Pitt, 'Can reverse discrimination be justified?' in eds Hepple and Szyszczak, *Discrimination: the Limits of Law*, (Mansell, London, 1992) Chapter 16.

16

GENDER DISCRIMINATION IN THE POLICE SERVICE[1]

Catherine Little

INTRODUCTION

Difficulties and tensions inevitably arise in the translation of the law into policy and practice. This chapter will illustrate explicitly the tensions between the following by examining the nature of gender discrimination in the police service:

(a) the legal discourse on discrimination and equal opportunities, of which the technicalities of the law are a part;

(b) the institutional discourse, that is, how the law is interpreted and formulated into policy by the organisation, and;

(c) the personal/experiential discourse, which relates to the individual's experience of discrimination in the work environment.

In order to understand the nature of gender discrimination in the police service, it is essential to examine the relationship between the structure of the organisation; the nature of the working culture within it; and the experiences at the individual level.

There are limitations to what anti-discrimination legislation can achieve. Such legislation could only ever create a slow change in the attitudes of individuals. What it was devised to achieve was certain 'rights' for individuals who suffered discrimination. The Sex Discrimination Act 1975 created legal recourse to those who had been discriminated against, according to their sex and marital status. The Act covers discrimination in the field of employment; education; and the provision of goods and services. It was intended to create 'equality of opportunity'. Certainly, in many areas of employment, the position of women has improved considerably. However, one area where this has remained problematic is in the police service. This chapter will address some of the reasons for this.

Furthermore, it will discuss gender discrimination in the police service in the context of the debate between 'equality of opportunity' and 'equality of outcome' (O'Donovan and Szyszczak, 1988).[2] The reason for this is that the

---

[1] This paper is based on the police service in England and Wales only.

[2] K O'Donovan and E Szyszczak *Equality and Sex Discrimination Law* (Basil Blackwell, 1988).

police service and the Home Office have consistently made the connection between equal opportunity policy and the quality of service to members of the public. It will be argued in this chapter, that if the police service are to achieve the aim of improving the quality of service, by addressing the problems of discrimination internal to the police organisation, then there needs to be a completely different approach than the present one. Furthermore, it will be argued that there needs to be 'vision' on the part of the police service, to accompany the putting the mechanisms into place for dealing with discrimination. There also needs to be an effective strategy for the implementation of equal opportunity policy. While there are limitations to the achievements of the anti-discrimination legislation, there is no particular reason why there should be lack of vision in the implementation of policy into practice. This is even more essential where there is the existence of 'institutional sexism'.

Following the enactment of the Sex Discrimination Act 1975, the police service was slow to adapt in making the necessary changes. External pressure forced the service into taking action to combat the problems of both race and sex discrimination. Research into the police handling of rape, sexual assault and domestic violence, heightened awareness of their failure to adequately respond to such cases (*Hanmer and Saunders*, 1984[3]; *Hall*, 1985[4]; *Edwards*, 1986).[5] Criticism was levelled at the police service, in terms of the poor quality of service, and the emphasis turned to examining problems within the service itself. The conclusion was that the police were unsympathetic to women who had been victims of rape and domestic violence.[6] This, along with the increase in litigation by policewomen necessitated tackling the internal problems of discrimination.

It is essential to understand the nature of gender discrimination in the police service in the context of the debate around the justification for discrimination against women. The justification for discrimination pivots on the argument that women do not possess the physical ability to perform 'operational' duties. The history of the struggle for the acceptance of women as police officers demonstrates the resistance to women and the reluctance on the part of the police service to integrate women into all duties. An issue to be considered, is what specific qualities and skills policewomen and policemen have to offer to the police service, and how they differ.

[3] J Hanmer and S Saunders *Well-founded Fear: A Community Study of Violence to Women* (Hutchinson, 1984).
[4] R Hall *Ask Any Woman: A London Inquiry into Rape and Sexual Assault* (Falling Wall Press, 1983).
[5] S Edwards *The Police Response to Domestic Violence in London* (Polytechnic of Central London, 1986).
[6] The result of the criticism of the police in such cases led to the establishing of dedicated units to deal specifically with domestic violence; and 'rape suites' where women were to be treated with more sympathy. These units were, and still are, staffed predominantly by women officers, which in itself goes against the spirit of the Sex Discrimination Act 1975.

STRUGGLE FOR WOMEN'S ACCEPTANCE INTO THE POLICE SERVICE

The history of women's acceptance into the police service is one fraught with conflict. The awareness of the need for policewomen was rooted in the campaigns of the Suffragette movement, which preceded the First World War and continued until the Second World War. Prior to this (from the 1880s) there were a very small number of women employed to work as 'police matrons', they were often the wives of serving police officers, who were employed to perform very specific tasks concerning women and children. The police matrons were not sworn officers, they performed an auxiliary role, with the type of work they performed being more similar to social work (for example, they were used to escort and guard women prisoners) (J Carrier, 1988).[7]

> The twin themes of protection and control (of women) were central to the strug-
> gle for women police[8]

> (Radford, 1989, p 18)

The more militant suffragettes who were members of the Women's Freedom League, focused their campaign around the concern about men's violence against women and the lack of protection afforded to them by the police and the courts. However, those in authority at the Home Office, were more concerned with the control of women entering the 'white slave trade'. It was recognised that the presence of women police officers on the street may deter women from becoming involved in prostitution. Policewomen would effectively be 'moral watchdogs' and act as a preventive moral presence (L Bland, 1985, p 24).[9] Despite recommendations of the Criminal Law Amendment Committee in 1914 (which supported the introduction of policewomen for this reason) the Home Office considered that the police matrons were sufficient.

At the outbreak of the First World War, women who had been campaigning for the recruitment of policewomen, formed the organisation of Women Police Volunteers (WPV). There was much internal wrangling in the WPV which centred on the nature of their role. The WPV was headed by two women, the militant suffragette, Nina Boyle and Damer Dawson, a former member of the Criminal Law Amendment Committee. Nina Boyle whose campaigning had focused on male violence, was very uncomfortable with the idea that the WPV should be controlling women by 'rescuing' them from prostitution. Damer Dawson, on the other hand saw the role of the WPV as a 'moral crusade' to protect women by controlling prostitution. Following the split between these two women, the WPV was succeeded by

[7] J Carrier *The Campaign for the Employment of Women as Police Officers* (Arebury, Aldershot, 1988).
[8] J Radford 'Women and Policing: Contradictions Old and New' in J Hanmer, J Radford and A Stanko *Women, Policing and Male Violence* (Routledge, 1989).
[9] L Bland 'In the Name of Protection: the Policing of Women in the First World War' in J Brophy and C Smart *Women in Law* (Routledge and Kegan Paul, 1985).

voluntary women's patrols, who were concerned predominantly with the moral welfare and rescue of women. It was the voluntary women's patrols which received official Home Office recognition in 1916. In many ways this was not surprising as these women were content to assist the authorities in the control of other women. Consequently, they were perceived as less of a threat to the power and authority of men (Radford, 1989).[10]

In short, the work of the voluntary women's patrols during the war effort was eventually recognised as valuable. Women were kept as auxiliaries during this time and were in the employment of the local authorities. They were seen to have very specific and limited roles to perform, which were viewed as appropriate to their gender. In 1918, the Metropolitan Police Force established a scheme for the recruitment of women police officers. This, along with the enactment of the Sex Disqualification (Removal) Act 1919, which meant that women could no longer be disqualified by sex or marriage from performing any public function, paved the way for the recruitment of policewomen. Local police authorities were encouraged by the Home Office in 1919 to recruit policewomen. However, this did not lead to standardisation. By the end of the Second World War, the recruitment of policewomen was still left to local discretion. There remained a great deal of hostility towards the recruitment of women and it was not until the end of the Second World War that the police force finally recognised the need for policewomen and the battle ended (Jones, 1986).[11]

There were very few changes for women in the police service until the enactment of the Sex Discrimination Act 1975. Prior to that, women were still organised in the specialist Policewomen's Departments, which had their own rank and promotion structure and different pay from their male counterparts. The nature of the work performed by policewomen at this time was to deal with women and children in 'moral danger', either as 'victims' or 'offenders'. The police service actively sought exemption from the Sex Discrimination Act, arguing that women could/should not perform all police duties. The police service compared itself with the Armed Forces who were exempt from the provisions of the Act, as Crown servants. Much of the debate around the integration of policewomen into all police duties centred on the notion that women were not physically capable of performing all duties. This is because of the over-emphasis on the need for physical strength as a pre-requisite for the job.

However, in accordance with the legislation, policewomen could no longer be discriminated against either directly or indirectly, on the basis of their sex and marital status. Thus:

'As a result of the Act, no distinction was to be made in either recruitment or deployment on the grounds of sex, thus challenging the notion that policing should be a mainly masculine occupation and heralding the removal of the traditional and well-established sexual division of labour.' (Jones, 1986, p 6).[12]

[10] Above n 7.
[11] S Jones *Policewomen and Equality: Formal Policy and Informal Practice* (Macmillan, 1986).
[12] Above n 10.

One would imagine that the creation of opportunity and equal treatment in employment would create a marked change in the position of police-women, and consequently the structure and nature of the police service. This, however, has not been the case.

NUMBER OF POLICEWOMEN

The increase in the number of women police officers has been slow but gradual. At the end of 1975 the percentage of women in the police forces of England and Wales was 5.2 per cent. By the end of 1982 it was 8.5 per cent (Jones, 1986, p 31).[13] As at the end of December 1993 the England and Wales average female strength was 13.2 per cent (Her Majesty's Inspectorate Constabulary figures). This ranges from 9.2 per cent in South Wales to 16.1 per cent in the West Midlands.

The other issue which relates to the number of female officers is their distribution across the senior ranks. The greatest concentration of policewomen is at the rank of Constable. As at the end of December 1993, out of a total of 16,571 female officers, 15,195 were Constables, 1,044 were Sergeants, 237 were Inspectors, 54 were Chief Inspectors, 27 were Superintendents, 11 Chief Superintendents, 3 were Assistant Chief Constables, and there were no female Deputy or Chief Constables. (HMIC figures).[14] At the start of the litigation by Assistant Chief Constable Alison Halford in 1990, she was then Britain's most senior policewoman. Pauline Clare was appointed Britain's first female Chief Constable in June 1995.

Problems of gender discrimination in the police service

The small number of women in the police service poses a problem in itself. However, merely increasing the strength is insufficient as this alone would not dramatically change the nature of the organisation. Arguably, it is more important to integrate women into the senior ranks where most of the decision making takes place. Here another argument emerges in the debate about the suitability of women for police management and 'leadership'.

The revelation of the operation of unofficial and unlawful quotas in the recruitment of policewomen was the most significant matter. Research conducted on behalf of the Policy Studies Institute in 1983 revealed precisely this (Smith and Gray, 1983, p 246).[15] Similarly findings were made by S Jones (1986, p 82)[16] who states that the justification for this is the perceived lack of career commitment by policewomen. While there have been clear breaches

---

[13] Above n 11.
[14] These figures exclude staff at the Police Staff Training college.
[15] D Smith and J Gray *Police and People in London* (Policy Studies Institute, 1983).
[16] Above n 11.

of the legislation in the past, there is presently no evidence to suggest that the police service still operates quotas in the recruitment of women.

One of the reasons for the low number of women in the service relates to the lack of applications. One can only speculate about why this is, as the reasons may be many and varied. It could be that the recruitment strategies employed by the service are not aimed directly enough at women. This was an issue raised by the 1992 report of Her Majesty's Inspectorate of Constabulary, on equal opportunities in the police service,[17] where concern was expressed over recruiting patterns, which they believed may have 'indirect discriminatory effects'. Furthermore, the HMIC's examination of recruiting literature 'revealed a considerable domination of white male images' (p 3). Publicity surrounding the litigation by Alison Halford did nothing to improve the image of the police service as an all-male bastion, in which policewomen are under-valued and discriminated against.

The pivot of official police discourse has been the view that women are not suitable for police work unless they are performing certain tasks best suited to their gender. Much of policewomen's work has been dealing in the areas of 'victims' of rape and domestic violence, liaising with Social Services regarding juveniles and 'victims' of child abuse. This over-emphasis on gender difference has led to women being stereotyped into this area of work and being effectively excluded from other potentially more interesting areas such as dog-handling, CID, traffic and so on. Evidence of this exclusion was found by S Jones (1986)[18] in her research on 'Medshire', a medium-sized non-metropolitan police force. She found that policewomen were being discriminated against in their deployment; promotion and general career development.

The research by Jones uncovered a disparity between formal policy and informal practice, in these areas. She illustrates this point in relation to selection criteria, where the informal policy is based on the 'people like us' criteria which may mean in practice, the same sex. She argues that this 'mark of infinity' is part of the masculine occupational sub-culture (Jones, 1986, p 131).[19] The underpinning of this type of informal policy is the attitude of male officers towards policewomen. Jones' research endorsed similar findings of the Policy Studies Institute (Smith and Gray, 1983).[20]

Furthermore, research conducted on the impact to the Sex Discrimination Act on the Scottish Police Force areas, also found that the advancement of policewomen was thwarted by the presence of informal barriers, resulting from the existence of a masculine culture (Wilkie, 1989).[21] Again in 1990, in a joint review of equal opportunities in the Metropolitan Police Force, the Equal Opportunities Commission revealed the exclusion of women from

[17] Her Majesty's Inspectorate of Constabulary *Equal Opportunities in the Police Service* (Home Office, 1992).
[18] Above n 11.
[19] Above n 11.
[20] Above n 15.
[21] D Wilkie *The Effect of the Sex Discrimination Act on the Scottish Police Service* (Centre for Police Studies, University of Strathclyde, 1989).

specialist duties such as firearms, dog handling, and so on, which were clearly discriminatory (Equal Opportunities Commission/Metropolitan Police, 1990).[22]

It could be argued that the over-emphasis on physical strength as a pre-requisite for the job is the main thing preventing the advancement of police-women. The important point here however, is that the Sex Discrimination Act 1975 (s 7(2)(a)) excludes 'physical strength and stamina' as a 'genuine occupational qualification', where this arises it is a matter for individual consideration. Clearly then, the argument by the police service, for the justification of discrimination on the grounds of physical strength is invalid, and if carried out in practice would be unlawful. The police service *are* capable of change, even if this is forced upon them by litigation. The Metropolitan Police Force jettisoned the height restriction placed on officers and there is now greater flexibility in relation to uniforms. One of the most important changes, resulting from litigation, is in relation to the arming of police-women. The decision in *Johnston v Chief Constable of the RUC* [1986] IRLR 263, led police force areas to train policewomen as firearms officers.

One of the major problems with the debate about the physical requirements of the police role is that the emphasis is only based on the 'operational' aspects of policing. Approximately 10 per cent of all police time is spent in dealing with operational duties in which public order is the focus. The majority of police time is spent in dealing with paper work, court work and so on. Although physical ability and stamina are often seen to be the main issues, there is also the moral/chivalry debate in which it is thought that women should not be exposed to such conditions. (Bryant, Dunkerley and Kelland, 1985).[23]

This pre-occupation with the need for physical strength also disregards the other essential skills that policewomen and policemen require to perform their function. This is as a consequence of the concentration on gender difference, whereas if gender similarity was the focus, it may be surprising to see how much common-ground there is between policewomen and police-men, in terms of the skills they each possess. One issue raised by the Alison Halford case is the suitability of women for senior management and their leadership ability. In the debate about gender discrimination in the police service, this is an issue that requires further research.

Physical strength is not the only 'skill' required for dealing with the public, and in public order situations it is the use of force by the police service which often flares the situation. This is evidenced by the clashes between the police and demonstrators which have occurred on numerous occasions.[24] Furthermore, in a review of research on assaults on police

---

[22] Equal Opportunities Commission/Metropolitan Police *Managing to Make Progress* (Metropolitan Police Service, 1990).

[23] L Bryant, D Dunkerley, G Kelland 'One of the Boys' *Policing* Vol 1, No 4, Autumn 1985.

[24] For example, the Poll Tax demonstrations and the demonstrations against the most recent Criminal Justice and Public Order Act 1994. The earlier, but most notable clashes in recent times, are those during the miners' strike in 1984.

officers, McKenzie and Moxey, 1993,[25] argue that it is often the case that police officers provoke attacks on themselves. This, they argue, is because they often lack basic policing skills and have an inability to communicate effectively in such situations. It seems that policewomen are, therefore, at no more risk than policemen from attack, and in fact, they are often better equipped in the necessary skills for dealing with such situations. Unless this pre-occupation with physical strength is surmounted, there will be little hope of the desired change in the quality of the service.

This leads to the next issue of high wastage rates of policewomen, and limited promotion to the higher ranks. Further justification on the part of the police service stems from the idea then, that policewomen are uneconomic to employ, bearing in mind the costs of training and so on.

Moreover, experience and length of service are important factors in the promotion of police officers. Therefore, women officers will only make it to the senior ranks if they are long serving officers. The cynical attitude here is that women use a job in the police service as a 'stop-gap between school and reproduction', despite the lack of evidence to support this. This is more likely caused by the inflexibility of the work pattern, particularly for those women with family responsibilities, shift work being one of the greatest problems (Bryant, Dunkerley and Kelland, 1985, p 241).[26] Many of these problems are now being tackled within the police service with a move towards job-share; part-time work; career breaks, and so on. Stone, Kemp and Weldon (1994),[27] make recommendations in their report on part-time working and job sharing, to move towards the introduction of a successful scheme.

Research by Coffey and Brown (1992)[28] on the career aspirations of policewomen challenged the traditional notion that policewomen lack career commitment. Among the most common factors highlighted in this research hindering the progress of women, were:

- perceived lack of service and experience;
- their gender;
- perceived sexist attitudes; and
- a belief that senior officers had blocked applications from women, to specialist departments.

Findings from this research are consistent with those previously mentioned.

[25] M Moxey, IL McKenzie 'Assaults on Police' *Policing* Vol 9, Autumn 1993.

[26] Above n 23.

[27] R Stone, T Kemp, G Weldon *Part-time Working and Job Sharing in the Police Service* (Police Research Group, Home Office, 1994),

[28] S Coffey, J Brown and S Savage 'Policewomen's Career Aspirations: Some Reflections on the Role and Capabilities of Women in Policing In Britain' *Police Studies* Vol 15, No 1, Spring 1992.

HOME OFFICE RESPONSE

The official response to the problems of discrimination came in the form of the issue of the Home Office Circular 87/1989 'Equal Opportunities Policies in the Police Service'. It was issued to all Chief Constables urging them to produce and implement a written equal opportunity policy and to provide the necessary procedures for the development and monitoring of such policy. The circular expressed concern about the relationship between the implementation of equal opportunities policies; the standard of professional conduct; public perceptions of the police; and the quality of services. It requested a genuine commitment to equal opportunities by chief officers and stated that the effects should be two-fold:

it should ensure that the best use is made of the abilities of every member of the force;

it should demonstrate the willingness of the police to show that all members of the service are firmly opposed to discrimination within the service and in their professional dealings with members of the public. (p 4.)

Despite the slow response of the Home Office to these issues, the circular was a significant step towards improving the quality of the police service for its own officers, and members of the public.

Since the issue of Home Office Circular 87/1989 debate about the role and position of policewomen has continued (Young, 1991;[29] Low, 1991;[30] Brown and Campbell, 1991;[31] Coffey, Brown and Savage, 1992;[32] Heidensohn, 1992).[33] Low, 1991, p 15, for example, states that the pressure to implement equal opportunities policies was 'met unenthusiastically, but politely, and a carefully measured and limited response resulted.' Furthermore, the litigation taken by Assistant Chief Constable Alison Halford raised serious questions about the effectiveness of equal opportunities policies. Furthermore, there came the alarming and serious allegation of PC Eileen Waters, that she was brutally raped by a policeman in police residences (*The Guardian* 8 February 1993).

In 1993 Anderson, Brown and Campbell published their research 'Aspects of Sex Discrimination within the Police Service in England and Wales'.[34] This was a fairly extensive piece of research which revealed that all forces in England and Wales had promulgated a written equal opportunities policy. Additionally, it showed that, every force now designates overall responsibility for equal opportunity issues to one individual, either a senior officer or a specific post holder. In some force areas these are held by civilians. Their findings effectively confirmed Her Majesty's Inspectorate of Constabulary's

[29] M Young *An Inside Job* (Clarendon, 1991).
[30] P Low 'Are Women That Different?' *Policing* Vol 7, Spring 1991.
[31] J Brown and E Campbell 'Less than Equal' *Policing* Vol 7, Winter 1991.
[32] S Coffey, J Brown and S Savage 'Policewomen's Career Aspirations: Some Reflections on the Role and Capabilities of Women in Policing in Britain' *Police Studies* Vol 15, No 1, Spring 1992.
[33] F Heidensohn *Women in Control: The Role of Women in Law Enforcement* (Clarendon, 1992).
[34] R Anderson, J Brown, E Campbell *Aspects of Sex Discrimination in the Police Service in England and Wales* (Home Office, Police Department, 1993).

data compiled in 1991. The research also exposed evidence of the sexual harassment of female officers by their male colleagues, another problem of gender discrimination to be added to the list.

These research findings are significant in echoing previous concerns about police culture (often referred to as canteen culture). In fact, Her Majesty's Inspectorate of Constabulary's 1992 report 'Equal Opportunities in the Police Service' expressed similar concerns. This was a thematic inspection of 12 forces selected to ensure a wide representation of different sizes, structures and stages of development in relation to equal opportunities. Much of the inspection was based on interviews, thus producing qualitative data, relating to the level of awareness and confidence in equal opportunities; knowledge of the procedures; and the effectiveness of training.

Among its conclusions, HMIC stated that the inspection revealed some chief officers and others were not committed to equal opportunities, which they saw as frustrating the progress of fair treatment for all officers. They also found evidence of some change in 'canteen' or police culture but this was mainly in relation to race relations issues. HMIC expressed concerns about the serious problem of sexual harassment of policewomen in the service and the effects of white male culture, which they stated is not clearly understood.

While HMIC found that there was no evidence that women are institutionally barred from opportunities, and all the mechanisms are in place for dealing with equal opportunities, there still appears to be problems. Consequently, HMIC emphasised the need to continue to train all officers in equal opportunities in the service. It identified sergeants and inspectors as the most important in requiring training because of the influence they yield in the force, and emphasised their key role in personally challenging 'unacceptable language and behaviour in relation to both race and gender issues'.

The resounding message which has emerged from the research into gender discrimination in the police service is that it is a problem that is not easily resolved. Again this is evidence of the tensions between the law, policy and practice. The mechanisms for dealing internally with discrimination in the police service are now in place. Despite this, there appears to be no evidence that the problems of gender discrimination in the police service are being conquered. This is because, despite every effort being made, all that HMIC can do is operate a system of checks on the progress of equal opportunities in the service. What HMIC cannot easily institute is the political or social will to implement changes. Consequently, this leads to the need to address the question of why gender discrimination remains such a problem in the police service. The answer lies in an examination of 'police culture'.

POLICE CULTURE AND THE POLICE ORGANISATION

The primary theme which has emerged from the above discussion of the research into gender discrimination in the police service, is that it is a serious problem which cannot be easily resolved. The enforcement of the sex dis-crimination and equal pay legislation, and the implementation of equal opportunities policy in the police service has done little to eradicate the problems. Undoubtedly, the nature of the problem is more deep-rooted than it appears and many of the problems policewomen encounter stem from the attitudes of their male counterparts (Graef, 1989,[35] Young, 1991).[36] However, it would be deluding to view the problem as one merely of atti-tude. The extent and nature of gender discrimination in the police service, demonstrates the existence of 'institutionalised sexism', as the effect of organisational policies, in practice, is discrimination against policewomen. In order to make sense of this, it is essential to examine police culture and the nature of the police organisation.

Many would argue that discrimination in the police service is no different to discrimination in any other organisation and that it merely reflects the general attitudes in society. In spite of this, the working culture within organisations is different. Police culture can be defined as being 'the rules, norms and values which construct and guide the attitudes and behaviours of police officers' (Brogden, Jefferson and Walklate, 1988, p 30).[37] Police culture is typified by the attitudes and behaviour of police officers, and this needs to be considered in relation to the structure of the organisation (Punch, 1983).[38]

Police culture is not created directly by the organisation, rather the nature and structure of the organisation facilitates the existence of such a culture. Furthermore, it would be misleading to assume that police officers are a homogeneous group of people, there is a deep dichotomy between the lower ranks and senior officers (Punch, 1983).[38] Clearly, apart from the low num-ber of women in the service, the nature of the police organisation differs from that of others. It has a hierarchical structure based on a militaristic rank system, with a management style based on a 'top/down' approach. Police officers also have access to the 'use of legitimate force', bestowed upon them by the power of law.

Police culture, among other things, is characterised by 'authority', 'discipline', 'obedience', 'loyalty', 'deference' and a sense of 'mission' (Reiner, 1985).[39] It is not just a job but a way of life this stems from the duty to 'serve and protect' the public. The characteristics are expedited by the structure of the police organisation. Within police culture, police work is often portrayed as 'violent', 'dangerous', 'tough' and 'exciting', a job unsuit-able for women. According to Reiner, 1985, p 89, this is part of the

[35] R Graef *Talking Blues: The Police in Their Own Words* (Collins Parvill, 1989).
[36] See n 27.
[37] M Brogden, T Jefferson and S Walklate *Introducing Police Work* (London, Unwin Hyman, 1988).
[38] M Punch *Control in the Police Organisation* (Massachusetts Institute of Technology, 1983, pp 227–51).
[39] R Reiner *The Politics of the Police* (Harvester Press, 1985).

'machismo syndrome'. The research by Smith and Gray, 1983,[40] found that a great deal of emphasis is placed upon these aspects, by policemen, resulting in an over-exaggeration of the need for physical strength. They saw this as a direct result of the existence of a 'cult of masculinity' in the police service. Moreover, according to Smith and Gray, p 51.

> '... certain themes tend to be emphasised in conversation in an exaggerated way: the prime examples are male dominance (combined with a denigration of women); the glamour (but not the reality) of violence and racial prejudice.'

It is these aspects, along with 'feats of drinking' which combine together to form a cult of masculinity. Holdaway, 1983, p 139,[41] also emphasises such 'folk narratives' as being central to the police occupational culture.

This dominant culture effectively marginalises policewomen, allowing the manifestation of a particular form of masculinity. Thus, what transpires is a 'culture of masculinity', typified by white, heterosexual, patriarchal power relations. This culture informs dominant police discourse, in which policewomen are peripheral. Policewomen are, therefore, continually perceived as unsuitable for the job, or seen to have a gender-specific role. Police culture is based on certain norms and values which inform attitudes and behaviour and ultimately institutional practices. If the norms and values are based on sexist, racist and homophobic prejudices, then the consequence of this culture is discrimination.

One further consequence of the existence of this male culture is that policewomen are disinclined to take action regarding sex discrimination and be seen to be breaking rank. This is a resulting factor of the centrality of 'loyalty', to the police culture. Low, 1993,[42] commenting on the *Halford* inquiry, emphasised the effects of loyalty and the 'conspiracy of silence' on policewomen. Policewomen are in a difficult position in relation to police occupational culture, in which masculinity dominates, as they never really 'fit in'. Policewomen are all too often perceived as threatening, if they attempt to behave like 'one of the boys', they are criticised as being unfeminine; if they do not challenge male culture, they are seen as passive; and if they seek promotion to the higher ranks, they are seen as too ambitious. Consequently, policewomen are in a 'catch-22' situation.

Finally, a further effect of police occupational culture is that such issues as equal opportunities and human resources are not prioritised within the service, resources are channelled into operational policing strategies. This results from the over-emphasis on the more dangerous and violent aspects of the police role, in addition to the real need to respond to the level of crime. However, under-resourcing of the implementation of equal opportunities policy demonstrates a lack of commitment to the improvement of the quality of the service.

[40] See n 15.
[41] S Holdaway *Inside the British Police: A Force at Work* (Basil Blackwell, 1983).
[42] P Low 'Reflections on the Halford Inquiry' *Policing* Vol 9, Spring 1993.

CONCLUSION

Gender discrimination in the police service, therefore, demonstrates the problems of the translation of law into policy and practice and the tensions inherent within this process. Existing research in this area has highlighted such difficulties and has demonstrated that the mechanisms for dealing with discrimination are now in place. The sex discrimination and equal pay legislation has not instigated much of a change in the nature of the police service, namely because it tackles the problem of gender discrimination in the workplace as an 'employment rights' issue. The equal treatment of men and women creates a meritocracy but does little to change the occupational culture. Individuals with a grievance can use the appropriate channels for dealing with discrimination – the ultimate end being litigation. However, the related problems have been raised in this chapter.

The emphasis in this debate now needs to focus on how the vision to bring about a genuine equality of opportunity for policewomen and the corresponding improvement in the quality of the police service can be developed. This depends very much on the way one defines 'equality'. The type of equality that will change the nature of the police service needs to be similar to that defined by O'Donovan and Szyszczak, 1988, p 7,[43] 'namely, equality as respect for others, avoidance of stereotypes and the viewing of the world from another's point of view'. This of course is difficult to implement. Legislation, and to a lesser extent equal opportunities policy, cannot achieve this alone.

The above can only be effected by individuals with vision, accompanied by clear organisational aims. It is essential that commitment is demonstrated by those in senior positions in the police service, a view echoed by the HMIC in its 1992 report. Baroness Jenny Hilton, formerly a Commander in the police service, similarly supports this view, in expressing concern and disappointment at the Police Federation's Statement of Intent on equal opportunities, she argued that the Statement 'ought to have emphasised the importance of language, ie the way police officers speak to one another'. Moreover, she stated:

> 'If police officers can learn to treat each other with sensitivity and imagination it is more likely that the public will be treated with courtesy and respect.'
>
> (*Police Journal*, January 1992, p 12.)

This is precisely the type of view that police officers and the police organisation needs to adopt to initiate change and improve the quality of service to members of the public. However, one of the problems with the nature of the organisational culture is that it does not empower individuals in the required way. Additionally, policewomen are too often marginalised by the masculine ethos of police culture. This is why the debate on the problems of gender discrimination in the police service is a circular one, and one that is

[43] See n 2.

difficult to surmount. One practical measure that could more easily be adopted by the police service, is a commitment to the training of all officers in equal opportunities, in the hope that change will arise through education.

McKenzie, 1993, p 172,[44] advocates a more punitive approach to police force areas which fail to effectively implement equal opportunities policy. This could involve the declaring of a specific police force as inefficient, for the purposes of the police budget allocated by central government. McKenzie argues that it is not enough to rely on 'good-will' alone and that the 'Thou shalt not discriminate' approach is inadequate unless a sufficient punishment can be applied. However, it is difficult to imagine that this approach will invoke any insight and vision, which it has been argued here, is essential to the successful implementation of equal opportunities policy. The threat of declaring a police force area as inefficient, may shake the police service into action but as we have already seen the mechanisms for dealing with discrimination are now in place, whether they are working effectively, brings us back to the starting point of lack of vision to create the necessary change in a masculinist police culture. Judging from the input that women have contributed to policing, both historically and more recently, maybe it is here that we can hold the greatest hope for the creation of the necessary vision to instigate change.

---

[44] I McKenzie 'Equal; Opportunities in Policing: A Comparative Examination of Anti-Discrimination Police and Practice in British Policing' (International Journal of Sociology of Law, 1993).

17

DISCRIMINATION IN CHILD MAINTENANCE

Peter Stone

THE (UK) CHILD SUPPORT ACT 1991

Few legislative measures in the United Kingdom have achieved so wide, deep and justified an unpopularity with almost everyone directly affected as the Child Support Act 1991.

It is not surprising that in approximately two years of operation this evil enactment has provoked an unusual degree of resistance, sufficient to force a number of largely cosmetic changes, while causing a great deal of hardship and anger.

A number of test cases have been brought or are pending. In one of these cases arguments based on European prohibitions on discrimination were offered, which will now be considered. Although the arguments did not succeed in that case, they may in due course be put to higher judicial bodies.

The *Green* case

In *Henry Green's* case[1] a Tribunal of Child Support Commissioners (comprising Chief Commissioner Machin and Commissioners Goodman and Hegg) were invited, in an appeal by a so-called absent parent from a Child Support Appeal Tribunal, to consider two distinct arguments as to the compatibility with European anti-discrimination law of the recent UK child support legislation.

The first of these arguments relied mainly on Art 119 of the EC Treaty and Council Dir 75/117, on equal pay. The appellant sought an order referring to the EU Court of Justice under Art 177 of the Treaty the question:

> 'Whether, in relation to an absent parent who is an employee, national legislation such as the (UK) Child Support Act 1991, taken with the ministerial regulations and orders made thereunder, is compatible with legislation of the European Union prohibiting gender discrimination (in particular, with Art 119 of the EC Treaty and Council Dirs 75/117 and 79/7), it being understood that the overwhelming majority of absent parents against whom maintenance assessments and deduction orders under such legislation are made are in fact male rather than female.'

[1] Case CCS/002/94, argued on 3 and 4 March 1995, and decided on 30 March 1995. The present writer represented Mr Green before the Commissioners.

The second European argument relied on Arts 8 and 14 of the European Human Rights Convention, on respect for family life and non-discrimination in relation thereto, as a guide to the construction of s 2 of the (UK) Child Support Act 1991, which provides:

> 'Where, in any case which falls to be dealt with under this Act, the Secretary of State or any child support officer is considering the exercise of any discretionary power conferred by this Act, he shall have regard to the welfare of any child likely to be affected by his decision.'

It was argued that, in view of Arts 8 and 14, s 2 must be read as requiring the Secretary of State to have *equal* regard to the interests of the various children involved and, therefore, that the Child Support (Maintenance Assessments and Special Cases) Regulations 1992 (SI 1992 No 1815) were *ultra vires* because they discriminated in favour of the children to be maintained under an assessment, and against children of a so-called absent parent's second marriage and his stepchildren.

Only a bare outline of the facts of *Green* is necessary to enable the arguments to be seen in context. Henry Green, the appellant, is an employee. The Child Support Agency (CSA) assessment was for Henry's two teenage children by his ex-wife, Susan, from whom he had been divorced many years earlier, and who was receiving income support. The amount payable under the assessment was more than three times the amount previously payable under the maintenance order made by the divorce court, and was more than one-third of what the CSA regarded as his net income. Prior to the CSA intervention, he was living with, and maintaining, his second wife, Thelma, together with a young child of that marriage, and Thelma's three children by her first husband. Under her divorce settlement Thelma was receiving maintenance for those children from her ex-husband, and the assessment against Henry effectively diverted much of that maintenance (and even the child benefit received for all the children in his household) to the children of his first marriage.[2] The consequence of the CSA intervention was to put such financial and emotional pressure on Henry and Thelma as to destroy their relationship, with the result Thelma eventually obtained a divorce from Henry and became dependent on income support.

---

[2] This was the effect of the Child Support (Maintenance Assessments and Special Cases) Regulations (SI 1992, No 1815), especially regs 11(2) And 12. The original version of these Regulations was in force at the time of the assessment against which the appeal was brought. Under the main formula, no allowances for Thelma and her children by her ex-husband were given in Henry's exempt income. Under the protected-income formula, small allowances were given for Thelma and those children, but the maintenance received from her ex-husband, and the child benefit received for all the children in his household, was included in Henry's disposable income. In contrast, the maintenance requirement included a substantial allowance for Susan, as carer of the children to be maintained. Thus the result of the combined formulae was to prevent Henry from properly providing from his earnings for his current household.

The equal-pay point

The argument that the (UK) Child Support Act, along with its implementing regulations, is incompatible with Art 119 of the EC Treaty and/or Dir 75/117, and is, therefore, invalid or inapplicable, involves four distinct issues:

(1) whether the relevant EC legislation has supremacy and direct effect;
(2) whether the UK child support legislation gives rise to indirect gender discrimination;
(3) whether there is sufficient justification for any such discrimination; and
(4) whether there is a sufficient connection between the making and/or enforcement of assessments of child support maintenance under the UK legislation and the pay or remuneration of employees.

In *Green* the Commissioners expressed no opinion on the first three of these issues, but decided the fourth against the appellant. They, therefore, refused to make a reference to the EU Court. They said merely that pay arises as a consequence of the relationship of employer and employee, and the obligation to pay child support is not covered by the definition of pay as set out in Art 119 either directly or indirectly. It is respectfully suggested that on these points they failed almost completely to address the arguments offered on behalf of the appellant.

Direct effect

As regards the first issue, there is no need here to rehearse the well established case law which establishes the supremacy and direct effect of EC legislation of suitable content. The direct effect of Art 119 is accepted,[3] and Dir 75/117 is principally designed to facilitate the practical application of Art 119, without altering the scope of the principle in any way.[4] Moreover, since the appellant was attacking a decision of a child support officer (a public official exercising statutory powers), it seems clear that the situation involved vertical, rather than horizontal, direct effect. It would, therefore, be enough that the UK legislation providing for such decisions was incompatible with precise and unconditional provisions of the Directive (even if it was not incompatible with the Treaty itself). The appellant was asserting that the Treaty and/or the Directive prevented the United Kingdom from empowering the official to make a binding order against him. In any event the appellant argued that the Treaty itself applied, and that the Directive, in referring to Art 1 to 'all aspects and conditions of remuneration', could be relied on by way of the clarification of the concept of pay, as referred to in the Treaty.

---

[3] See, for example, Case 43/75 *Defrenne (No 2)*, [1976] ECR 455; Case 69/80 *Worringham*, [1981] ECR 767; and Case C-262/88 *Barber* [1990] ECR I-1889.
[4] Case 96/80 *Jenkins*, [1981] ECR 911.

Indirect gender discrimination

As regards the second issue, the appellant relied on the fact that the over-whelming majority (well over 90 per cent) of so-called absent parents against whom assessments have been issued are fathers rather than mothers. Accordingly he relied on the case law establishing that direct discrimination against part-time workers, most of whom are female, amounts to indirect discrimination against women.[5]

Lack of justification

As regards the third issue, the appellant admitted, with emphasis, that the regulation in a reasonable way of the financial relationships between mem-bers of a family (including a broken family) is recognised by European Union law as a legitimate matter for national legislation, and that some measure of gender discrimination is justifiable under EU law for that pur-pose. It was further admitted that, in view of the fact that in most cases, upon marital or similar breakdown, the children remain in the mother's care, any reasonable system of child maintenance will almost inevitably involve some degree of gender discrimination. But it was submitted that, in view of various features of the current UK child support legislation, including in particular its provision for deductions to be made from earnings by means of an administrative act, without a prior application to and order of a court having power to consider all the circumstances of the case, the current UK legislation, insofar as it pursues any legitimate social policy capable of justi-fying some measure of gender discrimination, does so by unnecessarily oppressive and, therefore, disproportionate means. The obnoxious features of the then current UK legislation relied on included the following:

- It enables deductions to be made from the earnings of the absent parent, on the authority of an administrative act alone, without any prior application to or order by a court having power to consider all the circumstances of the case.
- It enables an administrative assessment to override a prior court order, includ-ing a court order made before the 1991 Act came into operation.
- It deals in isolation with maintenance by way of periodical payments, and ignores any prior or future transfer of capital designed to meet the needs of the child (or of the parent with care).
- It fraudulently disguises, as child maintenance, amounts which are in truth intended as maintenance of the mother, and ignores the rights and obligations of the parents towards each other under private law.
- It discriminates against children of second marriages, and against step-children, contrary to Arts 8 and 14 of the European Convention on Human Rights, as interpreted by the European Court of Human Rights in *Marckx v Belgium*.[6]

---

[5] See, for example, Case 171/88 *Rinner-Kühn*, [1989] ECR 2543.
[6] (1979–80) 2 EHRR 330. See also *Johnston v Ireland* (1987) 9 EHRR 203; *Inze v Austria* (1988) 10 EHRR 394; *Verniere v Belgium* (1993) 15 EHRR 488; *Keegan v Ireland* (1994) 18 EHRR 342; and *Kroon v The Netherlands* (1995) 19 EHRR 263.

- By ignoring such matters as the cost of travelling to work and existing debts (other than certain housing costs), it gives rise to enormous assessments which the absent parent is unable to pay.
- By backdating assessments to the date on which an enquiry form was sent to the absent parent, it enables administrative inefficiencies or malice to create arrears which the absent parent is unable to pay.
- By imposing an obligation to co-operate with the authorities in destroying her former partner and his new family on a parent with care receiving benefits from public funds, it treats her with contempt, and causes her unnecessary difficulties in exercising her parental responsibility for the children in her care.
- The consequences of the above points have given rise to unemployment, distress, mental breakdown, the breakdown of second marriages, and suicides.

Since the hearing in *Green,* some minor concessions to some of these criticisms have been made by the Child Support and Income Support (Amendment) Regulations 1995 (SI 1995 No 1045), and others are contemplated by the Child Support Act 1995. It is suggested, however, that such concessions are largely cosmetic, and that the fundamental objections to the UK legislation are not significantly affected.

Reliance was also placed on the European Court's ruling in Case C-343/92 *Roks,*[7] that even indirect gender discrimination cannot be justified by reference to budgetary considerations.

Connection with pay or remuneration

In relation to the fourth issue, the appellant relied on the wording of Art 1 of Dir 75/117, which applies the principle of gender equality to 'all aspects and conditions of remuneration' (ie of employees and derived from their employment). It was accepted that child maintenance is not itself 'pay' or 'remuneration'. However, it was submitted that, where the so-called absent parent is an employee, an assessment of child support maintenance against him under the relevant UK legislation, and/or a deduction from earnings order against him for enforcement of such an assessment, constitutes an 'aspect' or 'condition' of his pay or remuneration, within the meaning of the Directive, since part of his pay is charged or taken and his effective pay is thus reduced. It was pointed out that the income of the person assessed is the most important element in the assessment of child support maintenance under the 1991 Act and the Child Support (Maintenance Assessments and Special Cases) Regulations (SI 1992 No 1815), and in the case of an employee his earnings normally constitute all or most of his income. Reliance was also placed on the provisions on deduction from earnings orders (contained in the 1991 Act ss 31–32, and the Child Support (Collection and Enforcement Regulations (SI 1992 No 1989) Part III), which operate to intercept the earnings of the person assessed before they reach him.

[7] [1994] ECR I-571.

As regards case law reliance was placed on Case C-262/88 *Barber*[8] where the EU Court ruled that a pension paid under a contracted-out private occupational scheme falls within the scope of Art 119 of the Treaty, and that the principle of equal pay must be applied in respect of each element of remuneration, and not only on the basis of a comprehensive assessment of the consideration paid to workers. Admittedly in Case 192/85 *Newstead*[9] the EU Court had earlier drawn a distinction between gross pay and net pay, in ruling that European law did not prevent discrimination in respect of contributions to a widow's pension fund provided for under an occupational scheme which was a substitute for a statutory social security scheme. It was submitted that *Newstead* had effectively been overruled in *Barber*, which established that occupational pension schemes are within Art 119 after all, and that it would be absurd if occupational pensions were within Art 119 but contributions, whereby such pensions were bought, were not. It was emphasised that exclusion of deductions from earnings from Art 119 would offer an easy opportunity to employers who wished to discriminate. Reliance was also placed on the EU Court's decision in Case 171/88 *Rinner-Kühn*[10] and the House of Lords' decision in *Equal Opportunities Commission v Secretary of State for Employment*,[11] as establishing that the European legislation against gender discrimination is not rendered inapplicable by the fact that the discriminatory acts of the employer are authorised by national legislative provisions.

Thus it was submitted that a maintenance assessment and/or a deduction of earnings order against an employed person under the UK child support legislation constitutes an 'aspect' or 'condition' of, and gives rise to a (negative) 'element' in, his pay or remuneration from his employment, within the meaning and scope of Art 119 of the EC Treaty and Art 1 of Dir 75/117, as construed in *Barber*. A charge on, or deduction from, an employee's earnings for child maintenance is subject to evaluation for gender discrimination in the same way as a charge or deduction for income tax. Reliance could also have been placed on the EU Court's rulings in Case 175/88 *Biehl*,[12] and Case C-279/93 *Schumacker*,[13] that direct discrimination in income tax (for example, as regards allowances for dependants) on grounds of residence can amount to indirect discrimination on grounds of nationality, contrary to Art 48 of the EC Treaty and Art 7 of Regulation 1612/68.

The only authority apparently relied on by the Commissioners in rejecting these arguments was Case 80/70 *Defrenne (No 1)*,[14] which certainly establishes that benefits under a public social security scheme are not pay within Art 119. The appellant argued that *Defrenne (No 1)* has ceased to be authority

[8] [1990] ECR I-1889.
[9] [1987] ECR 4753.
[10] [1989] ECR 2743.
[11] [1994] 1 All ER 910.
[12] [1990] ECR I-1779.
[13] 14 February 1995.
[14] [1971] ECR 445.

for any wider principle, and that in any even it must be read subject to the subsequent Dir 75/117 and the subsequent decision in *Barber*. These arguments seem to have fallen on deaf ears.

The appellant did not ask the Commissioners themselves to decide the EU points in his favour, but to make a reference under Art 177. Given the difficulty and importance of the issues, and the state of the procedure, it is hard to see any justification for the refusal of a reference.

The Commissioners' refusal to refer seems even less justifiable in the light of the subsequent ruling of the EU Court (given on 13th July 1995) in Case C-116/94 *Jennifer Meyers v Adjudication Officer*, that a benefit with the characteristics and purpose of family credit is concerned with both access to employment and working conditions and falls, therefore, within the scope of Council Directive 76/207, on equal treatment for men and women as regards access to employment, vocational training and promotion, and working conditions. The Court emphasised that 'working conditions' are not confined to ones which are set out in the contract of employment or applied by the employer in respect of a worker's employment, but extend to benefits under a national social security scheme which are necessarily linked to an employment relationship.

The family-life point

A separate ground of appeal in *Green* invoked Arts 8 and 14 of the European Human Rights Convention, which confer the right to respect for family life without discrimination on grounds such as social origin, birth or other social status, as a guide to the interpretation of s 2 of the 1991 Act, which requires the Secretary of State, where in any case he is considering the exercise of any discretionary power conferred by the Act, to have regard to the welfare of any child likely to be affected by his decision.

Reliance was placed on the decision of the European Human Rights Court in *Marckx v Belgium*,[15] that Art 8, taken with Art 14, prevents a state which is party to the Convention from discriminating unreasonably against illegitimate children. It was submitted that, *a fortiori*, the Convention prevents unreasonable discrimination against children of second marriages, or against step-children, or children in respect of whom state benefit is not being paid. Since s 2 does not explicitly define the relevant weight to be given to the welfare of one child involved as against that of another child involved, it was argued that, in view of the requirements of the Human Rights Convention, s 2 should be construed as requiring the Secretary of State to have *equal regard* to the welfare of all children affected. In particular he cannot lawfully give preference to the interests of children of first marriages, or children in respect of whom state benefits are being paid, as against the interests of children of second marriages,

---

[15] (1979–80) 2 EHRR 330.

step-children of the person assessed, or children for whom state benefits are not being paid.

Since the Human Rights Convention was being invoked for the purpose of construing the words, 'have regard to', in s 2 of the Act, rather than for the purpose of introducing implied limitations as to the manner in which a statutory discretion should be exercised, it was submitted that such use of the Convention was consistent with the decision of the House of Lords in *Brind v Home Secretary*.[16] Reliance was also placed on the dictum of Thorpe J in *Biggin v Secretary of State for Social Security*,[17] which involved a deduction from earnings order, that s 2 is not satisfied by the Secretary of State merely noticing child welfare considerations in passing; he must give 'considerable weight' to the welfare principle.

Accordingly it was argued that various features of the Child Support (Maintenance Assessments and Special Cases) Regulations 1992 (SI 1992 No 1815), made by the Secretary of State under powers conferred by the 1991 Act, infringed this principle of equal treatment of children in different family or social security positions. In particular, improper discrimination between children arose (in the *Green* case) from provisions of the Regulations which made allowance for only half of a parent's compulsory occupational pension contributions in calculating his net income; from provisions which ignored completely any debts which were already owed by a parent at the time when the CSA first intervened against him, even if they had been incurred before the entry into force of the 1991 Act itself; and from provisions which gave no allowance in the so-called absent parent's exempt income under the main formula for step-children living in his household, while including maintenance received for them from their own father (and also child benefit received for them under social security legislation) in the so-called absent parent's disposable income under the protected-income formula.

The Commissioners short-circuited these arguments by ruling that s 2 had no application to the making of regulations. It was confined to the exercise of discretionary powers in individual cases, such as the making of a deduction from earnings order under s 31(2). They relied on the wording of s 2, referring to a case and a decision, as being inappropriate to general powers to make regulations. They relied also on the absence of any reference to child welfare both in the sections which conferred particular powers to make regulations, and in s 52, which deals with regulations generally. Accordingly they did not specifically advert to the Human Rights Convention.

Such a technical approach to matters of fundamental importance may be viewed as casting doubts on the ability of the English courts, in their current constitutional position, to offer more than illusory redress against oppression.

[16] [1991] 1 AC 696.
[17] [1995] 1 FLR 851.

18

PRE-EMPLOYMENT HEALTH SCREENING

Joanne Lunn

INTRODUCTION

This chapter is concerned with discrimination that may occur if job applicants are required to undergo health screening prior to employment. Discrimination may be said to occur when a person is treated differently from others for a reason which should not be considered relevant. In the context of pre-employment health screening a prospective job applicant may be rejected on the basis of not meeting health criterion, whereas another applicant may be accepted. This chapter will address the issue of whether such health screening is, or can be, unduly discriminatory.

It is accepted that pre-employment health screening may be justified in some circumstances, for example, for health and safety reasons. If, however, employers screen unduly, (ie for every job and with unnecessary high health criterion) this could result in inordinate discrimination between those who are considered fit and those who are considered unfit. This phenomena will evidently increase where applicants are disabled and may be particularly invidious where the disability is invisible, for example, epilepsy and mental illness. These two medical conditions will accordingly be used to illustrate the issues raised.

Pre-employment health screening should be contrasted with health surveillance, which may take place during the course of employment.[1]

First the practice and procedures of health screening, genetic testing, psychometric/psychological tests will be examined in turn. Secondly, employer fears and attitudes will be considered, as well as the ways in which these fears and attitudes may involve stereotyping affecting employment policies. Thirdly, statutory constraints on employers will also be explored, and fourthly the respective rights and duties of employers and prospective employees will be investigated.

---

[1] Control of Substances Hazardous to Health Regulations 1988 (SI 1988 No 1657) (as amended). In certain situations the employer may be under a statutory obligation to undertake both pre-employment health screening and health surveillance.

PRACTICE AND PROCEDURES

Employers may make an offer of employment conditional on the applicant satisfactorily undergoing pre-employment health screening, or they may only make an offer of employment once the applicant has been passed 'fit for work'. The normal practice is to make a conditional offer. The Court of Appeal has expressed the view, *obiter dicta*, that the test, as to whether an employee has satisfactorily passed a medical examination in pre-employment screening, is objective.[2]

The main purpose of pre-employment screening is to assess job applicants for the suitability or fitness for work. Employers may also have other reasons, for example, assessing susceptibility to certain hazards and providing the employer with baseline health data on employees which may be used to defend any future claims against them.

Employers have obligations[3] both to provide a safe system of work and to protect employees from exposure to hazardous substances.[4] In effect although employers have an obligation to protect employees from exposure to hazardous substance they may be concerned to screen out employees who are particularly susceptible at the recruitment stage. Baseline health data will also be of great importance to employers if they later wish to defend actions brought against them by employees for personal injuries. This is because the House of Lords has held, in *Gardiner v Motherwell Machinery & Scrap Co Ltd* [1961] 3 All ER 831, that there is a *prima facie* presumption that a disease is caused by work conditions if:

(a) the employee had not previously suffered from a disease;
(b) the employee contracts the disease after having been subject to conditions likely to cause it; and
(c) it is shown to start in a way typical of disease caused by such conditions.

Employers will, therefore, wish to have baseline health data to rebut this presumption by showing that the employee had previously suffered from such a disease prior to employment. *Prima facie* it is justifiable for employers to obtain baseline health data as this will not necessarily result in discrimination against the applicant, but merely be used as factual evidence as to the applicant's health at the start of the employment.

The procedures employers use for carrying out screening vary. Whatever method is used it is necessary to ensure that it does not lead to undue discrimination. The main method of carrying out pre-employment health screening is the use of a health questionnaire. Medical examination or interview may also be used.

Medical reports may also be obtained from the prospective employee's own general practitioner. The procedures for obtaining such reports are now governed by statute: the Access to Medical Reports Act 1988. This provides

---

[2] *Wishhart v National Association of Citizens Advice Bureaux* [1990] ICR 794.
[3] A discussion of the nature of these obligations is outside the scope of this paper.
[4] *Ibid*, n 1.

that the employee must be notified by the employer that the employer is proposing to make such an application. Prospective employees have the right to withhold consent to the employer's application.[5] They also have the right to request their medical practitioner to amend any part of the report they consider misleading or incorrect. If the medical practitioner agrees s/he are under a duty to amend the report accordingly or if s/he disagrees s/he must attach a statement of the employee's views to the report.

Notwithstanding the availability of these procedures it is probably impractical to obtain medical reports on all prospective employees and reports from the applicant's own general practitioner may be used in a more limited way, for example, if the initial screening reveals a potential problem.

Pre-employment health screening procedures do not normally provide applicants with a right to submit their own medical evidence or report.[6] If undue discrimination is to be avoided, employers should consider whether it is appropriate to adopt procedures that would allow prospective employees to submit their own evidence and/or report. Regard should also be given as to whether it is appropriate to obtain specialist reports.[7]

There is a need to address the use of genetic testing in pre-employment screening, as it is possible that this could form part of a pre-employment medical examination. A report by the Nuffield Foundation recognised that employers may want to use genetic testing to assess the risk of occupational diseases and 'to have access to genetic information about other diseases which may have implications for the employment relationship.'[8] Nevertheless, in practice, genetic testing does not significantly contribute to discrimination, as there is evidence that only one employer currently uses it in pre-employment health screening.[9] It will require further monitoring if it becomes more commonplace.

The Department of Employment have issued guidance on pre-employment health screening.[10] Employers should comply with this advice. It aims to establish good practice by setting out 'the circumstances in which pre-employment health screening may make a useful contribution to occupational health care and providing guidance on their conduct'.[11] Accordingly a decision to refuse employment should only be taken on carefully defined criteria specifically relating to the job in question.[12] This means that when occupational health practitioners are screening they should have a

---

[5] Access to Medical Reports Act 1988, s 5.

[6] This is in direct contrast to the procedures that need to be followed on dismissal. In order for the employer to ensure that a dismissal is procedurally fair he will need to ensure that the employee has had the opportunity to contend the employer's report or produce an independent medical report, *East Lindsey District Council v GE Daubney* [1977] IRLR 181.

[7] *Booth v Drake* [1986] Employment Appeal Tribunal/483/86 Transcript. As in ill-health dismissals where employers have an obligation to consider whether the occupational health practitioner should have obtained specialist reports.

[8] Nuffield Council on Bioethics, 'Genetic Screening Ethical Issues', December 1993.

[9] Above para 6.15.

[10] Health and Safety Executive, 'Guidance Note MS 20, Pre-employment health screening', 1982.

[11] Above para 2.

[12] *Ibid*, para 3.

clear idea of the tasks to be performed by the applicant in the particular post that s/he has applied for, and not merely the job title.

Where the prospective employee is disabled there is further guidance on health screening from the Health and Safety Executive.[13] It considers that health checks are not necessary for all jobs, nor for all people with disabilities but they should be used to dispel employers' doubts. Assumptions should be avoided, people with disabilities should not be excluded from jobs by employers because it is thought that health screening will automatically lead to their rejection.[14] Instead health screening could be used positively to dispel the employer's doubts.

Screening will normally be carried out by occupational health practitioners who are members of the medical profession, ie either nurses or doctors. As such they will be bound not only by legal considerations but also their own professional codes of conduct.[15] Occupational health practitioners may either be directly employed by the employer concerned or engaged on a consultancy basis.[16] To avoid discriminatory practices when screening these professionals should, irrespective of the relationship with the employer, exercise their professional judgment independently and in accordance with the guidance laid down by their professional bodies. At times, this may place them in a difficult situation. If they are employees they must not allow their duty of fidelity to conflict with their own professional judgment. Furthermore as in the case of all employees they will only be required to obey reasonable orders.[17]

EMPLOYERS' CONCERNS AND THEIR ATTITUDES

In order to evaluate whether pre-employment health screening is justified, it is necessary to consider the attitudes and concerns of employers that give rise to the process. Employers' concerns were identified by the Department of Employment[18] in the following terms:

(1) Safety at work.
(2) Attendance and health.
(3) Pensions schemes.
(4) Alterations to premises and equipment.
(5) Communications.
(6) Manual dexterity.
(7) Physical effort.

These need to be critically examined to consider their validity.

[13] Health and Safety Executive, 'Code of Good Practice on the Employment of Disabled People', 1984.
[14] *Ibid*, paras 5.17–5.19.
[15] Nurses Code of Professional Conduct, UKCC 1982.
[16] Kottow considers that if the relationship is one of employment this may conflict with the occupational health practitioner's duty of confidentiality to the applicant, as the occupational health practitioner may also feel under a duty of loyalty to the employer. MJ Kottow, 'Medical Confidentiality: an intransigent and absolute obligation', Journal of Medical Ethics (1986), Vol 2, pp 117–122.
[17] *Ottoman Bank v Chakarian* [1930] AC 277.
[18] HMSO (1994). The Allitt Inquiry.

Safety at work

Employers have a duty to provide a safe system of work.[19] This may give rise to concern as to the safety of employing particular employees if the employer considers that they represent a safety risk.

It is clear form the guidance available that care must be taken to avoid stereotyping and that in such circumstances screening should be used positively to dispel doubts. This issue is particularly observable in the case of employing sufferers of epilepsy and mental illness. There are obviously restraints on employing people in certain occupations if they suffer from particular disabilities.[20] A common feature of these occupations is that they potentially involve the safety of others. To this extent the employers' fears can be justified, on the basis that the employers' obligation to have regard for safety of others takes precedence over the individual's interest in obtaining employment.

Attendance and health

Employers may be concerned as to possible poor attendance, although research shows that in some instances their fear is unjustified.[21] In the case of mental illness attendance records may be no worse and indeed better as individuals fear discrimination.[22]

Pension schemes

Employers also fear increased costs to the pension fund. The Piercy Committee, as long ago as 1956, concluded that there was no reason why superannuation schemes need prejudice the chances of disabled persons obtaining employment.[23] Further evidence has demonstrated that if the employee satisfies the requirements of fitness for the job then most employers will admit all employees to the pension scheme.[24] However, admission of disabled employees to the pension scheme does not alter the fact that the employer may harbour concerns about the consequences for funding.

A report published in 1969 showed that reports to the Department of Employment, by employers making reference to difficulties about the

[19] *Ibid*, n 1.

[20] These are supported by statute in certain instances and will be discussed below.

[21] H Sands and S Zalkind, 'Effects of an Educational Campaign to change Employer Attitudes towards Hiring Epileptics', Epilepsia (Amst), 1972, 13:87–96. Sands and Zalkind reported that sufferers of epilepsy as 'a group are safe workers, that is, they lose no more work time than their non-epileptic co-workers, have a work-absence rate less than their non-epileptic co-workers, and have job-performance ratings which equal or are better than those of their co-workers'.

[22] J Solomon, 'Why Hire the Rehabilitated Mentally Ill?', Management Review, 1986, p 69.

[23] Ministry of Labour and National Service (1956), 'Report of the Committee of Inquiry on the Rehabilitation, Training and Resettlement of Disabled Persons', (Piercy Report.) Cmnd 9883. London HMSO.

[24] 'Occupational Pension Scheme Cover for Disabled People', HMSO Cmnd 6849, June 1977.

pension scheme as a reason for not engaging a disabled person, had been infinitesimal.[25] The report was concerned with resettlement and, it may be that, the experience of individual job applicants may differ.

If employers' fears regarding the pension scheme are translated into selection criterion, this would at first sight appear to contravene principles of equal treatment and as such could be criticised. The European Community Dir 586/378 requires the principle of equal treatment to be applied to occupational pension schemes. At the present time the principle of equal treatment only extends to men and women, *not to able-bodied and disabled*. The principle would be difficult to extend to disabled people as the European Court of Justice has held that equal treatment is not contravened if the difference in pension arrangements is due to the use of actuarial factors.[26] Furthermore funding arrangements to secure pension payments are outside the scope of the Treaty of Rome.[27]

Communications, manual dexterity and physical effort

The employers' concerns as to the applicant's ability may involve undue stereotyping and screening may be used positively in such circumstances to dispel doubts and avoid false assumptions being made.

STEREOTYPING

Employers' attitudes and concerns have been the subject of an in depth research financed by the Department of Employment.[28]

Employers were asked, *inter alia*, what disabilities would prevent employment, what problems they experienced with existing disabled staff and what problems they felt there would be if they were to employ applicants with certain disabilities in the future.

The employers' responses to what disabilities would prevent employment are shown in the pie chart (see (A) below). This shows that main concern of 39.6 per cent of the respondents was with mobility, which is traditionally the sphere on which employers focus. Only 6.7 per cent of respondents referred to mental illness and 11.2 per cent of respondents referred to epilepsy as preventing employment. These disabilities are nonetheless important as 2–6 million adults suffer mental illness[29] and there are over 350,000 epilepsy sufferers.[30]

[25] Department of Health and Social Security, 'People with Epilepsy', (1969) London HMSO.
[26] *Neath v Hugh Steeper Ltd* [1994] 1 All ER 929.
[27] Above.
[28] S Honey *et al*, 'Employers' Attitudes Towards People With Disabilities', 1993, Institute of Manpower Studies.
[29] D Thompson and R Chee, 'Mental illness the Fundamental Facts', 1993. The Mental Health Foundation.
[30] Brown *et al*, 'An epilepsy needs document', Seizure, 1993, 91–103.

Employers were asked what problems they had encountered with existing staff who suffered from, *inter alia,* mental disorders and epilepsy. Their main specified concerns were about 'job ability' and 'effect on staff' in relation to the presence of employees suffering from mental disorders in the workforce;[31] 'safety' and 'effect on staff' were referred to in relation to epilepsy sufferers, (see (B) below).

Employers' main concern in relation to both disabilities was the effect on other staff. In effect these responses represent employers' perceptions and not necessarily reality.

These findings can be contrasted with employers' responses when they were then asked what the problems would be if they were to employ people suffering from mental disorder and epilepsy. Their main concern in respect of employing people suffering from a mental disorder changed to 'stress' and 'dealing with the public'.[32] In respect of epilepsy their concern remained 'safety'. 'Driving' was also identified as an issue. (see (C) below).

This change in attitude demonstrates some inconsistency, as new reasons were identified. The introduction of driving as an issue can be explained by the fact that in the case of epilepsy, it would be a barrier[33] if the job entailed driving duties and, therefore, would not have been relevant for existing employees. No mention was made of effect on staff in respect of either of the two disabilities.

This research highlights employers' attitudes towards disability. If a comparison is made between their concern over existing employees and their perceptions as to barriers to employing future employees with specified disabilities it can be seen that employers' stated concerns change. This, in turn may help to identify certain prejudices or alternatively, it may be that this difference can be accounted for as the number of respondents differed.[34] In other words different employers were in fact responding.

NEGLIGENT HIRING

A particular concern for employers is that they may be subject to a claim of negligent hiring. A reason given for the increased use of psychometric tests in the United States in recent years is the growing number of actions brought against employers for crimes committed by employees. The action is based on the allegation that the employer should have been aware of the characteristics of the employee for causing harm because of the possibility of psychological testing. Employers on the other hand argue that they have fulfilled their duty by using psychological tests when recruiting, although the

---

[31] In the case of mental disorder a third concern was expressed categorised as 'other'. Due to the nonspecific nature of this concern it is difficult to assess its validity.

[32] The miscellaneous category of 'other' remained.

[33] Road Traffic Act 1988, s 92 and the Motor Vehicles (Driving Licences) Regulations 1987 (SI 1987 No 1378) reg 24(2) (as amended).

[34] No reason is apparent in the research findings for the different response rate.

mere absence of negative evidence may not be sufficient to discharge the obligation of reasonable care.

In this country the doctrine of negligent hiring has been successfully tested in the High Court in *Hicks v Pier* (1984) *The Times*.[35]

POLICIES

Employers' concerns are likely to be reflected in their employment policies. A review of the literature would appear to reveal that there has been a growing awareness of the problems of disabled people but the emphasis has been on those suffering from 'visible' physical disability rather than 'invisible disabilities' such as epilepsy and mental illness. Honey *et al* found that the largest single category of disabilities affecting mobility or physical dexterity.[36] The stated object of their research was to obtain a clear picture of employers' policies, what they currently do and why and the kinds of help and assistance employers needed. The research found that there was a problem of stereotyping the difficulties disabled people have. This in turn, further supports the argument that there needs to be a focus on the specific needs of a particular group of disabled when developing policies.

Despite the Department of Employment's 'Code of Good Practice On The Employment of Disabled People' 1993, there appears to have been little focus on the needs of sufferers of epilepsy and mental illness. The Code of Practice was, in fact, prepared after a consultation process. MIND responded with a policy paper which particularly addressed the needs of the mentally ill.[37] Their particular needs do not appear to have been addressed by the Code of Practice although it recognises mental illness as a disability.

There have been 'scattered' reports on policies regarding mental illness. In fact 'research into the overall attitude of management towards mental illness has been sadly lacking in the UK.'[38] More recent research has concentrated on the content of national policies (for reimbursing the employers) rather than on the existence and content of individual employers' policies, (giving employees the right to work).[39]

In respect of policies concerning mental illness research has already been carried out in the United States of a survey into corporate policies concerning

[35] (1984) *The Times*, 10 February, the negligence in this case related to the taking up of references. The principle of negligent hiring could, in the future be extended, to cover the failure to carry out adequate psychometric testing as is the case in America.
[36] *Irving & Irving v Post Office* [1987] IRLR 289 CA, at p 84.
[37] MIND, 'Employment and Training For People with Disabilities', Response by MIND to the government's consultative document, December 1990.
[38] B Price, 'Mental Illness: a case for company concern', *Personnel Review*, 1978, p 40.
[39] N Lunt and P Thornton, 'Employment policies for disabled people: a review of legislation and services in fifteen countries', 1993.

the 'psychiatrically handicapped'. The results were published in 1991.[40] It made three major findings:

(a) fewer than one in four responding companies currently had a corporate policy concerning the 'psychiatrically handicapped;

(b) physically handicapped employees are widely perceived to be more desirable than 'psychiatrically handicapped' employees; and

(c) firms without corporate policies concerning the 'psychiatrically handicapped' perceive more onerous barriers to implementation than do firms with such policies.

The first finding as to the incidence of corporate policy obviously raises the important issue as to what the current attitudes are which underpin the desirability of such policies. Equally important related issues are the content of the policies and the rationale behind them.

The concept of 'psychiatrically handicapped' was defined in the study as 'an individual with a history of mental illness, generally including at least one psychiatric hospital admission'. This definition was used in the United States where it is unlawful to discriminate against individuals with either physical or medical impairments.[41] The American findings were prefaced by an introductory statement that despite an increased emphasis on hiring the 'handicapped', there have been only scattered reports of employers' policies involving the hiring and promotion of 'psychiatrically handicapped' persons.

SELECTION CRITERIA

Employers' policies will be reflected in their selection criteria. Employers' selection criterion must not contravene the Sex Discrimination Act 1975 (as amended) and the Race Relations Act 1976 and where necessary they must also comply with statutory constraints concerning certain appointments. (These will be discussed below.) At the moment, an employer could only be challenged as to selection criteria if it became an issue in unfair dismissal. In which case the question of whether an employer behaves unreasonably in stipulating medical conditions for a particular employment must depend on the facts of the case.

The courts' attitude towards medical criterion was highlighted in the case of *O'Brien v Prudential Assurance Co Ltd* [1975][42] in which the appellant claimed unfair dismissal after he was dismissed from employment as a district insurance agent, when his employers discovered he had a long history

---

[40] JB Jones *et al*, 'A Survey of Fortune 500 Corporate Policies Concerning the Psychiatrically Handicapped', *Journal of Rehabilitation*, 1991, 31–35.

[41] Americans with Disabilities Act 1990,

[42] [1979] IRLR 140, it was not contended in the case that the policy of not appointing as district agents persons with long histories of serious mental illness is in itself, automatically a policy which is unreasonable.

of mental illness, which had involved hospitalisation over the years and which he had failed to disclose.

When he had applied for the job, he had been asked whether he had suffered from any illness or accident requiring protracted medical attention. The Industrial Tribunal found that he had deliberately omitted details of his history of mental illness. He had attended a medical interview and had answered the following questions in the negative. Has the applicant consulted a psychiatrist? Has the applicant been under the treatment of drugs? Has the applicant any history of nervous or mental disorder? It was found that he had deliberately given untrue answers.

The Industrial Tribunal was satisfied that if he had not concealed his history of mental illness but had given details of it he would not have been offered the job. The employers had a 'policy' of not offering appointments as district agents with long histories of mental illness on the basis that they visited clients' homes. The appellant's medical diagnosis was doubtful, ie it was doubtful whether he had suffered from schizophrenia in the past or present. The medical evidence was also doubtful as to his prognosis, being unable to predict whether he would exhibit symptoms in the future.

However his application for unfair dismissal failed. To dismiss an employee because of his background of mental illness and because he had deliberately withheld the facts from his employer amounted to 'some other substantial reason'.[43] On appeal, the Employment Appeal Tribunal upheld the original decision[44] and found that the practice of not appointing persons with long histories of serious mental illness was not of itself an unreasonable policy. It expressly stated that, where a person had a history of mental illness, their employer would always need to be looked at on the particular facts of the case.[45]

DUTY TO DISCLOSE RELEVANT MEDICAL HISTORIES

An issue in pre-employment health screening is whether applicants have a duty to disclose their medical histories. A contract of employment is not a contract requiring *uberrima fides*[46] and, therefore, there is no concomitant duty of disclosure.

However, a duty of fidelity is owed between employer and employee. Therefore, the question needs to be asked whether non-disclosure of medical histories during the screening process would amount to a breach of this implied duty of mutual trust and confidence. Where a relationship is fiduciary,

---

[43] Within the meaning of para 6(1) of Sched 1 to the Trade Union and Labour Relations Act 1974, now s 57(1)(*b*) of the Employment Protection (Consolidation) Act 1978.

[44] This should be compared with the position for employees when to request an employee to undergo a psychiatric examination could amount to a breach of mutual trust and confidence.

[45] *Ibid*, at p 143.

[46] *Bell and Another v Lever Bros, Ltd* [1932] AC 161 at 228.

silence would normally amount to a misrepresentation. However, it is clear in the context of an employer/employee relationship that employees are not required, as part of their duty of fidelity, to disclose their own past misconduct. This principle should apply, *a fortiori*, to past medical histories where no fault is attributable.

In any event Lord Atkin in *Bell and Another v Lever Bros Ltd*[47] specifically referred to the possibility of employers being able to question employees and thus raise the issue of *caveat emptore*. In the context of pre-employment health screening employers have the opportunity to question prospective employees through the use of the medical questionnaire. The employer could, in practice, insert an express statement that the contract was conditional on not only the current state of health but also past medical histories. An employer could, therefore, assert breach of the term if the employee then withheld relevant medical information. Alternatively an employee could defeat any claim by the employer, based on misrepresentation, by alleging that in effect the employer was not relying on the answers to the medical questionnaire but on the report produced by the occupational health practitioner.[48] If this argument were to succeed the employer's right to rescind the contract for misrepresentation would fail, as s/he will not have relied on the employee's statements.

FEARS OF PROSPECTIVE EMPLOYEES

Balancing rights

Pre-employment health screening has also been seen as a human rights issue by the European Parliament.[49] It has expressed its deep concern as to the increase in medical tests and controls carried out without any objective justification, and sometimes without the consent of the persons concerned. It was concerned that these tests were being used as a selection criteria for access to employment and which it considered were a flagrant example of discrimination.[50] This raises the issue of what may amount to a human right and in particular whether the right to work constitutes such a right. As a corollary of the right to work, the right to privacy is also at issue in view of the pre-employment procedures used.

Pre-employment health screening can presently be justified by employers on the basis that they are following statutory constraints or that there is a safety implication. Accepting this as a justification inevitably means that the public interest is allowed to override the particular individual applicant's interest in obtaining employment.[51]

[47] Above.
[48] *Attwood v Small* (1836) 6 Cl & Fin 232.
[49] Annual Report, 'Respect for human rights in the European Community', 1993.
[50] Above.
[51] This may also be classified as a public interest.

However, care should always be taken to make accurate assessments which should be based on specific job criteria to avoid undue discrimination. Employers should also consider whether all the job criterion are essential. In effect this would mean that the job specification could be modified if any of the criterion were not essential, which would in turn only be following what is currently set out a good practice by the Department of Employment in its recommended policy objectives in relation to the disabled.[52] This would make reasonable accommodation for the applicant's health.[53] If undue discrimination is to be avoided employers should take care, not to make assumptions and to refrain from using stereotypes where prospective employees are disabled.

As a final point the government have now announced (January 1995) its intention to legislate[54] to make it unlawful for an employer to treat a disabled person less favourably because of his/her disability, without justifiable reason.[55]

---

[52] *Ibid*, para 5.2.

[53] This would follow the American model in The Americans with Disabilities Act 1990, s 102(*a*) which prohibits discrimination against any qualified individual with a disability. 'Qualified individual', is defined in the Equal Employment Opportunities Commission regulations as 'an individual with a disability who satisfies the requisite skill and experience, education and other job-related requirements of the employment position such as an individual holds or desires, and who, with or without reasonable accommodation, can perform the essential functions of such position.'

[54] These were set out in 'Ending discrimination against disabled people, 1995', Cmnd 2729, London HMSO.

[55] The proposals specifically state that health and safety would be a justifiable reason, above, para 3.4.

(A)   **Disabilities which would prevent employment**

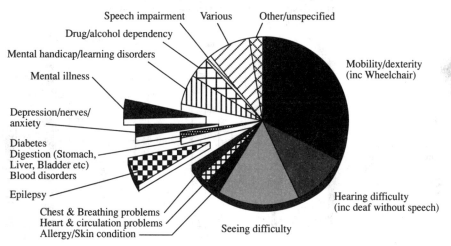

Data source: Honey *et al.*

(B)   **Problems associated with existing employees**

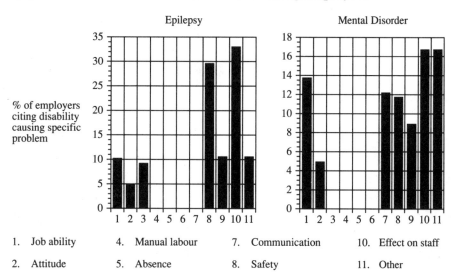

1.	Job ability	4.	Manual labour	7.	Communication	10.	Effect on staff
2.	Attitude	5.	Absence	8.	Safety	11.	Other
3.	Mobility	6.	Access	9.	Redeployment		

Data source: Honey *et al.*

(C)   **Reasons given by employers why epilepsy and mental disorder would prevent employment**

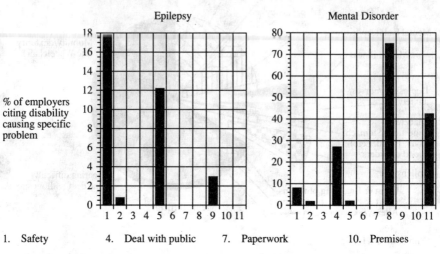

1. Safety
2. Fitness/mobility
3. Hazardous environment
4. Deal with public
5. Driving
6. Telephone
7. Paperwork
8. Stress
9. Manual Dexterity
10. Premises
11. Other

Data source: Honey *et al.*

INDEX

Sex discrimination – *contd*
  sexuality, adverse treatment due to, as, 62
  single sex recruitment, where permitted,
    31
  single-sex services, 8, 32
  unisex rating and *see* Social security
    schemes
  White Paper on Equality for Women, 14,
    49–50, 58–9
Sex Discrimination Act 1975, 8, 14, 16, 17,
  20, 22, 31–2, 34, 40, 41, 49, 52–3, 57,
  58, 198, 237
  effects of, 46
  safety factor not addressed, 32
  women in police force, effect on, 207, 208,
    210–11, 212
Sex Disqualification (Removal) Act 1919,
  210
Sexual orientation
  adverse treatment due to, as sex
    discrimination, 62
  dismissal for, 55–6
  same-sex relationships, 61–2
Sick pay, part-time employees, for, 26, 106
Single European Act
  effect in relation to non-EC nationals, 140
  purpose of, 139
Social Protocol, 38
Social security schemes
  Commission v Belgium (Case C-229/89), 27,
    194, 195
  costs –
    directives and, 186–7
    ECJ and, 187–192, *see also* European
      Court of Justice
    employer provided benefits, 186
    equalisation of pension ages, costs,
      182–3
    identifiable third parties, 184
    impact on the economy, 185
    insurance, 184–5, 186
    men, effects of equalisation on, 184
    moving from *status quo* group, effect of,
      179–80
    nature and incidence of, 178–9
    public interest, 185
    remedial, 179
    remedy and, 196
    removing discrimination, of, 177
    respondent and respondent group, 182
    status quo, of, 179
    to employers, of unisex rating schemes,
      183
    victim/victim group, to, 179–86
    see also unisex rating *below*
  developments in the Community, 177–8
  equalisation of pension ages –
    costs, 182–3
    effects, 180–1
  generally, 177

indirect discrimination –
  general principles, 192–3
  meaning, 192
  objective justification and, 193–5
  interest balancing approach, problems of
    judicial assessment in, 196–7
  justification of discriminatory benefits, 71,
    192
  objective justification –
    elements of, 192–3
    social policy objectives providing, 193–4
  Occupational Social Security Directive, 14
  pensions discrimination linked to age
    differences, 191
  retirement age differences, 191–2
  Social Security Directive (79/7), 14, 27,
    187, 189–92
  unisex rating –
    costs to employers, 183
    insurance companies, 184–5
    of contributors and benefits, 181–2
  see also Pension schemes
Students
  maintenance grants, national discrimination
    as to, 97
  see also Training
Sunday trading cases, 74

Tax arrangements, 71
Trade unions
  dismissal on grounds of membership, 43–5
  employees' membership rights, 43–5, 47
Training
  payments to part-time workers, 29
  vocational –
    European citizenship and, 94–5
    pay discrimination and, 27, 28
Treaty on European Union
  application to non-EC nationals, 141–3
  concept of European citizenship under,
    141–2
  Social Protocol, justification arguments for
    opt-out, 38

United Nations International Convention on
  the Protection of All Migrant Workers
  and Members of Their Families, 145,
  146

War veterans, 97
Webb v EMO Air Cargo Ltd, 21, 54, 55, 57,
  58, 68, 70
White Papers (UK)
  Employment for the 1990s, 38
  Equality for Women, 14, 49–50, 58–9
  Removing Barriers to Employment, 44
Worker
  EC concept of, 126
  see also Free movement of workers,
    Non-EC immigrant workers